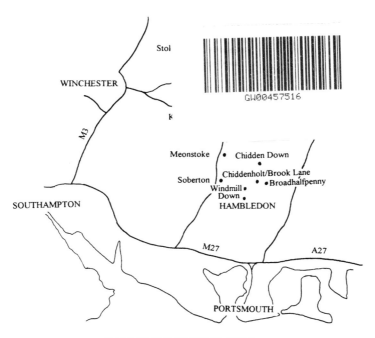

HAMBLEDON CRICKET GROUNDS

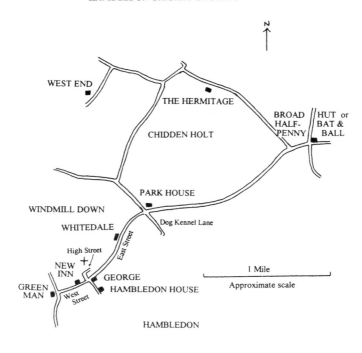

HAMBLEDON

HAMBLEDON

The Men and the Myths

ERRATA

P. x, line 25: for *Gouldstone* read *Goulstone*.
P. 98, line 3 & 17)
P. 99, line 24   ) for *1772* read *1775*.
P. 202, line 3: for *1851* read *1951*.
P. 204, line 15: for *Pertersfield* read *Petersfield*.

HAMBLEDON

The Men and the Myths

JOHN GOULSTONE

Roger Heavens
CAMBRIDGE
2001

Also available from Roger Heavens

An Index to Scores and Biographies (15 Volumes)
Cuckfield - Double Champions including Cuckfield Cricket - A brief History
*Henry Bentley's "Book of Cricket", with both supplements together with a
   new preface by David Rayvern Allen* (Numbered limited edition
   Facsimile)
Arthur Haygarth's Scores and Biographies (Numbered limited Edition
   Facsimiles -Volumes I to IX)

First Published November 2001

British Library Cataloguing-in-Publication Data
A Catalogue record for this book is available from
the British Library

ISBN 1 900592 34 7

Published by Roger Heavens
2 Lowfields, Little Eversden, Cambridgeshire, CB3 7HJ, England

Printed by E. & E. Plumridge Ltd.,
Linton, Cambridge, England

CONTENTS

LIST OF ILLUSTRATIONS

Front cover: The Hambledon Memorial erected in 1908 at Broadhalfpenny.

Between pages 96 and 97:

11. Gravestone of John Small (snr) at Petersfield - the only stone still standing in the churchyard.

12. The earliest surviving scorecard - obviously a forgery.

13. The bat presented to Richard Nyren - almost certainly a modern piece of cricket memorabilia. Nyren had left the Bat and Ball 20 years earlier.

14. The famous document restricting the width of the bat to 4¹/4 inches is almost certainly a forgery.

15. Nyren's signatures as a witness at the marriages of two Hambledon members in 1772 and 1780 bear no resemblance to the signature above.

Rear cover: Maps of Hambledon and district drawn by Gwyneth Fookes.

ABBREVIATIONS

acct	account
bapt	baptised
BCL	Bachelor of Civil Law
bur	buried
Capt	Captain
dau	daughter
DCL	Doctor of Civil Law
DD	Doctor of Divinity
DNB	*Dictionary of National Biography*
gns	guineas
IGI	International Genealogical index
JP	Justice of the Peace
MI	Monumental Inscription
MP	Member of Parliament
OED	*Oxford English Dictionary*
PC	Privy Councillor
PCC	Prerogative Court of Canterbury
S&B	*Scores and Biographies*
sic	as written

Books often referred to in the text are abbreviated to Author,
e.g. Snow, Haygarth, etc.
For full reference consult bibliography.

FOREWORD

BY ROBERT BROOKE

There has been renewed interest in recent years in the story of Hambledon cricket from the last quarter of the eighteenth century and its effect on the development of cricket and sport in general. Ashley Mote's books, *The Glory Days of Cricket* (1997) and his version of Nyren's *The Cricketers of my Time* (1998), and those of Sir Derek Birley and David Underdown, have explored the Hambledon story and arrived at historical and sociological conclusions. Some of these conclusions are fanciful, others no doubt sound, but it is well that the Hambledon story should be kept in view when considering the history and development of modern sport which today is such a preoccupation with the media.

Earlier cricket histories, especially the works of Pycroft, Haygarth, Ashley-Cooper and E.V. Lucas, will always be consulted by students of cricket and Hambledon history and some of them rank highly in the not inconsiderable annals of cricket literature. Certainly John Nyren's above work, which first appeared in a weekly periodical in 1852, delights the reader with some worthy prose.

Having contemplated the considerable wealth of Hambledon literature, the student and the general reader may well be wondering what John Goulstone's *Hambledon: The Men & The Myths* has to offer and why they should again wade through a well-known story. I am delighted to have the opportunity to provide a foreword to this work on the grounds that Goulstone has adopted the scholarly approach that we have come to expect from him in writing this latest book on the subject. It is evident and perhaps inevitable that a litany of errors has arisen in the chronicling of the events of an age when record keeping was not the science that it has become today but Goulstone has patiently applied the methods of the genealogist, archivist and historian in presenting a refreshing look at the subject and sweeping away so many of the Hambledon myths that have been perpetuated by previous authors, less inclined or able to research the subject in a studious manner.

To someone who has drawn attention to palpable errors, such as the celebrated batsman Richard Miller being continuously referred to as Joseph Miller; and Richard Newland being described as a surgeon which he never was, it must be so galling to see the mistakes repeated time and again. There are many, many others and it is evident that some of the writers and editors of the modern works on Hambledon - more especially and disappointingly the prize winning authors Sir Derek Birley and Ashley Mote - have failed their readership, and their 'tests' as historians, by ignoring Goulstone's earlier works. The minefield of labelling team either 'Hampshire' or 'Hambledon' (a minefield seemingly unappreciated by the above authors), is fully clarified along with many additional corrections.

I can unreservedly commend this book to those keen to have a more accurate record of the Hambledon story and to those who need to understand its origins and social and historical background. This book will be essential reading, in order that the many blunders of the current batch of approved cricket 'historians' will not be repeated and regurgitated yet again by the next generation of marketing experts and knights of the realm, anxious to make a name for themselves as cricket gurus. With Gouldstone beside them and an open mind, they might just have a chance of at last producing something original, worthwhile and acceptable.

Finally John Goulstone will always be recalled as the cricket historian who discovered the portrait of Lumpy Stevens and the details of the first known century in 1769. John Arlott once said of him: "He is of the type of archivist less often found in sport than in historical research circles, who go to basic chronicles - early newspapers, commissary court records and parish registers for their information."

This is a very important book: ignore it at your peril!

February 2001
Birmingham

INTRODUCTION

Once, hardly more than a quarter of a century ago, the history of sport was a subject left pretty well to the occasional amateur. Since then much has changed. For many it has now become a full-time profession. The expansion of old and proliferation of new universities across the country has brought with it a growth of interest in a hitherto academically neglected area of study. Professors of sports history have made their appearance, numerous journals have sprung up to accommodate a never ending stream of learned papers, university departments and 'centres' specialising in the history of sport have been established and every year sees an extensive programme of international conferences organised for the express purpose of providing a forum for the growing number of scholars wishing to exchange ideas and present the results of their latest research.

Inevitably, cricket history has taken its rightful place within this great hive of scholarly activity. And within this specialist field nothing, some might argue, has in its way proved more remarkable than work undertaken during the last twenty or so years by a succession of acclaimed social historians on the era of the great Hambledon Club immortalised through the pages of John Nyren.[1] Yet despite its undoubted influence on modern academic thinking, some critics have expressed misgivings as to whether this school of historical literature leans too far towards an imaginative reinterpretation as opposed to factual reconstruction of the past. And indeed there is much to support the argument that it represents something rather different from 'history' as understood in most other academic disciplines. In certain respects this corpus of modern scholarship has even assumed the characteristics of a new mythology - one which extends from cricket's alleged beginnings as a French game called *criquet* (in fact a 19th century neologism derived from a misreading of the word *etiquet*, denoting a small stick)[2] right through to the Victorian era. Thus in the case of Hambledon we have impossible dates, a membership bearing little resemblance to reality, anecdotes which belong to historical fiction rather than to proper history, and origin myths of which the assertion by an award-winning Marxist historian that it was formed in London and not in Hampshire is by no means the most bizarre.

One particular aspect of the modern Hambledon myth has been keenly promoted by Leicester University's 'Centre for Research into Sport and Society' whose radical reappraisal of 18th and 19th century cricket was announced to an audience of distinguished scholars at a congress held at Eastbourne in 1998 and formally published in May 1999.[3] The Centre's analysis of the 'historical evidence' has, it is claimed, revealed that at Hambledon spectators were so unruly that they often interrupted play during the 1770s and 1780s - and that at cricket matches in general they used to pose a serious threat to public order. '18th century cricket crowds', we are told, 'were characterised by regular and serious disorder' and matches were so violent that they frequently had to be abandoned. The Centre has also demonstrated, to its own satisfaction and to the satisfaction of wider academe, that John Nyren, along with Mary Mitford, was guilty of fostering a 'pastoral myth' of earlier cricket 'far removed' from 18th century reality and, by failing to emphasise its associated rioting and crowd violence, helped establish an enduringly false concept of the traditional village game.[4]

However, few who are in any way knowledgeable in this field will be surprised that what the Centre euphemistically calls its 'historical evidence' comprises much which is wholly irrelevant, much which has no verifiable historical basis, and much which is palpably wrong (such sophistry as the Duke of Dorset wielding his bat on a spectator during a pitch invasion by a Hampshire mob, and the Prince of Wales presenting 10 guineas to a woman injured at the Artillery Ground in 1750).[5] And as for Nyren and Mitford, the truth of the matter is that their writings accord fairly well with the way country cricket was commonly viewed in the 18th century. A theme of John Burnby's *The Cricketers. A Catch* published in 1782 is that it was a pursuit untainted by many excesses of the age: 'Then of Cricket, of Cricket, (we) will chearfully (sic) sing; for a Game of such Innocence, pleasure must bring' - effusive sentiments hardly compatible with a sport 'characterised by regular and serious disorder'. And that it was one of the more agreeable features of country as opposed to town life is the message of I. Ingledew's *To a Friend in London* which appeared in 1773: 'Here all is pleasant as a man can wish, We cricket play, to fairs go, or fish'. As regards spectators, according to *Box Hill* (1777), when 'a happy band near Dorking meet attired for sport on Cotman's pleasant green',

> From hamlets round: crowded booths are filled
> With motley groups of joyous young
> And old, who, as their favourites please
> Their plaudits give...

while equally instructive are the impressions of a visitor to the country recorded in a letter from the Scottish poet, James Beattie, who watched a contest between two parishes near Maidstone in 1784:[6]

> The people are fond of cricket-matches at which there is a great concourse of men, women, and children, with a good store of ale and beer, cakes, gingerbread, &c. One of these was solemnized a few nights ago in a field adjacent to the parish church. It broke up about sun-set, with much merriment, but without drunkenness or riot.

Here both letter and verse closely correspond to the image of a village cricket match watched by young and old alike as portrayed a couple of generations later by Mary Mitford. Quite plainly neither she nor Nyren (nor anyone else in the 19th century) 'invented' an idealised romantic idyll of cricket in years gone by as claimed by Leicester University. The fact of the matter is that while Nyren can be faulted on many points of detail there are no reasons for doubting that he and Mitford provide a reasonably accurate overview of the game and its social background during the late Georgian period.[7]

As may be gathered from the foregoing, one of the problems besetting cricket historiography is a tendency for overzealous and at the same time insufficiently informed scholars to make daring reconstructions of the past which are not solidly based on evidence. When backed by adequate knowledge such reconstructions may be useful as hypotheses pointing out possible directions to be taken by further research. But if such knowledge is entirely lacking and mere hypotheses and speculations are taken for probable realities or actual facts, scholarship is reduced to fantasy and fiction and made ridiculous. Therefore, as a corrective to the mythology with which academe has enveloped the subject, it might be worthwhile re-examining Hambledon cricket on the basis of reliable historical evidence - in a nutshell, the justification of the present study.

Before proceeding further, however, perhaps it should be explained that in this context 'evidence' does not mean the contents of Ford, Brookes or other equally unreliable secondary works. On the other hand it does of course mean primary sources such as John Nyren and Arthur Haygarth as well as publications based on a direct study of original texts, by for example H.T. Waghorn, F.S. Ashley-Cooper, G.B. Buckley and Ronald Knight. But besides drawing on these and other key published sources I have tried to incorporate 'evidence' from outside the standard literature. This includes information on the players and their family background taken from parish registers, principally via the International Genealogical Index (hereafter the IGI) whose Hampshire microfiches cover Hambledon baptisms and marriages, and church and churchyard inscriptions transcribed by members of Hampshire Family History Society. Other local archival sources at the Hampshire County Record Office, Winchester, among them Hambledon burials (not covered by the IGI), incidental marriage details (witnesses, etc), the six-monthly manorial court books, wills, overseers' accounts and insurance policies, have been carefully researched and published by Ronald Knight in his ongoing series *Hambledon's Cricket Glory.*

Except for those who achieved a measure of fame in other fields, less work has been done on the club members. The most comprehensive and accessible source is Ashley-Cooper's 'membership roll', an alphabetical listing of subscribers with in most cases a few brief biographical notes, included in his *Hambledon Cricket Chronicle* (1924). Despite some being duplicated, one omitted, others wrongly identified and one non-subscriber accounted a full member it remains a useful reference source. Of course, since 1924 much more data has become readily available. As well as the IGI and monumental inscriptions (MIs) there is now a far wider range of printed biographical guides and indexes, from the Westminster School and Cambridge University registers, the volumes of biographies of 18th century MPs produced by R.J. Thorne and others to such works as D. Syrett and R.L. NiNardo's *The Commissioned Sea Officers of the Royal Navy 1660-1815* published for the Navy Research Society in 1994 and P.J. and R.V. Wallis' *Eighteenth Century Medics* which came out in a second edition in 1988 (instrumental in identifying one of the 'original' members). For the present work material has also been collected from such sources as the *Victoria County History of Hampshire*, army lists, various editions of 'Burke's Landed Gentry', *The Complete Peerage*, *Dictionary of National Biography*, *The Gentleman's Magazine*, files of the *Hampshire Chronicle* and wills proved in the Prerogative Court of Canterbury (P.C.C.) Notwithstanding that later members with no really genuine Hampshire connections are accorded no more than token coverage, and despite the remaining gaps, hopefully the corrected and much enlarged 'membership roll' in chapter 12 will provide a better basis for future study of the family, social and political connections underlying membership of the Hambledon Club.

As for more specific cricketing documentation, a number of press notices cited by Waghorn, Buckley, etc., have been re-checked both at The British Library, Colindale and at St Pancras. In the process several 'new' references have come to light and are (re-)published here for the first time. It has also confirmed what has long been apparent - that a substantial amount of cricket data remains to be unearthed from 18th century newspapers, and that Hampshire in particular would benefit by a meticulous study of the *Reading Mercury, Salisbury Journal* and *Hampshire Chronicle* along the lines already undertaken with respect to the Norfolk newspapers by J.S. Penny. For checking several volumes in the British Library's rare books department and for a number of press extracts both re-examined and discovered at Colindale, as well as for extended loan of key items from his cricket library, my thanks are due to Prof. Michael Swanton and to Roger Packham. Finally it may be noted that statistics quoted (somewhat sparingly) in the following pages have been taken from K. Warsop's career figures, in *Hambledon to 'Over-Arm'*, on pages 29 to 30 of *The Cricket Quarterly*, volume 5 (1966-67).

Chapter One

ORIGINS

One of cricket's mysteries is why it took so long to be recorded in Hampshire when across the Sussex border - in places such as Sidlesham and Boxgrove, scarcely more than fifteen miles from Hambledon - the game is documented as far back as the early 17th century. As it is we have no record of Hampshire cricketers until 1729 when 'a great cricket-match' was staged in Penshurst Park between Kent and Sir William Gage's team said to have been drawn from Sussex, Surrey and Hampshire.[8] Fifteen years later the *Daily Advertiser* for 31 May 1744 stated that the players in a forthcoming trial, to select the England XI to oppose Kent at Coxheath near Maidstone and the return in London's Artillery Ground, would include two from Hamilton in Sussex. 'Hamilton' was a common misspelling of 'Hambledon' and as there is no parish of that name in Sussex we must be dealing with Hambledon in Surrey or else the one in Hampshire. Unfortunately we have no way of telling which. We do know, however, that the father of Edward Aburrow, a star of the great Hampshire team of the 1770s, formed one of the England side under the name Cuddy, a corruption of Curry.[9]

By 1756 Hambledon had built up sufficient reputation for its eleven to be matched against the powerful Dartford club in Kent. Very likely the first game was the one held on Hambledon's home ground, Broadhalfpenny Down, on 18 August when the loss of a pet dog caused one of the spectators, the young clergyman Richard Keats[10] from nearby Chalton, to insert a notice in the *Reading Mercury* of 6 September :

> LOST, At the Cricket-Match on Broad-Halfpenny, on Wednesday the 18th of August, 1756, A Yellow and White SPANIEL DOG, of the Setting Kind, about 18 Inches high, with a mottled Nose, and one very large Spot of Yellow on the Right Side, and answers to the

Name of ROVER. Whoever will bring the said Dog to the Rev. Mr. Keats, of Chalton near Petersfield, or give Notice where he may be had again, shall receive Five Shillings Reward, and all reasonable Charges.

On Saturday 28 August five of the parish opposed five of the best cricketers of the day in the Artillery Ground as a preliminary to meeting Dartford, eleven a side, on the Monday. Details were given in *The Public Advertiser* of 28 August 1756:

Artillery-Ground, London. This Day will be play'd a Match at Cricket with Faulkner, Joe Harris, John Frame, John Bell, and Daulering, and five Gentlemen of the Parish of Hambledon in Hampshire, for twenty Pounds a Side, the Wickets to be pitch'd at One, play or pay. And Monday will be play'd in the same Ground another match at Cricket between Eleven Gentlemen of Dartford Club, and Eleven Gentlemen of the Parish of Hambledon in Hampshire aforesaid, it being the deciding Match between the two Elevens for Fifty Pounds a Side. The Wickets to be pitch'd at twelve. The Game to be play'd out.

The second game was announced again on Monday 30 August, two days later, in a shortened notice beginning 'This day will be play'd in the Artillery Ground' then continuing as above: 'another match at Cricket', etc. However, readers had to wait until Friday the 3rd to learn the result:

Artillery Ground, London. Next Monday will be play'd a Match at Cricket, between the Gentlemen of London and the Gentlemen of Dartford, (who beat the Gentlemen of Hampshire three Matches Successively) for Fifty Pounds a Side, allowing London to have Brian, Smith, Durling, and Joe Harris. The Wickets to be pitch'd at Twelve o'Clock and the Match to be play'd out, and on Thursday next the Second Match will be play'd on Dartford Brim by the Same Gentlemen.

From all this we may deduce that Dartford and Hambledon played one another on Broadhalfpenny on 18 August and on Dartford Brent, sometimes called the Brim, on an unknown date, both winning once, then contested a third or deciding game on the neutral Artillery Ground on the 30th. The notice in *The Public Advertiser* for 3 September implies that Dartford proved victorious in London, thereby winning the overall match by two to one.

One important point about these games is that Hambledon was twice referred to as a parish team - not as a club as stated by Mote and Birley. This renders it all the more remarkable that as a mere rural parish Hambledon should be considered far stronger than a town which, despite its huge population of maybe half a million, required four given-men to face a side which Hambledon a few days earlier played on level terms. For Hambledon to be described as a 'club' we have to go forward eight years to 1764 when *The St James's Chronicle* for 15 September inserted the following immediately below a remedy for deafness and immediately above a report of a duel in Hyde Park:

> On Monday last the great Match at Cricket, so long depending between the Gentlemen of Hambledon, in Hants, called 'Squire Lamb's Club, and the Gentlemen of Chertsey, was played on Laleham Borough. Chertsey went in first, and got 48 Notches, Hambledon got 76. Second Innings, Chertsey headed 87, John Edmonds and Thomas Baldwin turned the Game, by getting upwards of 40 Notches: Time expired, and they postponed it till the next Morning when Chertsey went in and got 12 Notches. Hambledon went in, three out for four Notches, the next five got, won the Game. Chertsey had three Men much hurt, and Hambledon had two, Mr. Steward having his Finger broke, and his Knee Sprained. On this match great Sums of Money were depending. During the Cricket Match a Gentleman of Fortune at Weybridge was taken up by a Warrant for a Bastard Child, which caused a great deal of Diversion; the Gentleman drew his Sword on the officer, and afterwards presented a Pistol, and went off in Triumph.

It was deemed of sufficient national interest for news to be circulated as far away as East Anglia where the *Norwich Gazette* reprinted the report in slightly abbreviated form in its issue for 22 September. This was two days after the *St James's Chronicle* reported the second match:

> On Monday and Tuesday last was played the second grand Cricket Match, between 11 Gentlemen of the Hambledon Club in Hampshire, and the like number of gentlemen of the Chertsey Club in Surry, which was won by two Wickets.

> The first Match was won by the Hambledon Club, for which Reason a third and decisive one is agreed on for a very considerable Sum, which is expected will be played on Monday next.

In those days it was by no means unusual for clubs like Hambledon to take the field under the banner of a local patron. For example we have 'Esquire Steed's Cricket Club' in 1731; Mr Hesse's club in Lamb's Conduit Fields near London in 1736; Mr Toll's club in Middlesex in 1743; Squire Farrar's club in Thanet around 1770; and Hambledon's own opponents of the late 1760s and early 1770s, viz Horace Mann's club at Bishopsbourne and Henry Rowed's at Caterham. But who exactly was 'Squire Lamb?' To begin with, there was no family named Lamb living in Hambledon during the 18th century. We know, however, that the name must have been Land because this is how he features in the club song written not many years later by the Revd Cotton - 'Then why should we fear either Sackville or Mann, or repine at the loss of Bayton and Land'. While variant printings spell the name 'Lamb' or 'Lann' (to rhyme with Mann) 'Land' is the spelling in the version authorised by the club in 1781. Moreover Hambledon had only one gentleman of this name of the right age to have been backing a cricket club in 1764 - Thomas Land of Park House. He belonged to a family established in the parish since at least the 1670s. All the eldest sons were christened Thomas, and Goldsmith has identified the 'Squire' as the one who died in 1767.[11] However, by 1764 this particular Land had already passed his 80th birthday - far too old to have been actively promoting sport on this scale. The club's patron must have been his son, then a mere forty-nine. This is an outline family tree:

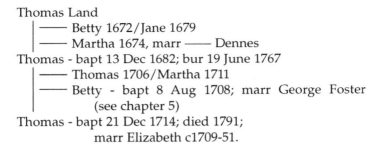

Thomas Land
   ├── Betty 1672/Jane 1679
   ├── Martha 1674, marr ── Dennes
Thomas - bapt 13 Dec 1682; bur 19 June 1767
   ├── Thomas 1706/Martha 1711
   ├── Betty - bapt 8 Aug 1708; marr George Foster
   │   (see chapter 5)
Thomas - bapt 21 Dec 1714; died 1791;
          marr Elizabeth c1709-51.

After being left a widower at the age of thirty-six, the younger Thomas Land became active in parish affairs and as late as the 1780s was still serving his term as churchwarden and overseer. In 1757 when a constable for the manor he subscribed (like his father) two guineas to the church ceiling fund. Also he was a JP and one of twelve customary 'Regarders' of the Forest of Bere - indeed, by neglecting to replace those who died, one of only two still holding office in 1789. In 1758 he bought the manor of Denmead Molyns in Hambledon for £460 and in 1759 acquired the lease of Park House, about a mile east of the village beside the lane leading towards Broadhalfpenny, where he resided for the rest of his life. Doubtless we will never know precisely why or when Land withdrew from the club after 1764, or whether a new, in a sense rival, club was formed by other gentlemen. Whatever the reason and whatever the circumstances, he afterwards concentrated more on his pack of hounds, hunting deer in summer and fox in winter. In W.N. Heysham's (Æsop) *Sporting Reminiscences of Hampshire (1745-1862)*, published in 1864, we read:

> Mr Land of Park House, Hambledon, kept a pack of fox-hounds, with which he hunted deer all the summer in the Forest of Bere. In the autumn he hunted cubs with the same hounds; after two or three days they would stick to their fox, and actually go through the deer they had hunted in the summer! ... Will James was Mr Land's huntsman ... Mr Geary of Fareham, the son of the king's head-keeper, who lived at Critch Lodge (the keeper's residence in the Forest of Bere), constantly hunted with Mr Land. He says that his

father frequently had great rows with Mr Land about hunting the deer, which he had no right or permission to do, as Mr Geary's father kept hounds on purpose to take them, and they were attended by the resident gentry. Lord Scarborough who was a keen sportsman and colonel of the York militia then stationed at Portsmouth, frequently hunted with him.

On his death in 1791 the *Hampshire Chronicle* for 27 June noted: 'Saturday [Saturday week] died, in an advanced age, Thomas Land, Esq. of Hambledon, one of the most celebrated fox-hunters in Great Britain'. Land left instructions for his executor to sell his hounds as soon as possible to the best advantage. His pack is still remembered in the name of Dog Kennel Lane leading to the woods opposite Park House - while the master himself is commemorated by a tablet inside Hambledon church to Thomas Land, died 18 June 1791 aged 76, and his wife, Elizabeth, who died 10 March 1751 aged 42.

His will, dated 11 June 1789, with a codicil of 19 January 1790, witnessed by Edward Hale, William Garratt and Richard Mathews, appointed his friends John Goldsmith, shopkeeper, and William Horn(e), yeoman, trustees of his lands. An anecdote concerning his later years tells how, when suffering from gout, he used to sit by his fireside near a basket of logs, one of which would be hurled at the door whenever a servant was needed.[12] But his bequests hint at a more kind-hearted side to his nature. To George Taylor he left money to compensate him for a fine levied on him for killing game. By his codicil he appointed one of his great-nephews executor in place of his niece because he thought the work might prove too onerous. And to his servants, Elizabeth Tulip and Elizabeth Colwell (who witnessed his father's will in 1767), he bequeathed £12 per annum each along with the late Martha Howard's house, its garden and orchard but not its field, rent-free for life, with his executor keeping the house in good repair at his own expense and providing them with a hundred good faggots every year.[13]

The principal legatees were his great-nephews, sons of his nephew George Foster - George junior, Francis and John, who was also his sole executor - and his niece Betty Gay. Betty was the former wife of a manorial tenant, Francis Clarke, who according to the court book died c1757, and had a daughter, Betty or Bete, who died in infancy about a year before she became a widow. She then married on 29 November 1762 George Gay who was buried in Hambledon churchyard on 14 September 1780. Land's household goods, furniture and stock of liquor in the cellar at Park House was shared equally by Betty, John and Francis; his tanyard at Havant passed to Francis; and the rents of a house and leasehold land at Blendworth, to the east of Hambledon, to Betty and Francis.

Although, so far as we can tell, he had nothing to do with the later club his testamentary papers indicate continuing links with some of the lesser lights of Hambledon cricket. William Horn must have been the Horn (or else his brother) who played for Hambledon Town *v* Surrey in 1773. John Goldsmith, Buck Stewart's brother-in-law, had a son who represented Hambledon and even once substituted for Surrey. Edward Hale was either the village surgeon, owner of the cricket ground on Windmill Down or his son, Edward junior, who as well as playing for Hambledon for a few years also subscribed to the club. And William Garratt must have been a brother or relative of 'Farmer' Edward Garratt who sub-let Windmill Down to the club and whose two sons turned out for Hambledon in the 1800s. Land's most significant cricketing connections, however, were with the Fosters. Under his father's will he had been entrusted with the upbringing of his great-nephews, the three Foster brothers, boys then aged between about six and nine, all of whom became useful cricketers, good enough to take part in some of Hambledon's minor matches of the 1780s and 1790s. The eldest, John, succeeded him at Park House and his son, another John, was a keen player and supporter of the game in Victorian times. He was described by a fellow cricketer in 1857 as being descended from a 'good old patron of this noble game'[14] - presumably an allusion to his collateral ancestor, his great-great-uncle, Thomas Land.

Chapter Two

THE HAMBLEDON CLUB
1767-1772

Two years after Land's involvement, the *Kentish Post* in June 1766 reported how 'the great subscription cricket-match, played on Thursday, between Sussex and Hampshire ... was won by the latter; though after the first innings the odds were 40-1 against Hampshire'. Rather than individual patrons, the word 'subscription' implies some kind of club or clubs with groups of subscribers financing each team. The account does not connect the Hampshire side with Hambledon. But a year later the *Reading Mercury* of 10 August referred to Hampshire beating Sussex on Broadhalfpenny Down and in early October there were two reports of an actual club.[15] The first reads:

> A few days since a grand match at cricket was played near Croydon, for 200 guineas, by a farmer with a gold-laced hat and ten others with silver-laced hats against eleven gentlemen of the Hamilton Club, which was won by the latter by a majority of 262 notches. It was remarkable that the Hamilton Club got two new hands from Hampshire, who kept in three hours and a half and got 192 notches, the greatest thing ever known.

while the second, dated 'Reading, October 3rd', relates to what seems to have been a two-day match lasting from 28 to 29 September 1767:

> On Tuesday last a great match at cricket, which has been so long depending, between the gentlemen of the Hambledon Club and a set of gentlemen belonging to a club in Surrey, was decided on Broad- Halfpenny, near Hambledon, who got 224 notches ahead. The match was began on Monday morning, but was not finished till Tuesday afternoon at three o'clock.

These look suspiciously like two notices of the same match, in which case 'near Croydon' should properly refer not to the venue but to the 'club in Surrey' which we know was led by Caterham's Henry Rowed, styled 'the golden farmer' from his wearing a gold-laced hat, who resided at Court Lodge, about five miles from Croydon. Another match took place a fortnight later at Caterham - suggesting a return match rather than a third or decider which would normally be arranged on a neutral ground:

> On Wednesday [14 October] ... a cricket-match was played on Catterham Common, near Bletchingley, in Surrey, between the gentlemen of Catterham and Hambledon, Hants, for £100 a-side, when the game was decided in favour of Catterham.
>
> (Waghorn 1899)

In September 1768 the *Reading Mercury* (on 5th and 12th) reported the Hambledon Club in action on Broadhalfpenny twice within the space of a week, first beating Kent by 'upwards of 100 notches', then Sussex by 7 wickets:

> Last Monday another great match at cricket was played on Broad Halfpenny between eleven gentlemen of the county of Sussex against eleven of the Hambledon Club for a large sum, which was won by the latter, who had seven wickets to go down ...

1769 saw further fixtures with the old rivals from Surrey:

> On Thursday the 29th of this instant June, will be played the first grand match at cricket by the gentlemen of the Hambledon, and Caterham Clubs. N.B. The wickets will be pitched at 9 o'clock upon Broadhalfpenny, near Hambledon, Hants.
>
> (*Reading Mercury* 12 June)

One may assume a return match was held in or near Caterham because, with both sides presumably winning once, a deciding game was required on a halfway ground at Guildford:

> The third match between the gentlemen of Hambledon and the gentlemen of Catterham, will be played at the Bason at Guildford, on Monday the 31st

instant. *N.B.* The wickets will be pitched at Ten o'clock.

(*Reading Mercury* 24 July)

The subsequent report, under 'Reading, August 5th' (see Waghorn 1899, pp. 68-9), is of especial importance in that it provides the first Hambledon team list:

> On Monday last began to be played at Guildford, in Surrey, the decisive grand match at cricket between the Hambledon and Catterham Clubs, which, after a long and vigorous contest, was determined on Tuesday evening in favour of the former. The utmost activity and skill in the game was displayed by each individual through the whole course of this match, but particularly the batting of Messrs Small and Boyton on the Hambledon side. There were near 20,000 spectators, and it is generally allowed by the best judges to have been the finest match that ever was played. The particulars are as follows, viz. :-

	1ST INNS	2ND INNS
Catterham	104	137
Hambledon	99	142

and four wickets to go down.

HAMBLEDON SIDE	CATTERHAM SIDE
Messrs Ridge	Messrs Rower
Hogflesh	Bellchambers
Bret	Stevens
Steward	Page
Nyren	Millar
Small	Smeale
Boyton	Wood
Glazier	Palmer
Suter	Shepherd
Purdy	Quiddington
Barber	Wessing

Nine of the Hambledon men are covered in either chapter 4 or (in the case of Ridge) 12. Of the others, nothing definite is known about Glazier while the only Purdy in the parish registers whose dates fit someone playing for the club in 1769 is William who married Elizabeth Hall on 29 September 1751. They had a son, another William, baptised on 5 May 1754 and a daughter, Sarah, on 18 June 1758 (both as Purdu), and as 'Purdy' William signed the record book of Hambledon's six-monthly manorial Court Leet and Court Baron on 3 October 1758 and 20 April 1762. If he was the Purdy in the 1769 team, he must surely have been in his forties and the veteran of the side, and therefore a probable survivor from the eleven which faced Dartford in 1756. The younger William is unlikely to have been the cricketer. He was only fifteen at the time and his name does not appear in the town or parish sides of 1773 and 1784 when he should have been nearer his peak. The father died in 1773 (buried 13 February) and according to the next court left a widow, Elizabeth, and son, William, 'about eighteen years of age', as next heir. His widow died in 1784 (buried 7 March) as a copyhold tenant with, as her heir, her son William, who had married Ann Tay or Tee at Hambledon in 1782. There is one other person in the register who might conceivably have been the 1769 Purdy. This is Joseph 'Purdey' from 'Ertham' in Sussex buried in Hambledon churchyard on 3 June 1770. Assuming this was Joseph christened at Eartham on 14 January 1739, he would have been thirty at the time of the Caterham match. His father, the Joseph 'Purdue' who married Elizabeth Palmer in Chichester Palace Chapel on October 9th 1738, had a second son, Richard, baptised at Eartham in 1746. This of course was the home parish of Hambledon's star player, Richard Nyren. So could there have been a cricketing connection between the two families?

According to the 'memoranda' - 'a small manuscript, written some years since by an old cricketer, containing a few hasty recollections and rough hints to players' - incorporated into *The Young Cricketer's Tutor*,

> about the years 1769 and 1770, the Hambledon Club, having had a run of ill-success, was on the eve of being dissolved. It had hitherto been supported by the most respectable gentlemen in that part of the county. They determined, however, once more to try their fortune, and on the 23rd of September 1771, having played the county of Surrey, at Laleham Burway, they beat them

by one run.

The trouble with the above scenario is that the club was then quite successful, at least against Caterham - winning a decider in 1769 and achieving a comfortable victory by about 54 runs in 1770. Furthermore, a year later, on 16 August 1771, the *Gazetteer and Daily Advertiser* reported:

> Tuesday last, after two days sport, ended the grand cricket match at Guildford, between the Hampshire lads, known by the name of the Hambledon Club, and eleven picked men from different counties, when the former were beat by very considerable odds. The Hambledon Club were reckoned the best cricket-players in England, and never beat before. Several thousand pounds were won and lost on this occasion.

Therefore in the late summer of 1771 the Hambledon men were hailed as the best players in England and, until suffering an unexpected reverse at Guildford, had evidently enjoyed a long run of success.

As for the 'most respectable gentlemen' said to be supporting the club at this time, one could have been the 'principal in the Hambledon Club' who umpired a women's match on Rogate Common on June 22nd 1768 and 'was so delighted with their activity that he made them a very genteel offer if they would play on Broad-Halfpenny common, which they likewise agreed to' (Waghorn 1899 p. 65). This was almost certainly George Ridge or his son, Thomas, who played against Caterham in 1769, both already members of the club at the time detailed records begin in 1772. In 1723 George's father became Lord of the Manor of Rogate, which later passed to his brother, Sir Thomas Ridge, who bought another Rogate manor, Fyning, before dying a bankrupt in 1765. Fyning remained in the family though Rogate had to be sold in 1770.

Apart from this we know nothing definite about Hambledon's backers between 1764 and 1772. But needless to say this minor difficulty has failed to deter some historians. Altham claimed that the Revd Charles Powlett was responsible for developing the club after his appointment as curate of Itchen Abbas in 1763, explaining that 'he, Dehaney, and some others of the first known membership were Westminster boys in the forties' so were 'in close touch with the "advanced" London game' and thereby responsible for 'pruning away' certain 'local peculiarities' in the game as played in Hampshire. Why cricket in London should be deemed to be 'advanced' compared to the rest of the country is left unexplained - along with the nature of these 'local peculiarities' and indeed the identity of the 'others' who attended Westminster School in the 1740s. Subsequent scholars have gone on to establish that the club was formed about 1750 by Charles Powlett; in the late 1760s with 'a clear London origin, in that a majority of its founders were former pupils of Westminster School'; during the 1760s by a group of London gentlemen, named as Charles Powlett, Lord Winchilsea, Charles Lennox and J.C. Jervoise; soon after 1763 by Charles Powlett, Philip Dehany and Charles Lennox; and about the same time by Powlett and Dehany, on this occasion managing without Lennox's assistance.[16] As we have already seen in the introduction, another 'authority' maintains that the club was not founded in Hampshire at all but in London!

Although all pretend to be factual accounts, none of the above is based on real evidence. One can only wonder in what other field of historical study would a 'recognised expert' seriously assert that a major club could be established in the mid-1760s by Lord Winchilsea, born in 1752, and Charles Lennox, born in 1764! On current evidence thirteen gentlemen can be positively identified as subscribing to the club before the minutes commence in June 1772:

H. Bonham	C. Powlett	C. Saxton
R. Cotton	J. Richards	B. Shelley
J. Cussans	G. Ridge	P. Taylor
J.T. De Burgh	T. Ridge	R. Turner
P. Dehany		

All were mentioned before 1775 without record of having been elected. Another thirteen who appear slightly later possibly joined during those periods when no minutes were kept or have not survived - lacunae covering almost the whole of 1775, August to September 1776 and June to July 1778. On the other

hand, apart from Samuel Leeke who was then only seventeen, all
may well have been members at the start of the 1772 season:

W. Bennett	P. Griffin	D.R. Karr
Duke of Chandos	J.C. Jervoise	R. Maidman
Lord Dunkellin	T.S. Jolliffe	Lord Northington
G.C. Garnier	W. Jolliffe	W. Skinner

More than half of the twenty-five lived within an easy hour's
ride from Broadhalfpenny Down. Four - Cotton, Richards,
Shelley and Turner - had houses in Hambledon itself. Ten -
George Ridge, Jervoise, Griffin, Garnier, Taylor, Bennett,
Dunkellin, De Burgh, Maidman and probably Skinner -
resided four to six miles away; and seven - Thomas Ridge,
Bonham, Cussans, the Jolliffes, Saxton and Karr - within about
eight miles. Yet none of the key Old Westminsters, except for
Thomas Ridge, was based in any realistic sense 'near'
Hambledon. In order to reach Broadhalfpenny Powlett and
Northington needed to travel about fifteen miles, Dehany
nearer twenty. Moreover in Ridge's case his most significant
old school connections were probably less with Westminster
than with Reynell Cotton's school in Winchester which he
attended in the 1740s (and which, slightly later, was attended
by Henry Bonham). Therefore everything points to
Hambledon being originally a local club, founded by local
gentlemen, and not a club established by former pupils of a
London public school residing fifteen to twenty miles away in
a quite different part of Hampshire.

Chapter Three

REYNELL COTTON'S
CRICKET SONG

The Rev Reynell Cotton, one of the senior and evidently most influential figures in the club, was the first attested president, nominated 'for the ensuing year' on 4 May 1773, and writer of what came to be recognised as the official club song. Baptised at Rudgwick, Sussex, on 16 April 1717, he was the eldest son of the incumbent, the Revd Richard Cotton, who the previous year had married Anne Reynell of Horsham at St Martin-in-the-Fields.[17] He attended Winchester College from 1730 to 1734, entered Corpus Christi, Oxford, in January 1735 and returned to Winchester where he became rector of St Lawrence parish from 1742 to 1768 and later an alderman of the city. Also, during the 1740s, he opened a school, later known as Hyde Abbey School, which he moved into new premises in 1772:[18]

> Winchester, June 17, 1772. The Rev. Mr. Cotton having taken an house in Hyde-street, in the suburbs of Winchester, is obliged to request the favour of a fortnight's holidays extraordinary, in order to prepare it for the safe and commodious reception of his pupils. He flatters himself that its healthy site, extensive outlet, and pleasant retirement, will more than compensate this loss of time.
>
> The new school will be opened on Monday the 20th of July, where (sic) Mr. Cotton will continue to prepare his scholars for the three public schools.

Annual reunions of former pupils were inaugurated two years later:

> The Rev. Cotton's SCHOOL, Winchester
> THE First Annual Meeting of the Gentlemen educated by the Rev. Mr REGNELL (sic) COTTON, is

appointed to be held at the George Inn, in the City of Winchester, on Wednesday, the 21st of September, 1774, when the Favour of the Attendance of all those Gentlemen, who are inclined to support this Institution, is requested.

STEWARDS

Cha. Wolfran Cornwall Esq	Rev. Mr Stephens
Rev. Mr Sturges	Mr John Wool

Tickets to be held at the Bar of the George Inn, at 4s. each - Dinner on Table precisely at Three o'clock.

(Hampshire Chronicle 15 August 1774)

Cotton's Hambledon connection can be traced back to 1751 when he married Susan Baddeley there on 15 June. Possibly Alexander Fitzgerald, son of 'Mr Cotton', baptised at Hambledon on 13 June 1758 was their son. Certainly it was their daughter Lucy - father 'Rev Mr Cotton' - who was christened on 5 October the following year. And perhaps there was a relationship with Leah 'Baddely' who donated 10s 6d to the repair of the church in 1757. Not generally appreciated by historians is that Cotton had his own copyhold house in Hambledon. This explains his regular attendance at club meetings during the summer of 1779 - on 8 June, 20 and 27 July and 3, 10, 17, and 24 August. Sadly, he died three months later on 29 October. The *Hampshire Chronicle* for the 30th reported: 'This morning (sic) died the Rev. Mr. Cotton, for many years the much esteemed master of an eminent grammar school in this city'. Afterwards *The Gentleman's Magazine* referred to him as 'an excellent preceptor and learned divine'. The subsequent sale of his Hambledon house with its contents was advertised a year after his death:

HAMBLEDON, HANTS.

To be SOLD by AUCTION by Mr BINSTEAD, on Thursday, the 15th of June instant, All the HOUSEHOLD GOODS and Furniture lately belonging to the Rev. Mr COTTON, deceased; consisting of four-post and other bedsteads, feather beds, blankets, quilts, glasses, china, books, exceeding good kitchen furniture of all sorts, a very good clock, and some Linen, with the brewing utensils. The sale to begin at eleven o'clock.

Also, on the same day, will be sold by Auction, between the hours of seven and nine in the evening of the above day, the Dwelling-house of the said Mr Cotton, situated in Hambledon aforesaid, consisting of a very good Dwelling house, 4 rooms on a floor; a very good barn, and upwards of three acres of pasture Land, held by a copy under the Lord Bishop of Winchester - For further particulars enquire at the house aforesaid, or of Mr Binstead, auctioneer at Easton, near Winchester.

(Hampshire Chronicle 12 June 1780)

Reynell had a son James who matriculated from his old college in 1769 at the age of seventeen and was apparently the 'Cotton jun' who played for the Gentlemen of Hampshire *v* those of Sussex in 1771 and Hambledon Town *v* Surrey on Broadhalfpenny in 1773 when the *Hampshire Chronicle* announced that 'Mr Bartholomew's notches are backed for a large sum of money against Mr Cotton's'. Cotton managed 0 & 2, his rival 5! James' absence from his father's will suggests he died young, sometime between 1773 and 1778. Reynell was survived by three daughters, Susan, Ann and the mentally unstable Lucy. His will (proved PCC), signed on 19 October 1778, divided his estate between them in equal shares. His friends (and former pupils) Thomas Ridge and Henry Bonham were appointed trustees of Susan's third, his brother-in-law, James Baddeley, gentleman of (Kings?) Worthy, Hampshire, trustee for that of Lucy - 'who is at this time in an insane state of mind' - to be used for her maintenance and only paid to her if she recovered her senses and 'continues in sound and perfect state of mind for a considerable time', and his friend John Smythe of Winchester, 'Doctor of Physic', his sole executor. Next day, the 20th, Susan married a young clergyman, Charles Richards, at St Bartholomew's, Winchester, the five signatories to the marriage settlement (which Reynell styled, 'Articles of Agreement') being Reynell and Susan Cotton, Charles Richards, Thomas Ridge and Henry Bonham. Bonham afterwards acted as trustee of James Baddeley's own will (PCC 1781-83) which left his estate, after his wife Lucy's decease, in trust to the three above-named nieces.

On 29 November 1779 his son-in-law, Charles Richards, advertised in the *Hampshire Chronicle* that he would be taking over as headmaster of Hyde Abbey School. He remained its master for the rest of his days, somehow combining tutorial duties with those of vicar of St Bartholomew's, Winchester, from 1797; rector of Chale, Isle of Wight, from 1806; and prebendary of Winchester and vicar of Wanborough from 1830 until his death on 20 January 1833. His most famous pupil, the future Prime Minister, George Canning, attended Hyde Abbey in the early 1780s. 'Flogging Richards', as he was known from his notoriously strict discipline, was present at Hambledon Club meetings as a non-subscriber on 8 June 1789 and 4 July 1796.[19]

A printed copy of a cricket song written by Reynell Cotton, headed 'Published by order of the Hambledon Club, June 5th, 1781', is in the MCC collection. There is nothing about the order in the minute for this particular meeting but the one for 19 July 1790 reads: 'Ordered that Mr. Cottons Cricket Song be Framed & glazed & hung up in the Cricket Club Room, & one Hundred Copys are printed'. There seems to have been an earlier, but now no longer extant, printing in the 1760s or early 1770s, sufficiently well known for a line from its final verse to be quoted by a newspaper advertising the Hampshire *v* England match at Guildford in 1777: 'The lovers of this noble science will have the opportunity, and perhaps the only one, ("for the heroes of Cricket, like others must die") of seeing all the capital players in England exerting their best endeavours for the amusement of a large and polite assembly'.[20] It was also the basis for a song published in the *Kentish Gazette* of 22 August 1772 to celebrate All England's victory over Hampshire in Bourne Paddock on the 20th. Four verses were altered to fit the home side:

Verse 3: What boasting of Castor and Pollux his brother,
The one famed for riding, for bruising the other;
Their lustre's eclipsed by the lads in the field,
To Minshull and Miller, these brothers must yield.

Verse 11: Minshull, Miller, and Palmer, with Lumpy and May,
Fresh laurels have gained by their conquest today;

Wood, Pattenden, Simmons, with Fuggles and White,
With Boorman will join and will toast them to-night -

Verse 12: With heroes like these even Hampshire we'll drub,
And bring down the pride of the Hambledon Club;
The Duke, with Sir Horace, are men of true merit,
And nobly support such brave fellows with spirit -

Verse 13: Then fill up the glass - he's the best that drinks most, -
The Duke and Sir Horace in bumpers we'll toast;
Let us join in the praise of the bat and the wicket,
And sing in full chorus the patrons of cricket -

The fact that the song appeared in print just two days after close of play is in itself good enough reason for supposing that it had been adapted from an existing work. And that this earlier work had a Hampshire origin may be inferred from the third line in verse 4 - 'Each mate must excel in some principal part' - containing the Hampshire dialect word for a player, a usage employed by the *Hampshire Chronicle* on 1 September 1777 with reference to Fareham 'with two mates' beating Portsmouth, Gosport and the Fleet and in 1788 when a score-sheet of a match at Kingston near Portsmouth included 'Hooper last mate 0' and 'Griffith last mate 1', and by the *Sussex Weekly Advertiser* in 1807, reporting how 'the Gentlemen of the Hambledon Club (with two given mates from Portsmouth)' beat Winchester 'with one given mate from the Mary-le-bonne Club' by 6 runs on Windmill Down.[21] The conventional Hambledon version was published in the *Canterbury Journal*, with acknowledgement to Cotton, on 12 October 1773. The text in its 1781 authorised version, omitting the chorus 'Derry down, &c' to be sung after every verse, reads:

ASSIST all ye Muses, and join to rehearse
An old English Sport, never prais'd yet in Verse;
Tis CRICKET I sing, of illustrious Fame:
No Nation e'er boasted so noble a Game.

Great Pindar hath bragg'd of his Heroes of old,
Some were swift in the Race, some in Battles were bold.
The Brows of the Victor with Olive were crown'd.
Hark, they shout, and Olympia returns the glad Sound.

What boasting of Castor, and Pollux his Brother,
The one fam'd for riding, for bruising the other ?
Compar'd with our Heroes, they'll not shine at all;
What are Castor and Pollux, to NYREN and SMALL ?

Here's guarding and catching, and throwing and tossing,
And bowling and striking, and running and crossing;
Each Mate must excel in some principal Part
The Pentathlon of Greece could not shew so much Art.

The Parties are met, and array'd all in white;
Fam'd Elis ne'er boasted so pleasing a Sight.
Each Nymph looks askew at her favourite Swain,
And views him half stripp'd both with Pleasure and Pain.

The Wickets are pitch'd now, & measur'd the Ground,
Then they form a large Ring, and stand gazing around.
Since Ajax fought Hector, in Sight of all Troy,
No Contest was seen with such Fear and such Joy.

Ye Bowlers take heed, to my Precepts attend;
On you the whole Fate of the Game must depend;
Spare your Vigour at first, nor exert all your Strength,
But measure each Step, and be sure pitch a Length.

Ye Fieldsmen look sharp, lest your pains ye beguile;
Move close like an Army in Rank and in File;
When the ball is return'd, back it sure, for I trow
Whole states have been ruin'd by one overthrow.

Ye Strikers, observe, when the Foe shall draw nigh,
Mark the Bowler advancing with vigilant Eye;
Your skill all depends upon Distance and Sight:
Stand firm to your Scratch, let your Bat be upright.

And now the Game's o'er, lo Victory sings,
Echo doubles her Chorus, and Fame spreads her Wings:
Let's now hail our Champions all steady and true,
Such as Homer ne'er sung of, nor Pindar e'er knew.

BUCK, CURRY, and HOGSFLESH, and BARBER and BRETT,
Whose Swiftness in bowling was ne'er equalled yet;
I had almost forgot, they deserve a large Bumper,
Little GEORGE, the long Stop, and TOM SUETER the Stumper.

Then why should we fear either SACKVILLE or MANN,
Or repine at the Loss of both BAYTON and LAND ?
With such Troops as these, we'll be Lords of the Game,
Spite of MINSHELL and MILLER, and LUMPY and FRAME.

Then fill up your Glass, he's the best that drinks most,
Here's the HAMBLEDON CLUB, who refuses the Toast!
Let's join in the Praise of the Bat and the Wicket,
And sing in full Chorus the PATRONS of CRICKET.

And when the Game's o'er, and our Fate shall draw nigh,
(For the Heroes of Cricket like others must die)
Our Bats we'll resign, neither troubled or vex'd,
And give up our Wickets to those who come next.

Various minor discrepancies occur in other texts, mostly with regard to personal names. For instance Land was also spelt 'Lamb' and 'Lann' (to rhyme with Mann) and Bayton as 'Boynton'. Its recurring emphasis on the works of Homer and Pindar, in verses 2, 3, 4, 5, 6 and 10, is consistent with the scholarly interests of an Oxford-educated headmaster and doubtless reflected the classical curriculum followed at Hyde Abbey School. Yet Cotton was by no means the first, nor the last, to extol cricket's superiority over the games of ancient Elis. The same sentiments were expressed in the epilogue to a play staged in Barrow, Suffolk, in 1744:

Of all the Joys our Parents did Partake,
From Games *Olympic*, down to *Country Wake*;
To one more noble they cou'd ne'er resort
Than CRICKET! CRICKET! ever active Sport.
(J.S. Penny; see Note 29)

And in a challenge from the Medway Volunteers, issued through the pages of the *Maidstone Journal* 12 June 1804, to play 'a game, far superior to the Olympic Games of the Heroes of ancient days'.

For reasons which are not altogether clear the song is sometimes accorded the date 1767. However the surviving text must be slightly later. For instance it refers to the loss of Bayton who played till at least 1769 and features Edward Aburrow alias Curry who, so far as one can tell, became a regular player sometime after 1769. Moreover the line 'Why should we fear either Sackville or Mann' is unlikely to have been penned in 1770 when Sackville (the Duke of Dorset) spent the whole of the year, and part of 1771 too, abroad on the Grand Tour. At the same time the song fails to mention Aylward, one of Hampshire's greatest batsmen, who first appeared in 1773. This narrows the probable date of composition down to 1771 or 1772. So maybe the strange anomaly whereby a work commemorating Hambledon cricket sings the praises not, as one might expect, of eleven players but of a mere nine has to do with those (the very same nine named in the song) who, assisted by Surrey's Yalden and Edmeads, beat England (including Minshull, Miller, Lumpy and Frame) on Broadhalfpenny by 53 runs and at Guildford by 72 runs in June and July 1772.

The identity of Bayton - 'Why should we ... repine at the loss of both Bayton and Land' - is a problem which remains unresolved. A contemporary batsman, whose name was usually entered in the scores as 'Boyton', had a career which, on the face of it, lasted from 1768 to 1776. He hit 8 & 36, the latter out of a total of 36 for 1 (three times the next highest innings in the match), for John Sackville's team *v* Horatio Mann's (5 a side) in the Artillery Ground in 1768 and played for Hambledon *v* Caterham at Guildford in 1769 when 'the utmost activity and skill in the game was displayed by each individual through the whole course of the match, but particularly by the batting of Messrs Small and Boyton on the Hambledon side'. In 1773 he was advertised for Sussex *v* Hambledon, a match cancelled because too few of the Sussex men put in an appearance. In 1776 he made 5 for England *v* Hampshire at Holt Common, near Farnham, and in 1777 (as Boynton) 1 & 13 for England *v* Hampshire on Broadhalfpenny Down.

If only one player was involved, one might deduce that he was a Sussex man who gained sufficient reputation to be chosen to play for the future Duke of Dorset in 1768 and to be recruited by the Hambledon Club by 1769, yet who in or before 1772 withdrew from the club and afterwards, apart from two appearances for England teams, restricted his cricket to local games within his own county. Now, the only Sussex cricketer named Bayton/Boyton whom we can identify with reasonable certainty is John, son of John and Mary Bayton, baptised at West Dean on 1 April 1722, who one assumes must have been the John Boiton of West Dean Warren who assisted Petworth & Midhurst *v* Slindon in 1754. Although rather too old to have been active himself in top-class cricket between the years 1768 and 1777, by his wife Elizabeth he had three sons: John christened on 28 December 1744, George on 29 January 1746 and James on 6 September 1751. The last was presumably the James whose marriage is recorded at Singleton in 1775. But in 1768 he was still only sixteen. His eldest brother might have been the John Bayton living in Hambledon from at least the early 1770s through to the 1790s, listed in directories as a baker and maltster in 1784 and simply as a maltster in 1793. By his wife Sarah (the vicar's daughter) he had three children between 1771 and 1774.[22] However it is hard to understand how the baker could have been the cricketer if he was residing in the village during the 1770s and at the same time being selected for Sussex and England teams against Hampshire. Equally significant is the fact that he was not chosen to play for Hambledon Town *v* Surrey in 1773. Purely on the assumption (and nothing more) that the Bayton of the song was closely related to Bayton/Boiton playing in Sussex in 1754, the only obvious alternative would be the middle brother, George, who was twenty-two when 'Boyton' appeared in the Artillery Ground and thirty-one when he played his last recorded match.

Chapter Four

OUR CHAMPIONS, ALL STEADY AND TRUE

Seven Hambledon players are so designated in the club song and along with the two heroes of the third verse comprise Edward Aburrow, William Barber, Thomas Brett, William Hogsflesh, George Leer, Richard Nyren, John Small, Peter Stewart and Thomas Sueter.

EDWARD ABURROW, one of the main supporting batsmen until his retirement from big cricket in 1782, played in about forty great matches finishing with an average around 10 and a top-score of 49 *v* Surrey on Broadhalfpenny in 1776. According to John Nyren 'he always went by the name of Curry' and was

> one of our best long fields ... being a sure and strong thrower, and able to cover a great space of the field. He was a steady and safe batter, averaging the same number of runs as Lear. We reckoned him a tolerably good change for bowling. Aburrow was a strong and well-made man, standing about five feet nine; he had a plain, honest-looking face, and was beloved by all his acquaintance.

He came originally from Slindon, the son of another Edward who in his day was perhaps an even more famous cricketer.[23] Edward senior appeared under the name Cuddy (a corruption of his alias, Curry) for England *v* Kent in the Artillery Ground match of 1744 immortalised by James Love whose *Cricket: An Heroic Poem* includes the lines: Next, his accomplish'd vigour, C——y tries; whose sheltring hand, the neat-form'd garb supplies' (Book II, 105-6). The family were notorious smugglers, running contraband from across the Channel via the Sussex coast. Edward senior himself spent a term in gaol while his brother, Henry Aburrow of West Meon, was hanged in Winchester about the time of his nephew Edward juniors birth. The following is a brief family tree:

Edward Aburrow alias Curry (Cuddy) married at Slindon
   8 June 1747 Elizabeth Coot
 | —— William bapt Slindon 7 Oct 1750
Edward bapt Slindon 24 March 1748; married at
   Hambledon 11 Oct 1773 Mary Moody, bur 6 March
   1774 after childbirth; married secondly Elizabeth,
   born c1760, died 22 July 1831 aged 71
   (MI Hambledon)
 | —— Molly bapt 3 March 1774
 | —— Ann 1781/Edward Callaway 1782-88/William 1784
 | —— Eliza 1786/Amelia 1789/Louisa 1795/Jane 1796

Along with Richard Nyren and Barber, the younger Edward formed a group of three key players who came from adjoining parishes in Sussex to Hambledon sometime after 1760. In his early teens, with his father again in prison, he must have had a troubled upbringing and it is by no means certain when he arrived in Hambledon, or why - to join relatives (Aburrows had been settled in the parish since the early 18th century), primarily to play cricket, or for some other reason? By 1769 he was already twenty-one, so it is surprising that his name is absent from that year's Hambledon team list. Perhaps he settled in the village only a year or two before his first recorded match in 1772.

According to Haygarth (*S&B* Volume I p 54) he followed the trade of shoemaker. But this is contradicted by Baker who in 1773 said that when Hampshire met England on Sevenoaks Vine the team (including Aburrow) contained four shoemakers whom he named as Barber, Yalden, Stewart and Small. It is fairly certain that his occupation was the same as his father's. On 24 April 1778 Edward Aburrow and Thomas Sueter appeared before the bench charged with 'having in … (their) custody and possession on the 27th February … at Hambledon … one fallow deer which had been unlawfully killed'. Both were found guilty but appealed and at the Quarter Sessions on 14 July their convictions were quashed. It may be noted that one of the JPs was club member the Revd Charles Powlett. Aburrow was then styled 'late of Hambledon' and 'a Taylor'. On the present state of evidence one cannot rule out the possibility that this was Edward senior. But there is no record of his having moved to Hambledon. At the manorial court held on 13 September 1781 Edward surrendered to the Lord of the Manor all his rights in a house or cottage, its surrounding land, a garden and about $^3/_4$ acre of ground to which he had a claim during the lives of Thomas, George and George Russell junior-conceivably acquired through his then recent marriage to Elizabeth (Russell?). In 1786-87 he served as parish constable and in 1790 owned sufficient property in Hambledon to qualify for a vote in the general election. Two years later, when described as a shopkeeper, he, Edward Hale junior and Thomas Pink were appointed joint-trustees and executors of the will of the wealthy village brewer Henry Coles, owner of Richard Nyren's *George Inn*, which they proved in London (PCC) in 1793. The same year a directory described him as a linendraper. Aburrow remained a prominent and respected figure in village life. Several times from 1793 he was an overseer of the poor and in 1824 became a member of the Select Vestry set up to run the parish on more efficient lines.

From his gravestone in Hambledon churchyard Haygarth transcribed the following inscription:

SACRED TO THE MEMORY OF
EDWARD ABURROW
who departed this life
The 6th day of October, 1835,
AGED 88 YEARS.

WILLIAM BARBER, a Sussex man, born at Midhurst in 1734, was apprenticed in 1747 to John Tupper, shoemaker of Graffham, four miles south-east of his native town. Two years after completing his term (assuming the normal seven years) Barber married Jane Birch of Walberton where he settled and worked as a shoemaker for at least six years. During his early to mid-twenties he must have established a reputation as a player in the then heartland of Sussex cricket, around the famous and adjoining parish of Slindon, and if Haygarth (*S&B* Vol I p 34) is correct 'was brought to Horndean by some gentlemen of the Hambledon Club who had seen him perform'. All we know for certain is that he was still living in Walberton on 30 August 1762, the day his third son was baptised in the parish church, but had moved to Hambledon (not Horndean which is in Catherington parish) by the time his daughter Mary was baptised in July 1767. Maybe he was noticed by the Hambledon backers when Hampshire played Sussex in 1766. At any rate he first appears in local records about the time we begin to get regular notices of a Hambledon Club the following summer. Haygarth also says that 'the Brett and Barber families intermarried'. This refers to the marriage of William's eldest son to Sarah Brett, presumably a sister of the bowler Thomas Brett, in 1779. The following is a brief family tree:

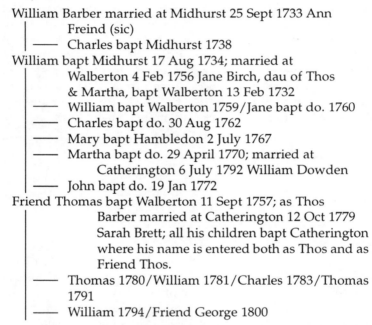

William Barber married at Midhurst 25 Sept 1733 Ann
        Freind (sic)
  —— Charles bapt Midhurst 1738
William bapt Midhurst 17 Aug 1734; married at
        Walberton 4 Feb 1756 Jane Birch, dau of Thos
        & Martha, bapt Walberton 13 Feb 1732
  —— William bapt Walberton 1759/Jane bapt do. 1760
  —— Charles bapt do. 30 Aug 1762
  —— Mary bapt Hambledon 2 July 1767
  —— Martha bapt do. 29 April 1770; married at
        Catherington 6 July 1792 William Dowden
  —— John bapt do. 19 Jan 1772
Friend Thomas bapt Walberton 11 Sept 1757; as Thos
        Barber married at Catherington 12 Oct 1779
        Sarah Brett; all his children bapt Catherington
        where his name is entered both as Thos and as
        Friend Thos.
  —— Thomas 1780/William 1781/Charles 1783/Thomas
        1791
  —— William 1794/Friend George 1800

As a bowler John Nyren coupled William's abilities with those of Hogsflesh, 'both good hands', both bowling with a 'high delivery, keeping a generally good length'. He played for the club till 1777 when he had reached the age of forty-three, latterly doing little with the bat apart from a highest score of 30 *v* Surrey on Broadhalfpenny in 1775. He generally went in last, or near to last, as seemingly the case against Caterham in 1770 when the diarist John Baker noted five Hambledon wickets collapsed for 7 or 8 runs 'but in last Barber and Brett brought it up to 132'. Baker also watched Hampshire, including Barber, against England at Sevenoaks in 1773, and after the match was over he 'walked away about town and called in on one Clouts a famous cricket-ballmaker, where Barber with whom some talk. (Said he was a shoemaker, so on the Hants side four shoemakers, vis. Barber, Small, Buck Stewart, Yaldon)'.

In or soon after 1771 Barber replaced Richard Nyren at the *Hut* (now the *Bat and Ball Inn*) overlooking the cricket ground at Broadhalfpenny where he acted as groundsman (compare the minute of 1773 that he 'shall take care that the Down is prepared'). The club paid the cost of his wine licence and built a 'bin' in his cellar, he in turn having responsibility for returning empty bottles to Mr Smith the wine merchant in Winchester. He and Richard Nyren set up booths for matches on Broadhalfpenny, and when a game was arranged on Kilmiston Down in 1775 Barber advertised that he would 'pitch several tents on the Down, where wines & provisions of all sorts may be had at the most reasonable rates'. For a while he had the task of hounding recalcitrant members for their arrears in subscription, being allowed ls 6d in the pound for all money collected.

Since his house stood just over the boundary in Catherington it is by no means certain that he would have been able to represent Hambledon parish during the 1770s. This may be why he was advertised for Hambledon Town *v* Surrey in 1773 but in the event did not play. However in 1776 'the famous Messrs. Small, Brett & Barber' appeared for Petersfield & Catherington *v* Alresford on Tichborne Down. In the early 1780s, after cricket was switched away from Broadhalfpenny to Windmill Down, he left the inn and moved to Horndean, a village on the main Portsmouth-London road. He died there in 1805 aged seventy-one and was buried in Catherington churchyard on September 10th.

THOMAS BRETT formed one of the Hambledon XI in 1769 when, to judge by his gravestone, he must have been about twenty-two. Three years later, for Hampshire *v* England in Bourne Paddock, near Canterbury, he bowled at one end while four took turns from the other, the *Kentish Gazette* (22 August 1772) reporting that 'Brett was much the best and swiftest bowler in the field'. At the beginning of the 1773 season he received an injury playing for Five of Hampshire *v* Five of England in the Artillery Ground and this affected his form when he returned to the ground for an eleven a side match between the same teams on 2-3 July. It was then noted that the Hampshire bowlers were out of luck and condition, the *Hampshire Chronicle* explaining that 'the reason Hants lost was owing to Mr. Brett's having received a violent blow from the ball when the last match of the five was played'. Doubtless this was a factor in Hampshire's subsequent poor season. However he was soon back to his best and in some thirty matches bowled more than one hundred wickets for Hampshire (his nearest rival, Richard Nyren, taking slightly fewer in about fifty), including seven clean bowled in one innings against Surrey at Laleham Burway in 1775. According to Haygarth (*S&B* Vol I p 39) he

> resided at Catherington, about five miles from Hambledon, where he had a farm called Fine Heads Farm, which had been in possession of his ancestors for many years. In 1857, however, no one of his name lived there, though in his time the family was so numerous 'that it ruled the village'. He seems to have left his native place for Portsmouth, that being perhaps the reason he left off playing for the Hambledon Club so young, being (in 1779) then but 31 years of age.

Not all of this can be true. There is no record of his baptism at Catherington but he married twenty-three-year-old Olive Collins (baptised 8 August 1750, the daughter of Edward and Deborah) there on Christmas Day 1773 and had a succession of children christened in the parish church: Mary 1774, Elizabeth 1777, Olive 1778, Anne 1780, Thomas 1781, Sarah 1783, Humphrey 1785, Jenny 1787. Then, on 26 October 1789, he married again, having taken out a Winchester licence in which he is described as a gentleman of Catherington aged twenty-one, his bride, Elizabeth Wheeler, as a twenty-year-old minor, marrying with the consent of her father, James, and brother, John Wheeler. His stated age signifies twenty-one or more, that is to say of full age. However, since Elizabeth's baptism is recorded at Catherington on 5 January 1774, her real age was almost certainly fifteen. Her mother, who married James Wheeler in 1764, was Ann Brett baptised at Catherington in 1745 thus doubtless a sister or at least a close relative of the cricketer. Therefore the probably forty-two-year-old Thomas and fifteen-year old Elizabeth must have been uncle and niece or else cousins. Furthermore only ten weeks after their wedding his young wife was delivered of a daughter, christened Sukey at Catherington on 3 January 1790. It was only then, after the birth of their child, and not, as suggested by Haygarth, around 1780 that he moved to the Portsmouth area. A number of Thomas and Elizabeth's children were baptised at Portsea - John in 1793, followed by Frances 1796, Henry 1798 and Maria 1801. Sukey Brett married John Sansom at Portsea on 13 March 1809, and Thomas, his eldest son, married Lydia White there in 1804 and had several children of his own. Haygarth transcribed the following from Thomas Brett senior's tombstone in Kingston churchyard near Portsmouth:

SACRED TO THE MEMORY OF
THOMAS BRETT,
Who Died December 31, 1809,
AGED 62 YEARS

WILLIAM HOGSFLESH, described by John Nyren as a 'good hand', a change bowler with 'a high delivery, and a generally good length, not very strong however, at least for those days of playing, when the bowling was all fast', was a native of Hambledon, baptised in the church on 11 November 1744, who played for Hampshire until 1775. His father, Francis, was born there in 1706 and was buried at parish expense on 13 September 1785. William had a younger brother, Francis junior (born 1746), who married Mary Lankester at Portsea in 1767 and lived in Hambledon until about 1776 when the churchwardens and overseers of nearby Boarhunt accepted his settlement along with his wife and four children - Mary aged about five, Francis four, Sarah two and William one - all born in Hambledon. William retired from county cricket when still only thirty. If he was the William who married Mary Bailey at Portsea in 1774 and then settled in the Portsmouth area he was probably the Hogsflesh named by the *Hampshire Chronicle* as one of the two bowlers for a combined Portsmouth, Gosport and the Fleet XI which lost to Fareham at Fratton in 1777. But on present evidence this could equally well have been William Hogsflesh born in Gosport in 1750. However he was mentioned, rather belatedly and with his name misspelt, by the anonymous author of *The Noble Cricketers* (1778), satirising the Duke of Dorset and Lord Tankerville, who wrote that 'I am inform'd that you [Dorset and Tankerville] have got a fresh cargo of bats and balls, and that Lumpy, Small, Horseflesh (sic), with several other equally respectable personages, are order'd to prepare their shins for another campaign'. According to Haygarth (*S&B* vol I p. 23) he lived latterly at Southwick, the parish adjoining Hambledon to the south, and was buried there on 29 April 1818 aged seventy-four (sic).

GEORGE LEER is said to have been a native of the parish, yet the registers contain few references to a Leer or Lear family and his absence from the team list *v* Caterham in 1769 suggests that he arrived in Hambledon when already in his early twenties. On the other hand, a few miles away at Warblington a Thomas Lear (born 1702, the son of George) had a daughter Martha in 1733, a son John in 1742 and another son, George, baptised on 1 April 1746. Was this the cricketer? If so it means he dropped out of the first-class game in 1782 at thirty-six, not as supposed at thirty-three. He played for Hampshire in 1772 and was featured in Hambledon's club song, almost certainly written the same year, as 'Little George' - the soubriquet used by John Nyren who describes him as 'our best long stop':

So firm and steady was he, that I have known him stand through a whole match against Brett's bowling, and not lose more than two runs. The ball seemed to go into him, and he was as sure of it as if he had been a sand bank. His activity was so great, and, besides, he had so good a judgment in running to cover the ball, that he would stop many that were hit in the slip, and this, be it remembered, from the swiftest bowling ever known. The portion of ground that man would cover was quite extraordinary. He was a good batsman, and tolerably sure guard of his wicket; he averaged from fifteen to twenty runs, but I never remember his having a long innings. What he did not bring to the stock by his bat, however, he amply made up with his perfect fielding. Lear was a short man, of a fair complexion, well looking, and of a pleasing aspect. He had a sweet counter tenor voice. Many a treat have I had in hearing him and Sueter join in a glee at the 'Bat and Ball', on Broad-Halfpenny.

He also recounts how, when Noah Mann was fielding 'behind the long-stop, that he might cover both long-stop and slip',

> now and then little George Lear ... would give Noah the wink to be on his guard, who would gather close behind him; then George would make a slip, on purpose, and let the ball go by, when in an instant Noah would have it up, and into the wicket-keeper's hands, and the man was put out.

His batting average was actually nearer 14. He scored more than 1,000 runs with three half-centuries for Hampshire - 79 *v* Kent on Broadhalfpenny in 1775, 69 *v* England at Laleham Burway in 1777 and 58 *v* England, again on Broadhalfpenny, in 1779. Also he hit 53 for England *v* Kent at Bishopsbourne in 1781. John Nyren calls him George Lear, which was the standard form in press notices of the period, also in parish records. But George seems to have adopted the spelling 'Leer' by the time he witnessed a marriage in Hambledon on 13 November 1775. He also signed as 'George Leer' at Hambledon on 7 August 1780 when he married Martha, the twenty-five-year-old daughter of Robert Taylor, by banns. No children are recorded in the registers, though a George and Martha 'Lears' had a son, George, christened at Buriton in 1787 (the G. Leer who about twenty-five years later appeared as a paid player for the new Hambledon club?). Haygarth (*S&B* Vol I p 55) states that he became a brewer in the next parish, Petersfield, but after his death on 1 February 1812 he was buried back in Hambledon churchyard where his gravestone gives his age as sixty-three (in fact sixty-five?).

RICHARD NYREN is one of the best documented cricketers of his era. Yet his family origins and early and final years have been veiled in mystery, myth and even deliberate obfuscation. As recently as 1987, Dr. Teresa McLean, a leading Oxford-educated sports historian still felt justified in claiming that Richard was the grandson of a Jacobite involved in the 1715 rising and son of another concerned in the one of 1745. This unthinkingly repeats a family tradition to the effect that the name was originally spelt 'Nairne' and that Richard was the son of a Jacobite Lord Nairne who died in exile in France in 1770 - a myth finally laid to rest (for serious historians at least) through the researches of Edmund Esdaile who in the 1960s established that Nyren (in its variant spellings: Nieren, Nyeringe, Niringe, etc) was an old Sussex name and that Richard was baptised at Eartham on 25 April 1734, the son of Richard senior who (as 'Niering') married Susan Newland on 3 January 1733. Susan's brother was the celebrated cricketer, Richard Newland, who kept a farm in the adjoining parish of Slindon and whose influence on the young Richard Nyren was noted by *his* son, John:

> He owed all the skill and judgment he possesed to an old uncle, Richard Newland, of Slindon, in Sussex, under whom he was brought up - a man so famous in his time, that when a song was written in honour of the Sussex cricketers, he was especially and honourably signalized. No man ever dared to play him.

The implication seems to be that Richard spent a few years living with his uncle (a widower and childless by 1745). However the fact that he came originally from Eartham has not prevented a photograph of The Grange, a grand house in Slindon, appearing in Mote's history of Hambledon cricket as the 'probable birthplace of Richard Nyren'.

More recent research by Roger Packham has confirmed, through a property notice in the *Sussex Weekly Advertiser* (19 June), that the Eartham connection was still maintained in the year 1758:

TO BE LETT OR SOLD

A Messuage or Tenement, Barns, Stables and other Conveniences thereto belonging, fifty-six Acres of Land, and One Hundred and Sixty Sheep Leases,

situate, lying and being in the parish of Eartham in the County of Sussex, and now in the Occupation of Richard Nyren.
Enquire of Mr John Boniface, of Eastergate; or George Woodall, Attorney, at Arundel, for further particulars.

This Richard was presumably the father. On 11 November following, his son, the cricketer, married Frances Pennycud in Eartham church. She was formerly a Quaker but afterwards a convert to Catholicism, perhaps due to her acquaintance (while in service?) with Barbara (c1720-97), Countess of Newburgh, whose family employed its own Roman Catholic priest at Slindon. A descendant, Miss Mary Nyren, informed E.V. Lucas that the Countess 'gave her a large prayer book, in which the names of her children were afterwards inscribed'.

Almost a year later, in September 1759, the twenty-five-year-old Richard Nyren made his first known appearance on a cricket field, playing as Nyland of Sussex for England against Dartford on Dartford Brent and at Laleham Burway. All we know about his play comes from John Nyren, writing a full seventy years later - the fact that he was left-handed (like his illustrious uncle), that he was 'a safe batsman and an excellent hitter', that, bowling with 'a high delivery', his balls were 'always to the length and provokingly deceitful', and that 'although a very stout man (standing about five feet nine) he was uncommonly active'.

It has always been assumed that he was originally a farmer. This is implied by John who calls him 'the proud old yeoman' and relates that he 'never saw a finer specimen of the thorough-bred old English yeoman than Richard Nyren'. He certainly came from farming stock. But there are reasons for believing (see below) that he may have been apprenticed to a baker. At all events, probably in the early 1760s he left his native county to become landlord of the inn, then known as the *Hut* (now the *Bat and Ball*), overlooking Broadhalfpenny Down, also, it is said, taking over a small farm. Soon afterwards he commenced a twenty-five-year-long career catering for Hambledon's home matches, hence his notice in the *Salisbury Journal* for 1 July 1782 advertising 'Kent, with Lumpey and Bedster, against England' (not Hambledon Club) on Stoke Down:

> Provisions, wines, tea, coffee, &c will be found in great plenty, as usual, at Nyren's. - He begs leave to return his warmest thanks to the public for the many favours he has received during the last twenty years, and hopes to be farther honoured on the 10th of July with the countenance and protection of all those Ladies and Gentlemen who wish to encourage the noble game of Cricket.

Richard's family raised initially at the *Hut* comprised John, the future cricket writer (born 15 December 1764); Richard, the father of a later John (died 1859) and grandfather of Richard Plantagenet Nyren of Caterham; William Laurence, buried at Hambledon on 8 May 1773; and four daughters, including Susan and Frances. Susan married Charles Farmer in an Anglican wedding at Hambledon on 24 August 1780, with Peter Stewart, presumably the cricketer, one of the witnesses, and on 21 November 1782 her parents stood as godparents to her daughter, Frances, baptised a Catholic at Horndean. Frances went through two marriages with William Silver on successive days in 1784 - a Catholic ceremony at Gosport on 26 December and an Anglican one at St Mary's, Portsmouth, on the 27th, and had daughters Henrietta (whose godmother was John's wife Cleopha Nyren) in 1794, Charlotte in 1796, Louisa in 1798 and Louisa in 1799, all christened at Portsea.

In October 1770 Richard was still at the *Hut* when the diarist John Baker dined 'at Nyren's house' on Broadhalfpenny. Sometime within the next two years he moved down into the centre of the village to take over the *George Inn*, possibly succeeding Henry Coles, a former landlord who seems to have bought the house when it came up for auction at the inn itself on 7 March 1768 as

> a commodious well brickt house with cellars to contain large quantities of liquor; a good kitchen, two parlours, a barr, and brew-house on the ground floor; five chambers and a dining room on the second floor with

garrets over them; two good stables with large hay-lofts, besides other convenient buildings; a good garden walled round and well planted with choice fruit-trees now in their prime.

It was in the dining room on the upper floor of the *George* where Richard Nyren used to hold annual cricket club dinners, such as the one advertised in the *Hampshire Chronicle* in 1773:

Cricket. A meeting is requested of the Gentlemen of the HAMBLEDON CLUB, at the GEORGE INN, at Hambledon, on Friday the First of October next, on Special Affairs. Dinner to be on Table at Three o'Clock.
Hambledon, Aug. 29. R. NYREN

And by 1779 he was combining innkeeping with another (his original?) trade. On June 19th his own landlord, Henry Coles, took out a Sun Life policy on the *George* 'in the tenure of Richard Nyren innkeeper & baker' - a dual occupation confirmed by a 1784 directory listing him as innkeeper and baker of Hambledon. He also held auctions there, like the one in 1777 of an estate at Boarhunt 'to be sold by auction, on Friday the 4th of July next, at the house of Richard Nyren, bearing the sign of the George, in Hambledon ... between the hours of two and four o'clock' (*Hampshire Chronicle* 23 June) and by 1793 had become the village post-master, as evidenced by his entry in that year's *Universal British Directory*: 'Richard Nyren @ George Inn (Excise and P.O.)'.

Very much the mainstay of the cricket team, for Hampshire Richard Nyren was credited with almost 100 wickets (in his own era bettered only by the much younger Thomas Brett) and about 1,000 runs at an average of 13, higher than anyone of his generation apart from John Small. His biggest score was 98 against Surrey in 1775. Moreover 'he was the chosen general of all the matches, ordering and directing the whole', and, it seems, in later years when no longer a regular player, continuing to act as captain from the boundary edge (see chapter 11, under Noah Mann). As secretary he also took a hand in the club's day-to-day affairs, inserting notices in the newspapers in this capacity in 1779:

The Members of the Hambledon Club are desired to

take Notice that the Meeting will be held on the 15th of June on Stoke Down, near the Grange. By order of the Stewards, R.Nyren, Secretary.

(*Hampshire Chronicle* 7 June)

and in 1788:

The Members of the Hambledon Club are earnestly desired to attend on Windmill Down on Tuesday, the 19th inst. N.B - The Venison will be on the Table at three of the Clock. - R.Nyren, Secretary.

(*Hampshire Chronicle* 18 August)

It is generally believed that, having reached the age of fifty-seven, Nyren sold up and departed the village. In Goldsmith we read that when he 'left Hambledon in 1791 the old club virtually broke up' but 'lingered on for another five years', while Mote declares that he moved to London in 1791, played cricket there and died in 1797 when his widow, Frances, returned to Hambledon to live in a cottage provided by her son John. To support this sequence of events it is maintained that he received a going-away present in the form of a five-inch-long model bat inscribed 'Richard Nyren - from old friends, *Bat & Ball* Hambledon. Sept 4th 1791'. According to an article which appeared in *The Cricketer* for 14 August 1937, the bat then belonged to the collector G.N.Weston of Kidderminster, although its later (1997) whereabouts are said to be unknown. It is therefore impossible to say whether the bat is genuinely old or, alternatively, a collectable produced to satisfy a more recent demand in the cricketana market. Nor is it possible to explain why the inscription mentions the *Bat and Ball Inn* when by 1791 Richard Nyren had been living for about twenty years at the *George*!

In any case, Nyren remained in Hambledon for several more years. Local records refer to his financial transactions with the parish overseers on 5 December 1792, 17 November 1794 and 6 April 1795. Three months later, in July 1795, he inserted a notice (which interestingly included the above wording, 'old friends') in the *Portsmouth Gazette*:

... Nyren begs leave to inform the Lovers of Cricket, that all sorts of Liquors and cold Provisions may be found at his Booth on the Down; and as the finest Players in England are engaged in this Match [Lord Winchilsea's v R. Leigh's XI], his old Friends, he trusts, will not forsake him, as they may expect to see the game played in the highest style of preference.

And that October the newspaper announced a subscribers' meeting at 'the house of Richard Nyren'. According to the club accounts, next year, on 4 July, the sum of 10 guineas was 'Paid Nyren'. And beneath an entry for 29 August 1796, alongside the sum of £33 2s is written 'By paid Nyren as on the other leaf'. The final entry in the minute book is for 21 September, so if his son John is correct he must have moved away not long after this date: 'When Richard Nyren left Hambledon the club broke up, and never resumed from that day. The head and right arm were gone'. It seems he only survived for a matter of months: a maternal grandson informed Haygarth (*S&B* Vol I p 3) that he died at Lee or Leigh in Kent on 25 April 1797 (Ashley-Cooper recorded that the death occurred at Leeds in Kent). Unfortunately Haygarth failed to locate a burial in either of the parish registers and so far no one has been able to verify the date. This leaves certain questions unanswered. Could the date or place be wrong? If not why did he leave for a distant village in Kent shortly before his death? Why was Haygarth's informant unable to say where his grandfather was actually buried? Could there be a confusion with the Lee and Leigh to the south of Hambledon? Did Nyren's departure have to do with his son John's removal from Portsea to London the same year?[24]

JOHN SMALL, linked with Richard Nyren in Cotton's song - 'What are Castor and Pollux to Nyren and Small' - was the great celebrity of the old eleven, one of those whose fame extended well beyond the cricketing counties of the South East. Thus in 1787 the *Leicester Journal* alluded to a local player as having 'gained as much fame as will contemporize his name with the Small's and Lumpy's of the day'. Concerning the Hambledon batsmen, John Nyren declared that 'the name of John Small, the elder, shines among them in all the lustre of a star of the first magnitude', while the less well informed author of *The Noble Cricketers*, who imagined his first name was

Sam, called him 'that wond'rous wight, yclep'd SAM SMALL' and urged the Duke of Dorset, 'degenerate dwindled to a cricket player',

> If the low sordid fame of cricketer,
> Your Grace, to nobler titles can prefer
> Yield up your native honours, yield 'em all,
> Then go, and reign the rival of SAM: SMALL.

This famous cricketer was the son of John Small who married Anne Turner at Empshott on 13 April 1735. He was born in that parish on 19 April 1737 (and baptised on the 26th) and when about six moved with his family five miles to Petersfield where he remained for the rest of his long life. Although doubtless taking part in neighbouring matches from the 1750s it looks as if he only began to play for Hambledon at the age of thirty - that is assuming that he was one of the 'two hands from Hampshire' who for the club against Caterham in 1767 'kept in three hours and a half and got 192 notches, the greatest thing ever known'. The following year he was mentioned by name for the first time. After beating 'eleven gentemen of the county of Kent' by over 100 runs it was observed that 'what is very remarkable, one Mr Small, of Petersfield, fetched above seven score notches off his own bat' (*Reading Mercury* 5 September 1768), while a week later a report ran:

> Last Monday another great match at cricket was played on Broadhalfpenny between eleven gentlemen of the county of Sussex against eleven of the Hambledon Club for a large sum, which was won by the latter, who had seven wickets to go down. Mr Small got above four score notches in this match, and was not out when the game was finished.
>
> (*Reading Mercury* 12 September 1768)

Against Caterham at Guildford in 1769 his and Boyton (Bayton)'s batting was singled out for special praise, and after Hampshire faced England in Bourne Paddock in 1772 the *Kentish Gazette* commented that Small's great success has crowned him the ablest batsman' and 'Lumpy had the honour of bowling out Small, which we are informed, had not been done for some years'. Then, when he made 38 & 136 not out *v* Surrey on Broadhalfpenny in 1775 the *Kentish Post* reckoned that 'Small must stand the best cricketer the world ever produced'. In the corresponding match the following year he scored 85.

It has been calculated that from 1772 to 1798, in what would now be termed 'first-class cricket' he totalled 3,357 runs, with ten half centuries as well as his 136, at an average of 16.70. This does not of course take into account the big scores made earlier when possibly at his peak. Sometimes there were wagers on his runs. Against Kent, Middlesex & Surrey on Broadhalfpenny in 1772 £500 was reportedly laid against Minshull in Small's favour 'when the former was beat by a very great majority, to the surprise of all present'. In the Surrey match on Broadhalfpenny the following year 'a very large sum' was 'depending between the batting of Miller and Small', and against Surrey on the same ground in 1776 'considerable sums' were laid on Small, Miller and Minshull's runs, though in the event neither of the last two played.

A memoir by Samuel Maunder published in 1827 observed that Small was considered the surest batsman of his day, and as a fieldsman 'was decidedly without an equal'. According to John Nyren 'he was the best short runner of his day, and indeed I believe him to have been the first who turned the short hits to account. His decision was as prompt as his eye was accurate in calculating a short run' But he has little else to say about his batting except that,with respect to shortish deliveries to the off,

> Old Small, one of the finest batsmen of his own day and perhaps of any other, always played such balls with an upright bat; he would pass his left foot across the wicket and this action gave him power and command over the ball. The upper edge of his bat was turned slightly back towards the wicket. The whole motion was performed by the wrists and arms and I never saw any batter who could use his wrists like this admirable old man.

John Nyren adds that 'he was an admirable field's-man,

always playing middle wicket … a remarkably well-made and well-knit man, of honest expression, and as active as a hare'. So correct was his judgment of the game', we are told, 'old Nyren would appeal to him when a point of law was being debated. Indeed, both appear to have captained the side in 1777 when the *Hampshire Chronicle* noted how, against twenty-two of Liphook, the superior 'skill of Small and Nyren in managing the field gave the victory to the Hambledon Club'.

He was also one of those who retained top form well beyond the normal span. At fifty-one, in a six a side match at Lord's in 1787, when described as 'the Ulysses of his party', he 'batted with great coolness and judgment' in making his team's highest score of 9. And after being out for 0 in the second innings, when 'the ball ran up his bat and so hit his wicket', one newspaper report followed his score with an exclamation mark. Next season in 'A Grand Alphabetical Match', again at Lord's, it was observed that the 'system which the new school have adopted appeared to most advantage in the hands of T. Walker and Small senior; the old school in Booker's who got 12 notches in 3 strokes'. Small made 43 runs in total, the most for his side, Walker 25. Two years after that, at fifty-four, he top-scored with 48 for Hampshire *v* Surrey on Moulsey Hurst.

In the late 1750s he married and had several daughters who died young - Dinah 1760-71, Ann 1762-66 and Ann c1774-76 - and two sons, John (see chapter 11) in 1764 and Eli in 1767. His wife Ann, who died on 22 November 1802 aged sixty-three, was also a cricket enthusiast. This is John Nyren's account:

> She, I think, took as much delight and interest in the game as he. Many's the time I have seen that worthy woman (every way deserving of so kind and excellent a husband) come galloping up the ground at a grand match, where he was to play (for … she always accompanied him to those high solemnities), and no player even could show more interest in the game than she, and certainly no one, as was natural, felt so much pride in her husband's fine playing.

John Baker in 1773 noted that he followed the trade of shoemaker. But a 1784 directory has John Small of Petersfield as 'salesman and haberdasher' consistent with the entry in Lord Winchilsea's account book for 14 August 1789 which reads: 'Small for breeches for cricketers 6 gns'. He also became famous for making cricket bats and balls and in the 1790s supplied equipment to the Hambledon Club whose outgoings in 1793 include the item: 'Paid Small for Batts & Balls 3 7 0'. In 1798 Winchilsea 'paid Small for Batts £1 10s.'

In 1783 Mrs Susanna Beckford, mother of club member Francis Love Beckford, appointed him gamekeeper to her manor about five miles north of Petersfield, according to Samuel Maunder:

> He held the deputation of the Manor of Greatham and Foley for many years, as game-keeper under Madame Beckford, and retained it under her son and successor, till the property was parted with, which did not happen till Small was nearly seventy years of age; yet, such was his strength and activity at that time of life, that before he began his day's amusement, he regularly took his tour of seven miles, frequently doing execution with his gun, which to relate would appear almost incredible.

From Maunder we also learn that Small was 'an excellent sportsman, and capital shot', equally famous for his prowess as an ice-skater among 'those who have witnessed his evolutions on Petersfield Heath Pond'. Moreover 'even during the last three or four years of his life he took the most active exercise as a sportsman, and frequently followed the hounds on foot'. His other interests included music:

> ... though we cannot say that his excellence as a musician was equal to his excellence as a cricketer, still, among his compeers he was pre-eminent; and, we have no doubt, that to the soothing power of music he was not a little indebted for the equanimity of temper he possessed, and the tranquil delight he felt in the company of his friends - for those who knew him can conscientiously declare that no man was more remarkable for playful wit, cheerful conversation, or inoffensive manners.

So early did he display his taste for music, that at fourteen years of age, he played the bass at Petersfield choir, of which choir he continued a member about seventy-five years, having performed on the tenor violin there within the last twelve months, and that too without the aid of spectacles. After what has been said it will not be a matter of surprise to hear that Mr. Small was highly respected by all the gentlemen who patronized cricket; and, as they knew nothing could gratify him more, they frequently joined in a concert with his musical friends after cricket was over for the day.

His two surviving sons, John and Eli, not only inherit his love for the game, but the first mentioned particularly excels in it, and both are equally celebrated for their musical attainments; indeed, during their father's life this musical trio ranked high among the performers at all the amateur concerts in the neighbourhood.

... he was not merely a player on the violin-cello and violin, ... he was both a maker and a mender of them! with pleasure should we descant on his mechanical, as well as his musical skill, and show that his proficiency in each, was the result of his own untutored ingenuity, proving that he had a natural genius for fiddle-making, as, well as for bat and ball-making. We should bring proof that he once made a violincello, aye, and a right good one too, which he sold for two guineas - nay, we should further prove, that the old instrument which his son, the present John Small, plays on at church every Sunday, (made by Andria Weber, Genoa, 1713) was thoroughly repaired by him, and an entire new belly put thereto ...

Samuel Maunder further relates how

In his younger days, Mr. Small was in the habit of attending balls and concerts; sometimes contributing to the delight of the gay votaries of Te[r]psichore - at others forming one of the instrumental band, which met for the gratification of himself and his amateur friends. Returning one evening with a musical companion from a concert in the neighbourhood, they were rather suddenly saluted, when in the middle of a large field, by a *bull*, who, in no very gentle mood, gave them reason to believe that, to insure their safety, they must either hit upon some expedient to allay his rage, or make a hasty retreat. Mr. Small's companion adopted the latter plan; but our hero ... boldly faced him, and began to play a lively tune. Scarcely had the catgut vibrated, when the bull suddenly stopped, and listened with evident signs of pleasure and attention. The skilful master of the bow, felt a secret satisfaction on discovering so unquestionable a proof of the influence of sweet sounds; and, continuing to play, while he gradually retreated towards the gate, quietly followed by the bull, he there gave his quadruped auditor an example of his agility by leaping over it, and unceremoniously left him to bewail the loss of so agreeable a concert.

And how

... in a five-of-a-side match, played in the Artillery-ground, he got seventy-five runs at his first innings, and went in the last mate for seven runs, which it is hardly necessary to say, were soon scored. On this occasion, the Duke of Dorset being desirous of complimenting him for his skill, and knowing that Small was as passionately fond of music as he was of cricket, he made him a present of a fine violin, which he played upon many years, and which is now made use of by his grandson.

Concerning the last, in John Nyren's book we read that Small 'was a good fiddler' who also 'taught himself the double bass' and the Duke 'having been informed of his musical talent, sent him as a present a handsome violin, and paid the carriage', whereupon 'Small, like a true and simple-hearted Englishman, returned the compliment by sending his Grace two bats and balls, also *paying the carriage'*.

His death occurred in December 1826. Shortly afterwards the Revd White, curate of Empshott, entered into his diary: 'Small the celebrated cricketer died'. His inscription in Petersfield churchyard reads:

SACRED TO THE MEMORY OF
JOHN SMALL,
Who died December 31, 1826,
AGED 89 YEARS.
Praises on tombs are trifles spent,
A man's good name is his own monument.

while his memoir ends with Maunder's suggested epitaph, 'an unlabored composition of quaint simplicity, just such a one as the parish clerk himself would indite':

Here lies, bowl'd out by DEATH's unerring ball,
A CRICKETER renowned, by name JOHN SMALL;
But though his name was *small*, yet *great* his fame,
For nobly did he play the 'noble game'.
His *life* was like his *innings* - long and good;
Full ninety summers he had DEATH withstood,
At length the *ninetieth* winter came - when (Fate
Not leaving him one solitary *mate*.)
This last of *Hambledonians*, old JOHN SMALL,
Gave up his BAT and BALL - his LEATHER, wax and all.

The author, who refers to his subject as 'our old friend John Small' – 'whose exploits were once the theme of universal praise' - also wrote *The Game of Life*; or, *Death among the Cricketers* (also published in 1827) in which he describes cricket as 'my favourite sport'. However the allusion to Small as 'this last of Hambledonians' and an introduction which states that 'the whole of the Hambledon club have now been bowled down by death' overlooks Tom Sueter who outlived Small by about six weeks and Edward Aburrow of the 'old eleven' who survived until 1835.[25]

PETER STEWART appears in the club song simply as Buck and in some old scores as Buckstewart or Bucksteward. Likewise in 1773 Baker, in noting that along with several other players he followed the occupation of shoemaker, called him Buck (not Peter) Stewart. Reviewing John Nyren's book in *The*

Gentleman's Magazine in 1833 the Revd John Mitford assumed that he acquired this nickname 'from his spruceness'. Although this proves that the OED is wrong in saying that this usage only became current about a hundred years ago, in the 18th century the word usually denoted someone with spirit, a merry lively person, as in *The Jovial Cricketters* published in *The Canterbury Journal* on 14 May 1776:

> Ye bucks and ye bloods, from the field now return'd,
> Come taste of the liquor so playfully earn'd;
> I'll give you a toast: May each cricketers name,
> For honour stand high in the annals of fame.

So quite likely he was 'Buck' because he was regarded as the village wag, consistent with John Nyren's story concerning what the minutes for 1773 call 'the machine to convey the cricketers to distant parts'. While travelling to an away match the 'caravan' (as Nyren terms it) overturned and Buck 'refused to come out, desiring that they would right the vessel with him in it, for that 'one good turn deserved another'. This repartee was admired for a week'.

Although never credited with a wicket, he was employed as a change bowler in 1772 when the *Kentish Gazette* of 22 August noted how, against England in Bourne Paddock, 'the bowlers for Hampshire were Brett, and at the opposite wicket Hogsflesh, Currey, Barber, and Buck Steward'. Nyren recalls that his usual place was in the long field where he

> was a steady man at his post; his batting, too, reached the same pitch of excellence; he would cut balls very hard at the point of the bat ... Buck was a dark-looking man, a shoemaker by trade, in height about five feet eight, rather slimly built, and very active.

Yet apart from his 31 *v* Surrey on Broadhalfpenny in 1773 the surviving scores (those from 1772 onwards) never credit Stewart with an innings of more than 15. The truth is that these were the twilight years of a long, and in the past presumably more successful, career. Christened at Hambledon on 26 July 1730, he was one of the youngest of the many children of Archibald Stewart who apparently came from Scotland in the early 1700s (one of Buck's brothers was Archibald Douglas

Stewart). In the baptismal register his surname is entered as Suard. It was also spelt Steward - by, among others, John Nyren himself. He appears again in the registers in 1757, witnessing the marriage of William Arnold and Elizabeth Luff on 16 May. And on 29 May 1765 he married Mary Goldsmith by a licence from the Bishop of Winchester which describes him as a bachelor of Hambledon, Mary as a spinster of the same, both aged twenty-one. This means of full age, twenty-one or over. Mary was actually thirty, having been born in 1734, and baptised on New Year's Day 1735. They had three children: Mary baptised on 13 April 1766, James on 15 January 1768 and Peter on 26 January 1770. Sadly, his wife died not long after the final birth and was buried on 2 March 1770. Their son James received £100 and Peter £50 under the will of their grandfather, James Goldsmith, dated 1777.

Now in his mid-twenties, it may be a fair assumption that Buck played for Hambledon against Dartford in 1756 - on Broadhalfpenny when Richard Keats lost his spaniel dog and later in the Artillery Ground, London. But he was not specifically mentioned until 1764, as the 'Mr Steward' representing Esquire Land's club who had 'a finger broke and his knee strained'. His name also appeared in the Hambledon team list against Caterham in 1769 while in 1770 Baker observed that he was batting for Hambledon against Caterham on Broadhalfpenny at the close of play on 4 October and still at the wicket at the after-dinner resumption on the 5th (when his partner, Richard Nyren, was bowled first ball). He continued to play regularly, not making much impact on the score-sheet, till at least the end of the 1774 season. In September that year Peter Stewart was appointed a constable at Hambledon's manorial court. Ten years later a directory listed him as a publican in Hambledon, yet there is no mention of him in another published in 1793. According to Haygarth he kept the *Green Man* on the western edge of the village and was buried in the churchyard on 15 February 1796.

Several sources say that his brothers played cricket for various Hambledon teams. With the probable exception of James, his son born in 1768, these were his nephews, in one instance great-nephew - sons and grandson of his older brother William. It may even have been a nephew - probably Peter, possibly James – rather than Buck who appeared for Hampshire between 1776 and 1779. By 1776 Buck was forty-six whereas Peter junior and James were respectively twenty-one and eighteen. So unless historians are able to come up with fresh evidence we will never know with absolute certainty the identity of 'Stewart' who played just once for Hampshire scoring 15 & 7 both not out against England on Moulsey Hurst in 1776, then returned on three occasions in 1777-79 to make 3, 0 not out, 4, 2 and 6. On the other hand there can be no doubt that 'Young Buck Stewart' advertised for Hampshire against the Alresford & Odiham clubs in the *Reading Mercury* of 27 May 1782 and 'Stewart' for Hampshire *v* Kent in 1783 belonged to the next generation of cricketing Stewarts.

THOMAS SUETER's family settled in Hambledon seemingly during the 1740s and remained in the parish for at least three generations. His father, John, is named many times in the manorial court book from the 1750s onwards. He also contributed half a guinea to the church ceiling fund in 1757 and served as constable in 1763:

John Sueter, born c1719, died 21 July 1784 aged 65; married
   Elizabeth (Betty), bur 1 June 1793 aged 77.
—— Elizabeth 1744, bur 3 March 1793; married 31 Oct
   1773 John Duncaster of Kingston (Thomas Sueter
   a witness); perhaps the Duncaster bowled out for 0
   in each innings for Mechanics of the Isle of Portsea
   v Portsmouth White Swan club 1789.
—— Edward 1748
—— John 1746, possibly John Suter' who married Sarah
   Collins at Chalton 15 May 1769; the John of
   Catherington qualified to vote at Hambledon 1779?
   Sarah, wife of John Sueter, left a daughter Sarah as
   heir to her copyhold property in Hambledon 1790.
Thomas 1750-1827; married 13 March 1772 Ann Merritt.
   —— Thomas 1773/John 1774/Ann 1777/Kitty 1779-79/
   Edward 1780/Maria 1782/William 1785
   —— Elizabeth 1775; married 1796 John Read of Idsworth
   (witnesses Thomas Sueter and Mary Aburrow).
Sally bapt 29 Feb 1788; married 9 Oct 1815 Henry Thresher.

Baptised on 17 April 1750, Thomas played as a nineteen-year-old for Hambledon *v* Caterham in 1769 and, so far as one can tell, took part in all of the county's principal matches until 1784. In all he scored about 1,400 runs for an excellent average of 15, including innings of 67 *v* England on Broadhalfpenny in 1774 and 66 *v* Kent on Stoke Down in 1781. He also hit 58 & 56 for the Duke of Dorset's XI *v* Sir Horace Mann's XI in Bourne Paddock in 1781 and 74 in a five a side game against Kent at Moulsey Hurst in 1774. His play was later recalled with relish by John Nyren:

> he was one of the manliest and most graceful of hitters. Few would cut a ball harder at the point of the bat, and he was moreover an excellent short runner: He had an eye like an eagle - rapid and comprehensive. He was the first who departed from the custom of the old players before him, who deemed it a heresy to leave the crease for the ball; he would get in at it, and hit it strait off and strait on; and, egad! it went as if it had been fired. As by the rules of our club at the trial-matches no man was allowed to get more than thirty runs, he generally gained his number earlier than any of them.

Behind the wicket he was evidently equally impressive: 'what a handful of steel-hearted soldiers are in an important pass, such was Tom in keeping the wicket. Nothing went by him; and for coolness, and nerve in this trying and responsible post, I never saw his equal'. Nyren goes on to say that 'as a proof of his quickness and skill, I have numberless times seen him stump a man out with Brett's tremendous bowling'. However this must have been in minor games. In big cricket he is credited with just one stumping, and then only after Brett's retirement. He adds that 'I have seldom seen a handsomer man than Tom Sueter, who measured about five feet ten', with

> so amiable a disposition, that he was the pet of all the neighbourhood; so honourable a heart, that his word was never questioned by the gentlemen who associated with him; and a voice, which for sweetness, power, and purity of tone (a tenor), would, with proper cultivation, have made him a handsome fortune. With

what rapture have I hung upon his notes when he has given us a hunting song in the club room after the day's practice was over!

In 1778, about the time he was serving as parish constable, Sueter was found guilty, along with fellow cricketer Edward Aburrow, of receiving a deer illegally killed that 24 April. But their convictions were quashed on appeal to the Quarter Sessions on 14 July. Strangely, the Sessions records give his occupation as 'yeoman', though in directories he appears as 'carpenter and joiner' in 1784 and as 'carpenter' in 1793. As a general builder he was responsible for the club-house on Windmill Down. The relevant minute for 13 May 1783 reads: 'the gentlemen present having seen & examined the several plans produced this day by Mr. Sueter for a building on the Downs recommend a brick building to the consideration of the gentlemen at the next meeting'. In addition he worked part-time as gamekeeper - in 1786 appointed keeper to the Manor of Denmead and Glidden in Hambledon by a former club member Joseph Bettesworth, in 1787 to the Manor of Hinton Merchant by John Richards and in 1793 to the Manor of Hormer. From 1773 onwards his attendance as a juror is recorded in the local manorial court book - and in 1777 as a constable - and in 1780 he was one of those chosen by lot to serve in the militia, though a paid substitute took his place.

We have no record of Sueter on the cricket field during the 1787 season. Then, in 1788-89 he only appeared for teams outside the county and in 1789 and 1790 played *against* Hampshire. Conceivably he stopped attending the club's practice games and instead accepted an engagement with another club which gave him a new county qualification. Because he represented or was advertised to play for Surrey in each of these seasons it has been assumed that he was living in that county, even (on the basis of a supposed 12-month residential qualification) that he had settled there by July 1787. Yet throughout this period it seems that Sueter continued to live and work in Hambledon. His youngest child was baptised at Hambledon towards the end of February 1788; a stone set into Hambledon church tower bears the inscription: 'Thos Sueter, & Richd Flood; builders, A.D. 1788'; and he signed the manorial court book as a juror on 22 September 1789.

Despite advancing years, he showed good form with the bat during his final seasons. For Surrey he hit 59 *v* Kent in Bourne Paddock and 23 & 33 not out *v* Hampshire at Moulsey Hurst, and in 1790, 39, top score of the match, for the Left *v* Right handers at Lord's. Nonetheless after 1790 he gave up major cricket, though turning out for Hambledon Town *v* West Sussex in 1791. If, as has been suggested, his change of allegiance arose from a difference with the Hambledon Club it had been patched up before 19 September 1791 when an entry in the accounts reads: 'pd Thoms. Sueter for sundry works done at the house £4 2s'. Under 28 September 1792 he received £2 11s 8d 'for sundry Artles', while his work for the parish is attested by a churchwarden's voucher for 3 December 1792, 'To Thos Sueter for work done at the Poor House'. In 1798 he became an adjutant in the newly formed Hambledon Volunteer Infantry. He died at Emsworth, in the house of his daughter, Mrs Sally Thresher, in 1827 but was buried in his native village where about thirty years later Haygarth (*S&B* Vol I p 126) copied the following inscription from his headstone:

SACRED TO THE MEMORY OF
THOMAS SUETER
Who departed this life
The 17th day of February, 1827,
AGED 77 YEARS.

Chapter Five

SOME PARISH FAMILIES

For several years, after local players of the calibre of Stewart, Hogsflesh and Sueter were reinforced by such cricketers as Nyren, Aburrow, Barber and Leer, Hambledon parish was powerful enough to enter the field against an entire county. Yet as in the case of the parish side of 1756, most historians still confuse the 'town' team with the Hambledon Club. This is despite the fact that its games are clearly distinguished from those of the club in notices such as the one published by the *Hampshire Chronicle* on 26 July 1773:

> On Friday the 30th of July will be played a MATCH on Broad-Halfpenny, Hambledon Town against the County of Hants, for Twenty Guineas a Side. - The wickets to be pitched at Ten o'Clock. On Wednesday the 4th of August will be played a Match on the same Down, Hambledon Club against All England, for Five Hundred Guineas a side. And on Monday the 16th of August will be played a Match on the said Down, Hambledon Town against the County of Surry (sic), for One Hundred Guineas a Side.

With regard to the Surrey match the same newspaper for 16 August 1773 commented: 'the Hambledon Eleven are greatly improved, and excellent sport is expected'. The visitors proved too strong, but the village or parish was far from disgraced, scoring 103 & 51 to Surrey's 131 & 24-4. The following year the parish again opposed the rest of Hampshire:

> On Wednesday the 14th instant a great CRICKET-MATCH will be played on Broad-Halfpenny Down, between the County of Hants, and the Parish of Hambledon, for Fifty Guineas. - Great Sport is expected, and the skill of the victorious Alresford boys will be tried for the first time.
>
> (*Hampshire Chronicle* 12 September 1774)

And further matches between the sides were announced in 1775:

> A great Cricket-Match will be played on Kimpston Down, near the Milberrys on Monday the 4th of September, between the County of Hants, and the Parish of Hambledon, for Fifty Guineas. - Barber from Broad Halfpenny will pitch several tents on the Down, where Wines & Provisions of all Sorts may be had at the most reasonable Rates, and the Ladies who honour him with their Company will be as much at their Ease as if they were in their own Dressing Room.
>
> (*Hampshire Chronicle* 28 August 1775)

and in 1778:

> On Saturday May the 30th, a purse of FIFTY GUINEAS, given by the Gentlemen of the Hambledon Club, will be played for at Cricket, on Itchin Stoke Down, near the Grange, Hants: the County of Southampton, against the parish of Hambledon, the famous Noah Man being allowed to play for the parish. The wickets to be pitched at ten o'clock, and the match played out the same day. All sorts of provisions and liquors to be had on the down.
>
> (*Hampshire Chronicle* 25 May 1778)

The last was briefly noted by the diarist John Thorp of Preston Candover as 'a Crickett match upon Stoke Down with Hambleton (sic) Club'. Modern authorities describe it as Hambledon Club v Hambledon Parish. But this is incorrect. It was not the club but the county which opposed the parish of Hambledon. As well as these county games many lesser fixtures were advertised - enough to suggest a regular programme of village or parish contests quite separate from those organised by members of the Hambledon club. Below are just a few examples from the files of the *Hampshire Chronicle*:

> On Saturday the 25th of June instant, will be played a match on Shasbury Green, near Bursledon-Ferry, eleven of a side, Hambledon against Portsmouth, for eleven Guineas a side. The wickets to be pitched at Ten o'Clock. (20 June 1774)

On Tuesday, May the 25th, a great Cricket Match will be played on Broad Halfpenny Down, between the parish of Hambledon and the Alresford Club, for Fifty Guineas, and on Tuesday, the 1st of June the parishes of Hambledon, and North Chapel, in Sussex, are to play on Broad-Halfpenny Down, for one Hundred Guineas. The Return Match will be played on the New Ground, near Alresford Town, on the 28th of May; and the Return Match with North Chapel will be played at that place, on the 18th of June. - The wickets will be constantly pitched at ten o'clock, and the matches played out.

(24 May 1779)

This is to give notice to all gentlemen cricketers and others, That on Friday, June 16, there will be a match played on the Nythe, near Alresford, The Parish of Hambledon against Alresford, for Eleven Guineas a side. To begin exactly at ten o'clock..

(12 June 1780)

The 1780 notice does not appear to have been re-published before. Indeed a brief perusal of the 18th century papers suggests a significant number are still either unknown or have only been reproduced in abridged form, omitting important details.

There is no way of telling who exactly supported the local team, though we may guess that they included Hambledon's more prosperous tradesmen and farmers, possibly even Thomas Land himself. All we have are the clues provided by names which appear in the few score-sheets surviving from the 1770s, 1780s and 1790s.

The following names help identify some of the Hambledon parish families: HORNE, dismissed for 0 & 1 when brought in as an apparently late substitute for Hambledon Town *v* Surrey in 1773, must have been one of two brothers, twenty-five-year-old John or twenty-year-old William, descended from John and Catherine Horn living in Hambledon early in the century:

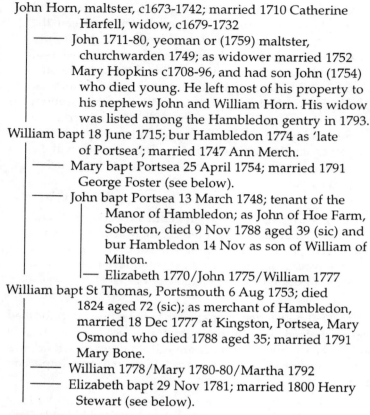

John Horn, maltster, c1673-1742; married 1710 Catherine
      Harfell, widow, c1679-1732
    ——— John 1711-80, yeoman or (1759) maltster,
        churchwarden 1749; as widower married 1752
        Mary Hopkins c1708-96, and had son John (1754)
        who died young. He left most of his property to
        his nephews John and William Horn. His widow
        was listed among the Hambledon gentry in 1793.
William bapt 18 June 1715; bur Hambledon 1774 as 'late
      of Portsea'; married 1747 Ann Merch.
    ——— Mary bapt Portsea 25 April 1754; married 1791
        George Foster (see below).
    ——— John bapt Portsea 13 March 1748; tenant of the
        Manor of Hambledon; as John of Hoe Farm,
        Soberton, died 9 Nov 1788 aged 39 (sic) and
        bur Hambledon 14 Nov as son of William of
        Milton.
       ——— Elizabeth 1770/John 1775/William 1777
William bapt St Thomas, Portsmouth 6 Aug 1753; died
      1824 aged 72 (sic); as merchant of Hambledon,
      married 18 Dec 1777 at Kingston, Portsea, Mary
      Osmond who died 1788 aged 35; married 1791
      Mary Bone.
    ——— William 1778/Mary 1780-80/Martha 1792
    ——— Elizabeth bapt 29 Nov 1781; married 1800 Henry
        Stewart (see below).

William Horn (1753-1824) was a friend and trustee of Thomas
Land who in his will described him as a yeoman, though he
appeared in the 1784 directory as 'maltster'. A prominent
figure in Hambledon parish life, he was chosen several times
to serve as churchwarden and overseer of the poor, as well as
constable in 1788. In 1798 he held the rank of captain in the
Hambledon Volunteer Infantry. On at least one occasion the
club hired his horses to roll the cricket ground, hence the
account entry in 1792: 'Horn's team for rolling the Down 15s'.

John GOLDSMITH (1733-1805), another of Thomas Land's
friends and trustees, then described as a shopkeeper but in
1777 both as a grocer and a tallow-chandler, was brother-in-
law to the cricketer 'Buck' Stewart who married his sister Mary

(1734-70) in 1765. By his wife Mary (*née* Row) whom he married on 16 March 1765, he had a son John who scored 15 & 0 for Hambledon *v* West Sussex in 1791 and, making up the number, 3 not out & 8 for Surrey *v* Hampshire on Windmill Down in 1792. This second John, baptised 1 April 1766, lived at West End, north of Hambledon village, where he entertained the celebrated William Cobbett at least twice during the 1820s, and died on 15 March 1845. His gravestone also records the death of his wife (formerly Hannah Hatch), whom he married in 1792, on 13 October 1840 aged 72.

In all probability 'COTTMAN' who made 1 & 3 for Hambledon *v* Petworth in 1784 was a son of Thomas, a customary tenant of the manor, who died in 1780. So the cricketer was either the seventeen-year-old Thomas (born 1767) or the fifteen-year-old John Binstead Cotman (born 1769), recorded as a surgeon and apothecary in 1793, who in 1821, as a bachelor and 'gentleman', was licensed to marry Mary Ann Cotman, aged forty, spinster of Weston Corbett.

MULLINS who, with 3 & 0, scored one run fewer than Cotman in the Petworth match seems to have been the thirty-five-year-old Henry Mullens, a 'common brewer' and yeoman, or else a younger brother, George (born 1756) or John (born 1761). Their father George senior (1717-1805) was a well-to-do Hambledon mercer, and their sister Martha (born 1751) was the wife of John Fleetwood, Deputy Clerk of the Peace, of Winchester. On 17 December 1781 Henry married Elizabeth Coles, then aged thirty. Her father, Henry COLES, attended the match between Hambledon and Caterham on Broadhalfpenny in 1770 and dined with the diarist John Baker at Nyren's *Hut*. Elizabeth was also granddaughter of Thomas Coles, landlord of the inn - 'the Hutt & Premise on the Edge of Broadhalfpenny in possession of Thomas Coles... in the parish of Catherington' - when it was conveyed from John and Elizabeth Walker to John Smith on 17 September 1740. Elizabeth Coles was also an aunt of the cricketer Edward Bennett:

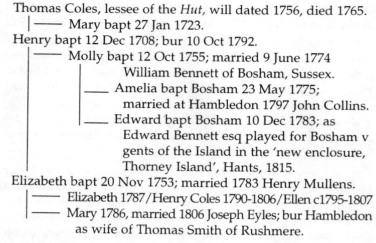

Thomas Coles, lessee of the *Hut,* will dated 1756, died 1765.
| —— Mary bapt 27 Jan 1723.
Henry bapt 12 Dec 1708; bur 10 Oct 1792.
 —— Molly bapt 12 Oct 1755; married 9 June 1774
 William Bennett of Bosham, Sussex.
 —— Amelia bapt Bosham 23 May 1775;
 married at Hambledon 1797 John Collins.
 —— Edward bapt Bosham 10 Dec 1783; as
 Edward Bennett esq played for Bosham v
 gents of the Island in the 'new enclosure,
 Thorney Island', Hants, 1815.
Elizabeth bapt 20 Nov 1753; married 1783 Henry Mullens.
| —— Elizabeth 1787/Henry Coles 1790-1806/Ellen c1795-1807
| —— Mary 1786, married 1806 Joseph Eyles; bur Hambledon
 as wife of Thomas Smith of Rushmere.

Henry Coles gave a guinea to the church ceiling fund in 1757 and at the time of its sale in 1768 the *George Inn* was described as 'many years occupied by Mr Henry Coles' (*Reading Mercury* 29 February 1768). It was probably he who bought the property at the auction held there on 7 March and installed Nyren as landlord around 1770-71. Baker in 1770 called him a brewer, which was his trade in 1779 when he took out a Sun Life policy (9 June) on the *George* 'in the tenure of Richard Nyren Innkeeper & Baker Bricked & Tiled', also on a house in Finchdean late in the occupation of William Padwick, innholder. The following year he bought another policy (22 April) covering his own household goods, thatched storehouse and malthouses, the 'house & stable adjoining called the George Inn in said Parish in the tenure of Richard Nayern', the *George Inn* in Portsdown and the *Bell Inn* in Horndean.

In the 1784 directory Coles was a common brewer and distiller and again a common brewer when he signed his five-page will, followed by a codicil, on 5 August 1792. His legatees were his 'dear wife Elizabeth', his daughter Molly Bennett and her daughter Amelia Bennett, and his daughter Elizabeth Mullens and her husband Henry, yeoman of Hambledon, with, as trustees and executors, Edward Aburrow, shopkeeper, and Edward Hales jun, gentleman, both of Hambledon, and Thomas Pink, yeoman of Barton Farm near Winchester. Henry died two months later and his executors proved the will in London in 1793 (PCC).

Henry Mullens, who was baptised on 17 December 1748 and served as a lieutenant in the Hambledon Volunteer Infantry (1798), is chiefly of interest in connection with the *Bat and Ball Inn*. As 'that small messuage tenement or dwellinghouse commonly called or known by the name of the Broadhalfpenny Hutt ... in the parish of Catherington' it was sold on 2 April 1772 by William Flood, shoemaker of Bramdean, and his wife Ann to the Earl of Clanricarde for £185. The Earl left it to his sons, Henry and John (both club members), who on 26 April 1788 sold the property for only £126 to Thomas Butler, gentleman of H.M. Dockyard, Portsmouth, and Henry Mullens, brewer of Hambledon. The release described the premises, 'formerly in the tenure or occupation of Thomas Coles afterwards ... Thomas Parrott lately of William Flood', as a 'small messuage tenement or dwelling house commonly called or known by the name of Broadhalfpenny Hutt together with the stable yard and backside thereunto belonging adjoining to Broadhalfpenny aforesaid and the Common there in the parish of [Cat]herington'. The document is endorsed by Butler under the date 1794 'This Day I relinquish my part in the House on Broadhalfpenny known by the sign of the Batt & Ball in the favour of Henry Mullins' - suggesting it had been renamed, perhaps by Mullens himself, soon after being bought from Clanricarde's family.

Against Petworth in 1784 the first three in the batting order were T., J. and G. FOSTER who together made more than half the runs in Hambledon's second innings. Because there were at least two Foster families in 18th century Hambledon, it is difficult to identify specific individuals. But in this case it seems a reasonable guess that the last two were the brothers John and George, then in their mid-twenties. We have no record of a T. Foster around this time but, bearing in mind that Ts and Fs were often confused in early texts, we might be justified in assuming that this was Francis, a third brother, still playing for the village in the 1790s. John, George and Francis were Thomas Land's three great-nephews and principal legatees. As far back as 1671 Martha Land married Thomas Foster in Hambledon church. But the main family connection arose through the marriage of George Foster of Blendworth (baptised there 24 August 1696) to Betty Land at Hambledon on 21 December 1727. As well as a younger son, Francis (1733) who seems to have died young, they had a son, George, baptised at Blendworth on 5 December 1728. This second George married in the same church in 1753 the seventeen-year-old Mary Heberdon (born Hambledon 1736) who sadly went insane while still in her twenties. The 1762 court book for Hambledon notes that Mary, sister of the late John Heberdon (1733-61) and wife of George Foster had been a lunatic for the past six months. She must have been Mary, widow (wife?) of George Foster, buried 18 December 1762 who at the next court (5 April 1763) was called Mary Foster, wife of George, who died leaving a son John aged four as next heir. In 1759 George Foster was one of those charged with enclosing manorial land, and in April 1764 with building a stable on the land which was ordered to be taken down. He was evidently dead by 1767 when his grandfather, the older Thomas Land, made his will (see note 11) authorising his son, Thomas jun, to pay for the education of George's three sons, apparently the three who went on to play against Petworth in 1784:

George Foster, born 1696; married 1727 Betty Land 1708-80
        who when buried at Hambledon 21 March 1780
        was named as Betty Foster and as Elizabeth,
        wife (widow?) of George Foster of Blendworth.
   —— Francis 1733
George, born Blendworth 1728; married 1753 Mary
        Heberdon 1736-62.
   —— George, born c1760, died 30 Aug 1811 aged 51;
        married 1791 Mary Horn, died 17 Sept 1829.
   —— Francis, born c1761; died 19 July 1847 aged 86.
   —— Mary, bapt Hambledon 23 May 1762 (died young?).
John, bapt Blendworth 4 May 1759; died Hambledon
        3 Jan 1848 aged 88; married 1792 Fanny
        Hammond, died 1853 aged 79.
John, bapt Hambledon 2 May 1803; died Hambledon
        3 May 1858; married Mary, died 19 May
        1844 aged 32.

The above George (c1760-1811), overseer of the parish in 1792, was recorded as a farmer in 1793. He scored 0 & 12 v Petworth in 1784 and 0 & 2 not out v West Sussex in 1791. His brother Francis (c1761-1847), presumably the T. (sic) Foster who top-scored v Petworth with 24 & 41, made 5 & 21 v West Sussex in 1791 as 'F. Foster' and was perhaps the Foster who scored 3 & 7 not out for Hampshire against England on Sevenoaks Vine in 1789. Although listed as a tanner of Hambledon in 1793 he inherited Thomas Land's tanyard in Havant where he later resided, making 3 & 1 for Havant v Hambledon in 1815. On 24 November 1791 he married Sarah Hatch (died 1805 aged 46) by whom he had Francis (1792-1801) and Ann (1796-1805). He took a second (?) wife, Ann Green, at Havant in 1825 and according to his monumental inscription at Hambledon died there in 1847.

John Foster (1759-1848), credited with 5 & 27 v Petworth, was Land's sole executor who moved into his house near the road leading to Broadhalfpenny Down and resided there until his death in his late eighties, presumably being the 'Forster' named by Thomas Smith of Droxford, writing in 1857 (see *S&B* vol I pp 114-5), as one of the new Hambledon club's chief supporters from the 1800s to 1825. On 6 October 1792, as a farmer of Park House, he married Fanny or Frances Hammond (baptised 2 March 1774), the eighteen-year-old daughter of Henry, a Hambledon currier, at St Mary's church, Portsea. Their son John (1803-58) must have been the 'Foster esq' who was run out for 17 and who bowled five first innings wickets for Hambledon v Midhurst in 1829, and the one who assisted Hambledon v South Hants club in 1844 when 'three beautiful catches made by Foster, Hall and Lee called forth loud applause' (*Bell's Life*). Under the enclosure award of 1857-61 he received a plot at Brook Lane, the site of the present Hambledon cricket ground, and Thomas Smith noted that although Windmill Down had been broken up 'hopes exist [in 1857] that it [the club] may again be established on a new ground, lately offered by a descendant of a good old patron of this noble game, Mr. Forster'. As already noted, the 'good old patron' can hardly have been anyone other than John Foster's collateral ancestor – his great-great-uncle, Esquire Land, Hambledon's backer in 1764. Foster died, while President of

Hambledon Cricket Club, the year after Smith wrote his letter. A monumental inscription can be seen on the family's chest-tomb in Hambledon churchyard.

Equally prominent in the old parish elevens were the STEWARTS, starting with the famous Peter 'Buck' Stewart (see page 48) who made 31 & 0 for Hambledon Town v Surrey in 1773. There is some uncertainty about the Stewart who represented Hampshire in the later 1770s and Hambledon in 1784. However we do know that the cricketing Stewarts of the 1790s were named Henry, James and John. The following (by no means complete) tree sets out their relationship to 'Buck' and various other family members:

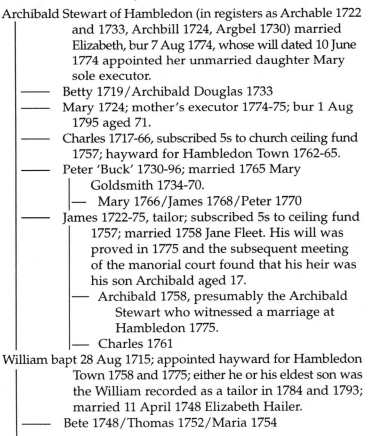

Archibald Stewart of Hambledon (in registers as Archable 1722 and 1733, Archbill 1724, Argbel 1730) married Elizabeth, bur 7 Aug 1774, whose will dated 10 June 1774 appointed her unmarried daughter Mary sole executor.
—— Betty 1719/Archibald Douglas 1733
—— Mary 1724; mother's executor 1774-75; bur 1 Aug 1795 aged 71.
—— Charles 1717-66, subscribed 5s to church ceiling fund 1757; hayward for Hambledon Town 1762-65.
—— Peter 'Buck' 1730-96; married 1765 Mary Goldsmith 1734-70.
   — Mary 1766/James 1768/Peter 1770
—— James 1722-75, tailor; subscribed 5s to ceiling fund 1757; married 1758 Jane Fleet. His will was proved in 1775 and the subsequent meeting of the manorial court found that his heir was his son Archibald aged 17.
   — Archibald 1758, presumably the Archibald Stewart who witnessed a marriage at Hambledon 1775.
   — Charles 1761
William bapt 28 Aug 1715; appointed hayward for Hambledon Town 1758 and 1775; either he or his eldest son was the William recorded as a tailor in 1784 and 1793; married 11 April 1748 Elizabeth Hailer.
—— Bete 1748/Thomas 1752/Maria 1754

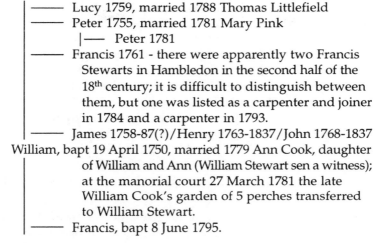

——— Lucy 1759, married 1788 Thomas Littlefield
——— Peter 1755, married 1781 Mary Pink
   |——— Peter 1781
——— Francis 1761 - there were apparently two Francis
       Stewarts in Hambledon in the second half of the
       18th century; it is difficult to distinguish between
       them, but one was listed as a carpenter and joiner
       in 1784 and a carpenter in 1793.
——— James 1758-87(?)/Henry 1763-1837/John 1768-1837
William, bapt 19 April 1750, married 1779 Ann Cook, daughter
       of William and Ann (William Stewart sen a witness);
       at the manorial court 27 March 1781 the late
       William Cook's garden of 5 perches transferred
       to William Stewart.
——— Francis, bapt 8 June 1795.

The younger Peter Stewart, baptised 10 July 1755, was married by banns to Mary Pink on 24 April 1781. His age was given as twenty-five, hers as twenty-five, and they had a son, Peter, baptised the following 7 October. She was mentioned in the will of her father, Robert Pink, yeoman, buried 26 February 1784. It was this Mary, not the wife of 'Buck' Stewart as stated by Haygarth (*S&B* Vol I p 43), whose gravestone stands in Hambledon churchyard - bearing an inscription to Mary, wife of Peter Stewart, late of Portsea, died 1798 aged forty-three. Whether this Peter was the owner of a freehold in Wickham residing in Hambledon in 1779, or the landlord of *The Neptune and Mars* in Broad Street, Portsmouth, recorded in a 1784 directory, is unclear. But it looks as though he must have been the Peter Stewart of Portchester qualified to vote in Hambledon in 1790, and therefore perhaps the 'Steward' who umpired a match in White Swan Field, Portsea, in which four of the White Swan club beat ten mechanics in 1789.

The 'Barber' or 'Young Buck' Stewart active as a cricketer in the early 1780s was presumably either this Peter or else his younger brother, James, baptised 15 January 1758, recorded as a shopkeeper in 1784. However as he was no longer listed in the 1793 directory maybe this was the James, son of William Stewart, buried in Hambledon on 7 August 1787 after being 'drowned bathing'. If so, the James Stewart who on Windmill

Down for the town of Hambledon scored 0 & 1 - and took two wickets - *v* West Sussex in 1791, and 17 & 1 *v* Brighton in 1792 can hardly have been anyone other than the son of Buck Stewart born in 1768. Since James appeared as given-man for Hambledon in 1791 he might possibly be identified with the Stewart of Portchester who assisted Portsmouth against a combination of Petersfield, Hambledon and East Meon in the last match staged by the old club on Windmill Down in 1796, and the Stewart who played for Portsea's White Swan club *v* Brockenhurst in 1797 (or was this Peter?). It may be noted that a James Stewart married Ann Green at Portsea in 1799 and had four children, Elizabeth, Harriet, Sarah and Peter, christened at Portchester in 1804.

Perhaps the best cricketer of the generation after 'Buck' was Henry, baptised on 5 August 1763, the one most likely to have been the Stewart who scored 7 & 13 *v* Petworth in 1784 when a couple of months short of his twenty-first birthday. Henry hit 37 & 47 for Hambledon Town against West Sussex in 1791 and 10 (plus four catches in an innings) for Hambledon *v* East Meon & Meonstoke in 1800. For Lord Winchilsea's XI *v* T.A. Smith's XI on Perriam Down in 1793 he failed with only 1 & 0. He may have been Stewart (Stuart 1789) who for Hampshire made 2 & 3 *v* Surrey on Perriam Down in 1788, 4 & 0 *v* Kent at Bishopsbourne in 1789, 3 & 4 *v* MCC on Stoke Down in 1797 and 1 & 3, both not out, *v* England on the same ground in 1806. As a bachelor of Hambledon he married by licence on 4 December 1800 Elizabeth Horn (see page 58), spinster, probably daughter of William Horn, Thomas Land's trustee. Henry died on 12 March 1837, followed by Elizabeth in 1848 aged 72.

In the same two matches involving Hambledon Town, Henry's brother, John, baptised 6 May 1768, managed just 4 & 0 in 1791 and 3 in 1792. Either he or James could have been the J. Stewart who made 3 for Hampshire *v* Kent on Dartford Brent in 1792 and 21 & 14, along with seven wickets and two catches for Smith's XI *v* Winchilsea's XI on Perriam Down in 1793. John married Mary Edicar, spinster of Hambledon, in 1801 and became licensee of the *New Inn* in West Street where the club held its anniversary meeting in 1804. Until the 1820s he catered for the new cricket club and conducted much of its routine business, collecting subscriptions, paying the players, etc. In 1824 he was appointed to the new Select Vestry established to run the parish.

According to his gravestone he died in 1837 aged sixty-nine. His nephew Francis, born in 1795, must have been the Stewart (initial given as F. in 1815 and 1818) who for Hambledon scored 3 & 6 *v* Portsea in 1814, 2 & 1 *v* Portsea and 2 *v* Havant in 1815, and 37 (top-score of the innings) *v* Portsmouth & Portsea in 1818, and the 'Steward' of Hambledon who according to *The Annals of Sporting* assisted Cosham *v* Fareham in 1823.

68

Chapter Six

CLUB AND COUNTY

Given the standard of much modern scholarship, perhaps no one should be surprised at finding Hambledon Town being identified with the Hambledon Club, or even at finding the boys' eleven which faced the boys of Petersfield & Buriton in 1781 being mistakenly styled 'the mighty Hambledon team'. More serious in some respects is the failure, even by Mote, to recognise the distinction between club and county. Some historians, notably Rowland Bowen, have pointed out that many of the sides termed 'Hambledon Club' should really be called 'Hampshire' as per contemporary newspapers and the early collections of printed scores. In numerous 18th century sources the same eleven went under both titles - a discrepancy perhaps most easily explained by the fact that club members arranged the matches and provided financial backing for the county team. We have an early example of this dual-nomenclature from 1768 (compare *Reading Mercury* 5 September, Waghorn 1899 p. 66) with the home side described in one report as a *club*:

> Last Tuesday the second great match at cricket was played on Broadhalfpenny between eleven gentlemen of the Hambledon Club against eleven gentlemen of the county of Kent for a considerable sum, which was won by the former by upwards of 100 notches; but what is very remarkable, one Mr. Small of Petersfield, fetched above seven score notches off his own bat.

and in another as a *county*:

> ... on Broad-Halfpenny a match of cricket between the counties of Kent and Hampshire, when the former were beat by an amazing difference of notches. The game on the close stood as follows:-

	HAMPSHIRE	KENT
First innings	131	141
Second innings	194	40
	325	181
	181	
Difference in favour of Hampshire	144	

For several years, when its chief rivals were other clubs such as Caterham and Chertsey, the team was mostly styled 'Hambledon Club'. In 1770, 1771 and 1772 Baker used this form - and again in 1774: 'on broad halfpenny Hambledon Club (having Lumpy to bowl) v. all the world'. In 1771 the *Gazetteer and Daily Advertiser* (16 August) referred to 'the Hampshire lads, known by the name of the Hambledon Club' and to 'the Hambledon Club' being considered 'the best cricket-players in England'. But in 1772 the *Kentish Gazette* (6 June) described that year's five a side game in the Artillery Ground as being 'between five men of Kent and five of Hampshire', inserted the scores under the headings KENT and HAMPSHIRE, and observed that 'we are also credibly informed that another great match is engaged; Hampshire against Kent, to be played in both counties, 11 on each side'.

The team which faced Kent (otherwise England) on Broadhalfpenny and at Guildford in 1772 had the alternative title 'Hampshire and Sussex' and the same year another Guildford match was called Surrey *v* Hampshire. Also in 1772, the epic contest in Bourne Paddock watched on the first day by an estimated 15-20,000 crowd, was announced by the *Kentish Gazette* (22 August) as 'the long and great depending MATCH of CRICKET, the gentlemen of HAMPSHIRE against ALL ENGLAND', and reported in such terms as 'the match of cricket between Hampshire, who had the choice of two men, and All England ...; the betts at pitching the wickets were ... in favour of Hampshire; ... The bowlers for Hampshire were ...', with the scores entered under 'Hampshire' and 'All England'. Two weeks later the paper published a version of Cotton's cricket song containing two lines which distinguished between the county and club:

> with heroes like these even Hampshire we'll drub,
> And bring down the pride of the Hambledon Club.

In 1773 the *Hampshire Chronicle* of 12 July styled a London fixture 'the great cricket match, Hampshire against All England', with its scores likewise headed HAMPSHIRE and ENGLAND - together with the comment: 'it is thought the reason Hampshire lost was owing to Mr Brett's having received a violent blow from the ball when the last match of the five was played'. 'The last match' relates to 'the grand match of cricket in the Artillery Ground, Hampshire against All England for £100, single wicket, five a-side' (Waghorn 1899 p. 90), which was only much later re-titled 'Hambledon Club' against England. The same summer the so-called 'Hambledon' team which played on Sevenoaks Vine was advertised as 'Hampshire' in the Kent papers - a nomenclature followed by Baker when he wrote: 'to see cricket match on Monday at Sevenoaks between Hampshire and All England ... [England] headed Hants in all 100 ... Hants went in and got but 49 more'. It should be noted that a well-known score-card of this match, headed 'Hambledon Club with Yalden against England', is a late 19th or 20th century forgery. It must have been printed after 1862 because its title, along with certain obvious errors - the initial J. accorded to Richard Miller and T. to John Wood of Surrey, and Small entered as 'J.Small sen' - are copied from *Scores and Biographies*. Again in 1773, the *Hampshire Chronicle* for 29 September published a 'letter from Egham' relating how:

> This neighbourhood, the residence of many families of gentility and fortune, has been much enlivened by our races, and a great cricket-match at Laleham Burway, near Chertsey ... The cricket match began on Thursday, when the Hampshire men got only 38 notches. The first innings the Surry (sic) men got 120. It was continued only a short time on Friday, on account of the rain, and was concluded on Saturday. It was a match between Surrey and the Hambledon Club, in Hampshire, and ended in favour of Surrey, who had eight wickets to be put down ... the Surrey men are exceedingly elated, having before beat the men of Kent, and it is said, they

will next year play against all the world.

But although the visitors were termed 'the Hambledon Club', the scores were entered under 'Hampshire' and 'Surry' (sic). Another report called it 'the cricket-match ... between Surrey and Hampshire, with two men given to each - viz., Miller and Minshull to Surrey, Frame and Bayley to Hampshire' (Waghorn 1899 pp. 114-5).

On 13-14 July 1774 Hampshire easily beat Kent with a number of given men on Broadhalfpenny and according to the *Salisbury Journal* (Harris & Ashley-Cooper p. 22):

> As soon as the game was over the Kentish gentlemen gave up the next match and forfeited the money; they then challenged the county of Hants. to play two matches for 1,000 guineas on condition that Lumpy and two other men from any part or England, except Hampshire, might play for Kent; this challenge was then accepted, and both matches are to be played before harvest.

Two games were arranged: at Sevenoaks on 8 August and on Broadhalfpenny on 15 August. The former was described by the *Public Ledger* of 11 August as being between the 'Duke of Dorset and ten men on the side of Kent, and - Ridge Esq and ten men on the side of Hampshire'. The following year the Duke changed sides. Thus a match on Broadhalfpenny now called 'Hambledon' *v* England was actually advertised by the *Hampshire Chronicle* of 10 July 1775 as 'the greatest cricket-match that has ever been made in Hampshire, the Duke of Dorset, with ten Hampshire Men, against any eleven Men in England'. And in 1776 the 'Hambledon Club' which is said to have met England on Sevenoaks Vine on 26 June was styled 'Hampshire' by the Hampshire and Kent newspapers, and also by the diarist Richard Hayes who recorded how he went to Sevenoaks 'to see Hampshire play with All England at Cricket' and how

> Hampshire got 241 runs ... Hampshire with All England. I was there ... the Hampshire men beat All England by getting as many runs in one innings nearly as all do. did in both their innings.   (Hayes Diary)

Similarly the next game on 2 July, according to the *Hampshire Chronicle*, again involved Hampshire, though this time *v* Kent not England:

> On Tuesday next will be played at Broadhalfpenny, the third great cricket match of the year, for 500 guineas, between the counties of Hants and Kent, the latter being allowed two from Surrey. The players for this county are ...

In the edition for 8 July the scores were headed 'Hampshire' and 'Kent'. Yet when the teams next met, at Sevenoaks on 15 July, the *Kentish Gazette* (13 July) announced:

> The Second GREAT MATCH, on SEVENOAKS VINE, will be played on Monday, July 15, 1776, HAMPSHIRE against ALL ENGLAND, For a Thousand Guineas. Wickets to be pitched at Ten o'Clock. Just published, Price 1d. A LIST of the GENTLEMEN CRICKETERS, who finished playing at BROADHALFPENNY, July 5, with the State of the Game. Sold by J. PRATT, Scorer; and at the Printing-Office, Sevenoaks. A Correct List of the ensuing game may be had within Half a Hour after the Game is finished.

Pratt, the scorer (whom we know later officiated at Hambledon in 1783), seems to have been responsible for this notice. A year later, on 2 June 1777, the *Reading Mercury* notified its readers that forthcoming matches arranged by the Hambledon Club included Lord Tankerville and ten of Hampshire *v* England to be played on the Vine and on Broadhalfpenny. The first was advertised two days later (4 June 1777) in the *Kentish Gazette:*

> On Sevenoaks Vine, on Wednesday, the 18th of June inst., will be played the first match for a thousand guineas. Hampshire (with the Rt. Hon. Earl of Tankerville) against All England. The wickets to be pitched at ten o'clock, and to be played with three stumps, to shorten the game.

Ironically, despite the extra stump, it still lasted for three days with Aylward compiling his great innings of 167 and Hampshire totalling an unprecedented 403. News of the return, starting on 7 July, appeared in the *Hampshire Chronicle* with the only acknowledgement of the county's latest triumph a brief note that they 'play better than usual':

> On Monday the 7th the second great cricket match of the year will be played on Broadhalfpenny Down near Hambledon, Hants, the county of Hants against any eleven in England. The Earl of Tankerville being allowed to play for the County. Players for England, Duke of Dorset, Minshall, Miller, Pattenden, Bullen, Yalden, White, Bowra, Lamborn, Wood, Lumpy; players for Hants Lord Tankerville, Small, Aylward, Sueter, Lear, Nyren, Aburrow, Veck, Francis, Taylor, Brett. The Hampshire men play better than usual, and lovers of cricket may see the twenty best players in England brought together.

In modern sources this, along with the Sevenoaks game, is usually treated as Hambledon Club *v* England whereas Tankerville, one of the 'Hambledon' side, was really a given-man for Hampshire. The next great match, already noted by the *Reading Mercury* on 2 June, was the Duke of Dorset and ten of Hampshire *v* England at Laleham Burway. It started on 22 July and finished on the 26th with Hampshire winning by 30 runs. The *Hampshire Chronicle* advertised the return as a 'great cricket-match' - 'the Duke of Dorset, with ten Hampshire men, against any eleven in England' - for 1,000 guineas 'on Kimston (sic) Down, near the Millbury's', with the teams listed under the headings 'Players for Hants' and 'for England'. However, according to its 4 August edition Tankerville specifically notified members of the Hambledon Club, evidently responsible for making the Hampshire games, that he would not be going through with the fixture:

> The Earl of Tankerville having given notice to the Gentlemen of the Hambledon Club that he intends to pay forfeit, there will not be any Cricket Match on Monday next at Kimpton.   Hambledon, August 1, 1777

Afterwards three new matches were arranged - at Guildford, Broadhalfpenny and the Artillery Ground. All are titled 'Hambledon Club' *v* England in *S&B*. However in this case we know the correct nomenclature not just from press notices but because scoresheets for all three are preserved in the Duke of Dorset's private papers. In every one England's opponents are 'Hampshire'. The Broadhalfpenny sheet states that the game was for a purse donated by the gentlemen of the Hambledon Club. So if the home team was the Club, as now often claimed, we would have the strange anomaly of a side playing for its own prize-money! At the end of the season the *Hampshire Chronicle* reported:

> The Gentlemen of the Hambledon Club have this year made ten great matches, of which they have won seven, received a forfeit for one and lost two ... they have undertaken to play Lumpy, with ten Hampshire men, against Kent including three of Surrey, supported by the Duke of Dorset. This will be the first match next year.

We have no record of this fixture. But interestingly towards the close of the 1778 season the *Morning Post* for 5 October gave notice that members of 'the Grand Cricket Club' had established a fund in order to reward 'such players who distinguish themselves in the great county match', adding: 'it is said the hero of the capital match to be played tomorrow at Chertsey, between Hampshire and Surrey, will be entitled to the first prize'.

It is worth noting that some 'Hambledon' matches of the early 1780s were arranged as Kent *v* England - i.e. those on Stoke Down and in Bourne Paddock in 1781 and those on Sevenoaks Vine and on Stoke Down in 1782. A printed score-card of the Sevenoaks game in fact reads 'His Grace the Duke of Dorset &c. against All England', with the teams headed 'The Duke's men' and 'England', while Richard Nyren advertised the return as follows in consecutive editions of the *Reading Mercury* for 1 and 8 July:

> On Wednesday July 10th will be played on Stoke Down, near the Grange, Hants. the second great Cricket-Match of the year, the county of Kent with Lumpey and Bedster, against England - All sorts of cold provisions and excellent wines, tea, coffee, &c. will be found at Nyren's tents on the down.

Below he listed the names of the 'players for England' and 'players for Kent'. Almost all the 'England' men came from Hampshire and later in the summer they reverted to their normal county designation for two games, including the historically significant opening match on Hambledon's new ground:

> On Wednesday the 7th of August inst. will be played a Match of Cricket, on Windmill-Down, near Hambledon, - HANTS, with Lumpey, against ENGLAND. - The wickets to be pitched at 11 o'clock.
>
> (*Reading Mercury* 5 August 1782)

Also in 1782 we have the team's county status affirmed by no less a source than the club's own records. The minutes for 5 September refer to 'the match between the Club & Sussex' - which had previously been described by the *Hampshire Chronicle* as Hampshire against Sussex. Then at the end-of-season meeting at the *George* on 17 September, with respect to 'those players who intend to play in the county matches in the ensuing year', the club ruled that 'all those players who play in the County Eleven shall receive on the Practice Day four shillings if winners, & three shillings if losers.' A notice for a match in 'the ensuing year' involving 'the County Eleven' ran:

> On Wednesday the 6th of August will be played at Bourne, The great Match of Cricket, For one Thousand Guineas, Made by the Duke of Dorset and Sir Horace Mann against the Gentlemen of Hampshire. Hampshire with Lumpey against Kent with Bedster and Yalden. The last being a Tye Game great sport is expected …
>
> (*Kentish Gazette* 30 July 1782)

Thus from the early 1770s, when regular matches began to be staged against major county or England XIs, until the mid 1780s, when for two seasons there were no important eleven a side games in Hampshire, we have no overwhelming reason to suppose that teams fielded under the aegis of the Hambledon Club or its members represented the actual club, even though they were sometimes styled 'Hambledon Club' in much the same way that, say, Kent or England might be called 'the Duke of Dorset &c' or 'the Duke's men' according to whoever happened to be financing the team. Hambledon-based sides were regularly termed 'Hampshire' throughout this period - for example by the Kentish newspapers - and were viewed as 'Hampshire' by the match scorer (Pratt of Sevenoaks), by cricket's then leading patron, the Duke of Dorset, and, as 'the county eleven', by the Hambledon Club itself. But 'Hampshire' was misleadingly changed to 'Hambledon Club' in *Scores and Biographies* and again in *The Hambledon Cricket Chronicle*, while score-sheets given by Waghorn and Buckley retain their original titles. Thus Buckley provides the full scores of 'Hampshire', not Hambledon, *v* Surrey at Laleham Burway in 1776. Yet, perhaps inevitably, some books still follow the amended mid-Victorian versions (complete with apocryphal T. Wood) rather than the properly titled 18th century scores.

After the hiatus of the mid 1780s, when no teams took the field, county teams continued to be fielded from a pool of players paid for practising on Windmill Down. But strangely these are not re-labelled 'Hambledon Club' in *Scores and Biographies,* even though Mote identifies the Hampshire side as 'Hambledon' in two six a side games in 1788, thereby contradicting *inter alia* the *Daily Universal Register* of 26 August which reported that

> The single Wicket Match, at Cricket between Lord Winchilsea and five of All England, and Mr Talbot and five of Hampshire, ended on Saturday. Hampshire won, with five wickets to go down.

The same newspaper announced that in Bourne Paddock an alphabetical match, made by Lord Winchilsea and Sir Horace Mann with the Duke of Dorset, would be held that day - and 'after the Alphabetical Match, Kent and Hampshire are to play for 500 *l.* single wicket'.

The continuity between pre- and post-1785 county sides is perhaps most clearly demonstrated by the minute for 30 September 1788 which effectively replicates that of 17 September 1782 by instructing that those receiving payment for playing on the Down are 'forbidden to engage themselves to play in any county or other great matches without the permission of the stewards of the Hambledon Club' (unless engaged by any member of the club or by the Duke of Dorset or Sir Horace Mann) and 'that Nyren do acquaint the players who give in their names to play in the county eleven with the above order'. This confirms that the same relationship between club and county was maintained from the 1770s right through to the 1780s, and explains why a team could still be styled both 'Hampshire' and 'the Hambledon Club' - because the players represented the county but were financed by the club or its members – as shown by the *Hampshire Chronicle* of 25 July 1791:

> Last week a match of cricket was played on Windmill Down, between All England and the Hambledon club, which terminated in favour of the former. The state of the game was as follows: England, first innings, 137; second, 143; total 280 - Hampshire, first innings, 137; second 76; total 213. The bets were at first nearly even; before Small was out in the first innings 5 to 4 in favour of Hants - at the beginning of the second innings, they were in favour of All England; and towards the conclusion, rose to 10 to one. The gentlemen of the Hambledon Club were uniformly dressed in sky-blue coats with black velvet collars, and the letters C.C. (Cricketing Club) engraved on their buttons.

That this particular fixture was arranged under the auspices of the Hambledon Club is borne out by two entries in its accounts: a note that Richard Nyren supplied members with forty-four bottles of port and fourteen of sherry during the three days, and a payment in respect of the ladies' dinners 'for the three days of the match July 13 &c.'

At Moulsey Hurst in 1786 a so-called Hambledon team, backed by Lord Winchilsea and 'the gentlemen of the Hambledon Club', allegedly beat Kent, supported by Sir Horace Mann, by 35 runs. But the match was really between 'the Rest of the Alphabet' and those whose surnames began with the letters A, B or C (also termed the 'ABC Club'). This illustrates the difficulty of deciding the correct title of sides (from 1786 onwards) containing players belonging to (i.e. paid by) the club many if not most of whom (the Walkers, Beldham, Noah Mann, etc) lacked a Hampshire birth or residential qualification. For example Haygarth's (*S&B* Vol I p. 65) 'Hambledon Club' which played Kent on Sevenoaks Vine in 1786 was styled 'England' by the *Kentish Gazette* and 'Hampshire' by the *Daily Universal Register*: 'The grand match at cricket between Kent and Hampshire will be played next month. Great bets are laid on this match' (26 May). But the return was 'England' *v* Kent according to both the *Gazette* and the *Register*: 'On Saturday last the grand match of cricket, Kent against All England, was played at Windmill-Down, in Hampshire, which was decided in favour of the latter' (22 July). And later in the year, at Bishopsbourne, Kent's six a side opponents were either Hambledon Club, England or (despite including Noah Mann and the two Walkers) Hampshire: 'On Friday last was terminated the grand select match at cricket, at Sir Horace Mann's seat in Kent, six of a side, Hampshire against Kent' (12 September). Although Kent won by just one wicket, the last report went on to state, quite wrongly, that the visitors 'won easy, having several men to spare' and that 'Aylward unfortunately knocked down his own wicket the first innings, which is supposed to have given the game so hollow in favour of Hampshire'.

At Lord's on 2-4 August 1787 six of Kent opposed six backed by 'a number of Hampshire gentlemen', nowadays called 'Hambledon Club' or 'Hambledon' but 'All England' according to the *Register* of the day:

> Thursday last, the Grand Cricket Match at single wicket, between Kent and All England was begun to be played in the Mary le bone Field ... for 500 guineas a side. Kent went in first, and got 53 notches, the first innings; when All England went in, and scored 8 notches; when the game was given over for that day.
>
> (3 August 1787)

or 'Hampshire' according to another issue of the same paper:

> Kent was at the end of their second innings 39 a head, and the odds rather against them, from their small majority. Hampshire went in last, and only scored 16 notches. Small on whom they most depended, was got out by the force of Clifford's [error

for Brazier's] bowling. - The ball struck the bat, which gave way to its force, and hit the wicket before he scored one. The grounds were attended all three days by much good company, and the play afforded excellent diversion to the amateurs of the same.

(7 August 1787)

A week later, according to Mote, 'Hambledon' beat Kent on Coxheath by 2 wickets. It omits to note, however, that in the *Maidstone Journal* of 14 August the visiting eleven was 'All England' with no mention of 'Hambledon', while the *Canterbury Journal* of the same date reported how

All England in the first innings, batted with extreme judgment, and in a stile more than usually superior; they headed Kent 116 runs. With this disadvantage Kent went in for its second innings ... and when Bullen, who was the last man, went in to Crosoer, they wanted one run to avoid being beat in one innings. A general damp seemed to spread itself through the spectators, and the most extravagant odds were laid. The game now took a sudden turn, the ball repeatedly flew to the booths, and great judgment and expertness were used in the playing; and after getting 39 runs each, Crosoer was caught out. All England, in its second innings, was not near so successful, eight men being put out for the runs got by Crosoer and Bullen, but the game terminated in favour of All England, by two wickets to go down.

Shortly afterwards, on 14 August, a match 'made by Lord Winchilsea and the Hampshire gentlemen against the Duke of Dorset and Sir H. Mann' commenced in Bourne Paddock. The *Daily Universal Register* described it on the 21 August 1787 as 'The Hambledon Club against All England'. Yet although the visitors included six players resident outside the county the same report also called the sides 'Hampshire' and 'All England', with the game ending in a 'majority in favour of Hampshire 266'. And likewise the *Canterbury Journal* on the same day (21 August 1787) noted that 'the state of the game from the beginning ran much against All England, an evident superiority being distinguishable in the Hampshire men, who,

80

from having the advantage of a constant practice together, have arrived to an unequalled degree of perfection'.

To take just one further instance, in what is reckoned to be the first full match by the Hambledon Club at Lord's, only five Hampshire men were among the eleven which beat thirteen of England by 6 wickets in 1789. Nevertheless a newspaper while calling them 'eleven of the Hampshire Club' still headed the scores ALL ENGLAND and HAMPSHIRE (*Daily Universal Register* 3 July). From these notices one possible inference is that in those days county qualification had as much to do with belonging to, that is to say being paid by, a club in a particular county as with residence. This would explain why men such as the Walkers, Beldham and Wells from Surrey and Noah Mann from Sussex who practised together on Windmill Down could be considered qualified for sides titled variously 'Hambledon Club', 'England' or 'Hampshire'. It used to be supposed that a strictly observed 12-month residence was a necessary preliminary to playing for a county. But the evidence is not very persuasive. As we have already seen, Tom Sueter represented Surrey for several seasons, even playing against his own county, yet parish and other local records suggest that throughout this period Hambledon remained his only permanent home.

Chapter Seven

THOMAS WHITE
AND HIS MONSTER BAT

Over and over again cricket historians relate how a certain Shock White turned up to play against Hambledon with a bat as broad as the wicket and thereby prompted the game's law-givers to limit the width to the present 4¼ inches at their meeting on 25 February 1774. This is the White who is featured twice by John Nyren, first as a change bowler - 'Shock White, another bowler on the England side; - a good change, and a very decent hitter; but take him altogether, I never thought very highly of his playing. He was a short, and rather stoutly made man' - then, towards the end of the narrative, as 'White of Ryegate' - 'several years since (I do not recollect the precise date) a player, named White, of Ryegate, brought a bat to a match, which being the width of the stumps, effectually defended his wicket from the bowler: and in consequence, a law was passed limiting the future width of the bat to 4¼ inches'. However the Reigate man, the one who played in the big matches of his day, was Thomas White (c1740-1831) who had no connection with the player who went under the name Shock. The real Shock White was mentioned by the *Whitehall Evening Post* on 28 September 1761:

> On Monday next will be played a Match of Cricket, Eleven of a Side, in Laleham Borough, between Chertsey and Eight of Hampton, Charles Sears, Shock White, and John Haynes, for Twenty Guineas a Side. The Wickets to be pitched at half an Hour past Ten precisely, and the Match to be play'd out.

Then, twelve years later, he was twice described as coming from Brentford, a Thameside parish about six miles downriver from Hampton. On 11 August the *Daily Advertiser* announced:

> On Monday next, in Tothill-Fields, will be played a Match of CRICKET, by ten Gentlemen of Westminster,

and Shock White, from Brentford, against eleven
Gentlemen of London, for Twenty Pounds a side. The
wickets to be pitched at Eleven and the Match played
out.

and on the 18th:

The Match of Cricket that was begun to be played on
Monday, in Tothill-Fields, Westminster, between ten
Gentlemen of Westminster, and Shock White of
Brentford, against eleven Gentlemen of London, for
Twenty Pounds a Side, will be played out this Day, in
Tothill-Fields. The Wickets to be pitched at Eleven
o'Clock, and the Cricketers to meet at the Bricklayers
Arms, the Corner of Stretton-Ground, near the Fields.

On the very same days, the 16th and 18th, Thomas (of Reigate)
was in action twenty-five miles away on Sevenoaks Vine,
scoring 59 in his first innings for Surrey *v* Kent. There is no
instance of the Surrey White being called Shock during his
career, and when the subject of a lengthy article in *The Sporting
Magazine* in 1828, evidently written by someone who knew
him reasonably well, his familiar cognomen was given as
'Daddy', with no mention of 'Shock'.

Confusion between the Brentford and Reigate players may
have arisen as early as July 1787 when the Eton College
magazine, *The Microcosm*, observed that 'a cricketer will, in
pouring over a page of Horace, lose the trophies which await
him as hero of The Hampshire and bulwark of the White
Conduit, and exchange the invigorating commendations of a
Small, Shock White, or Lumpy for the dull drudgery of
blundering through ten years of scholastic labour' (as quoted
by Pycroft in *The Cricket Field*). Nine years later *The Sporting
Magazine* (Dec 1796 p.153) reported that 'Shock White of
Brentford' amassed no fewer than 197 runs in July 1771 while
batting for Surrey & Kent in an otherwise unrecorded match *v*
Middlesex & Hampshire on Sevenoaks Vine. This at least
confirms that Shock came from Brentford in Middlesex,
though there is something not quite right about a report 25
years after the event which has him playing against his own
county. Maybe the writer confused Shock with Thomas, or

even with someone else altogether - someone like, say, John Ions, another batsman whom *The Sporting Magazine* (Oct 1795 p. 22) says made 197 runs in a single match, though in his case for London *v* Kent in 1783.

John Nyren adds a footnote to the wide-bat affair. 'I have a perfect recollection of the occurrence', he says, and 'subsequently a frame of the statute width, was constructed for, and kept by the Hambledon Club; through which any bat of suspect dimensions was passed, and allowed or rejected accordingly'. If he remembered quite clearly an incident on the cricket field which led directly to a clause restricting the width to 4 1/4 inches being incorporated into the revised laws in February 1774 (when he was still only nine) the obvious inference must be that the incident took place on his local ground, that is to say on Broadhalfpenny Down, sometime the previous summer. And in this case the likeliest occasion would have been when White contributed 69 to Surrey's convincing 9-wicket win at Hambledon on 4–5 August 1773. When White returned on 26 August to play for Surrey *v* the Town of Hambledon he managed only 4 & 3, and in September, for Surrey *v* Hampshire, scored 30 & 10 on Laleham Burway and 2 on Broadhalfpenny. Conceivably his less impressive form after the beginning of August might be explained by his having to revert to a normal bat under new Articles of Agreement, drawn up for the later matches, which, to prevent a repetition of what was deemed unfair play, had an extra clause inserted to restrict the bat-width to a hitherto customary 4 1/4 inches. However, a problem with this is a paper, formerly in the collection of J.W. Goldman and now one of the archival treasures of the MCC, according to which the bat episode occurred two years earlier in 1771. It reads:

In view of the performance of one White of Ryegate on September 23rd that ffour and quarter inches shall be the breadth forthwith.

this 25th day of September 1771 [signed]
Richard Nyren
T. Brett
J. Small

The paper is a slip cut from the lower part of a larger sheet, as shown by loops of two letters written above overlapping the top edge. Since the letters 'e' and 'r' in the text and in the signature are near identical, the writing seems to be that of Thomas Brett, or at least of the person who signed 'T. Brett'. Yet it needs to be treated with some caution. The document contains no information which could not have been obtained from all too familiar sources. Indeed the entire contents could have been lifted from *The Young Cricketer's Tutor* itself. Apart from brief allusions to Barber and Hogsflesh, Nyren, Small and Brett are the first three players to be featured. And, perhaps more suspiciously, the text bears an uncanny resemblance to Nyren's so-called 'memoranda' - 'one White of Ryegate' seems to echo Nyren's 'a player named White, of Ryegate', and by a quite amazing coincidence 23 September 1771 corresponds to the date given in the preceding paragraph where we are told that 'the Hambledon Club ... had a run of ill-success ... [but] on the 23rd of September, 1771, having played the County of Surrey ...'

The text also poses problems of its own:

a) Why did one of the younger men, Thomas Brett, then about twenty-four, draw up and sign the paper instead of a senior player such as Stewart or Barber? Moreover how can we square Brett the 'cricket legislator' with the player who possessed very little 'general knowledge of the game', the player whose 'judgment of the game', according to Nyren, 'was held in no great estimation'?

b) The diarist John Baker did not live in Surrey yet knew White's full name when he wrote on 16 June 1773: 'The Ryegate went in and Thomas [not Shock] White and another got about 19'. Baker was merely a spectator. It is odd therefore that those who actually played with him, such as the experienced cricketers Small and Nyren, were unaware of the full name of one of Surrey's leading and senior players.

c) The match in question lasted from Monday the 23rd to Tuesday the 24th, so the visitors from Hampshire must have travelled some forty miles home during the evening or night following the second day's play. It is hardly likely, then, that three of their number, including Small living eight miles from Hambledon at Petersfield, and Brett living at Catherington, would reconvene on the Wednesday.

d) The return match was arranged for Broadhalfpenny on 30 September. This along with the one on the 23-24 September would have been subject to articles of agreement covering any disputed points of law. So the conditions already agreed and signed could not have been altered by one side immediately after the first game.

e) John Nyren stated that he possessed 'a perfect recollection of the occurrence'. It is scarcely feasible that this could relate to Chertsey in September 1771. If so we would have to accept that the team took six-year old children to away matches even when this meant round-journeys of maybe eighty miles. On the other hand it is quite reasonable to suppose that as an eight-year-old he watched and recalled, with at least some degree of clarity, a match played just a couple of miles from his home in Hambledon village.

f) Is Nyren's signature genuine? Two examples, in his capacity as witness to the marriages of his fellow cricketers, Thomas Sueter and George Leer, can be found in the Hambledon parish registers (reproduced by Ronald Knight, vol. 7, opp. p. 6; vol. 11, cover and opp. p. 58). In contrast to the upright and roughly scrawled 'Richard Nyren' of 1771, we have a sloping and neatly written 'R. Nyren' in 1772 and 'Richd Nyren' in 1780. It might just conceivably be argued that the 1771 capital 'R' bears a crude resemblance to those in the registers. But otherwise there is little similarity. An obvious difference is the distinctively written 'y' of the 1771 hand compared to those with normal loops written in 1772 and 1780.

Insofar as I am aware, none of the published accounts provides the paper with an acceptable provenance before the 1930s when it found its way into the possession of a wealthy collector (when reproduced on page 516 of *The Cricketer* in 1936). Nor it seems has there yet been a scientific analysis of either the paper or the ink. It might though be possible to establish its authenticity by matching the other signatures with those on unquestionably genuine documents of the period. But even if it could be authenticated, a paper signed by three players belonging to the same team would not represent, as claimed, the passing of a 'law' by a committee of the Hambledon Club. Any such ruling may have applied to practice games on Broadhalfpenny. But that is about all. The conventional view that the club constituted cricket's law-makers is not based on sound evidence. It seems to have been inspired by John Nyren's reference to Tom Walker's new-style bowling being banned (around 1788?) 'by a council of the Hambledon Club' called for that purpose. At best this can only mean certain figures in the club, perhaps senior players, deciding what would be permissible at their own practice matches. There is nothing in the minutes, nor anywhere else, to suggest that the club possessed special legislative powers, powers which it later conceded to the M.C.C. The law makers prior to the formation of the M.C.C. appear to have been based at the *Star and Garter*, London (see Rait Kerr p. 114).

Chapter Eight

THE HAMBLEDON CLUB
1773-1796

Besides sponsoring the Hampshire team, the club's aspirations to county status may be inferred from the fact that some of its home matches were held on a second, more central, ground near Winchester. As early as 1773 the *Salisbury Journal* of 7 September advertised an end-of-season fixture between the club and Sussex to be played thirty miles away at Andover during the town's annual races. But it had to be cancelled when only seven of the 'visitors' showed up. The five Hambledon subscribers reported at the meeting were 'Mr Powlet' (presumably the Rev Charles), Lord Northington, Lord Dunkellin, the Duke of Chandos and Peter Taylor. Of these, two in particular - Powlett and Northington - perhaps with Dehany, are likely to have been the members chiefly responsible for Hambledon's adoption of a new ground on Stoke Down, about five miles from Winchester, a mile from Powlett's rectory in Itchen Abbas and, in the other direction, a mile from Northington's country seat, the Grange. Hambledon parish played Hampshire there in 1778 (the year his lordship was club president) and during the next three seasons Stoke Down hosted three major games compared to Broadhalfpenny's two. England *v* Kent followed in 1782, then Hambledon or Hampshire *v* England (six a side) in 1784 and further great matches down to 1806.

In 1777 the club arranged for Hampshire to play England eight miles away on Kilmiston Down, but the match had to be called off after Lord Tankerville paid forfeit. Earlier still, in 1776, Broadhalfpenny was replaced for the second of three home games by 'the new made ground called Childer (sic) Holt, near Broadhalfpenny', otherwise 'the sheep common called Chidden Down and Chidden Holt'. The *Salisbury Journal* informed its readers that this common being private property 'tis hoped that no person will presume to erect booths or pitch tents without the consent of the owners of the soil. The Cricket Ground has been made at great expense, is sheltered from all winds, and is much more commodious in every respect than the ground at Broad Halfpenny Hill.

Though many evidently considered Broadhalfpenny too open and windswept, Holt Common for whatever reason proved unsatisfactory and Hambledon continued to play on the old ground until 1781. After the club's opening meeting on 4 June 1782 it switched to nearby Soberton:

The Gentlemen of the Hambledon Club are desired to take Notice, That their Meeting on Tuesday next, the 11th Inst., will be held on Soberton Little Down, instead of Broadhalfpenny. (*Hampshire Chronicle* 10 June 1782)

and on 18 June finally moved to Windmill Down, about a mile nearer the village but like Broadhalfpenny also 'commanding a delightful and extensive prospect of a fine sporting country'. Nyren recalled how 'the playing-ground was changed from Broad-halfpenny ... at the suggestion of the Duke of Dorset and other gentlemen, who complained of the bleakness of the old place'. And whereas Haygarth reckoned that 'Windmill Down is certainly too small, and the sides too steep for effective fielding', for Nyren it was 'one of the finest places for playing on I ever saw. The ground gradually declined every way from the centre; the fields-men therefore were compelled to look about them, and for this reason they became so renowned in that department of the game'.

A year later the club approved plans for what was almost certainly the first permanent building specifically for cricket - what would now be called a pavilion but at Windmill Down first known as the 'lodge' or 'booth', then 'the house' - a brick-built club-house designed by Tom Sueter which continued to be repaired and improved.[26] In 1784 it was 'ordered that a bell be hung in the Lodge under direction of the stewards' and in 1787 a Venetian blind was to be placed in the west window and a '*dulce Lenimen*' provided for the steward. A substantial sum, £13, was paid to Charles Clay and Henry Holt in 1791 'for Bricklayers work' at the House; windows were attended to in 1792 (2s paid to 'the glazier') and doors mended and a coat of whitewash applied in 1794. Its thatched roof is mentioned in the records of the new club in the 1800s. And in 1793 the *Universal British Directory*, after noting that Broadhalfpenny and Windmill Downs were 'well known to gentlemen cricketers of London and Kent, for the numerous grand matches they have played thereon', stated that

> On the said Windmill-down is a new building erected, for the selected gentlemen of the cricketing club to dine and enjoy their beverages in; which assembly annually meets in May and continues weekly, every Monday, till the season for partridge shooting commences.

As for the financial resources required to support this sort of venture, before 1783 it is unlikely that the club's annual income exceeded £100. But then it increased substantially because of a decision at the end of that season, perhaps partly to offset the cost of building, to raise the annual subscription (presumably from two guineas) to three guineas. As records are incomplete it is impossible to give an accurate estimate of the number of members during the 1770s and 1780s. However we do know that the latest figure from Birley, who claims that 'assiduous' research (what assiduous research?) has established that the club once boasted a membership of 157, is no more sensible than the declaration by Marqusee that by 1773 its members included eighteen aristocrats, two MPs, two knights and, as presidents, the Duke of Chandos and Lord Darnley (then aged six!). About the time that the club-house was being erected the overall membership may have been in the region of 40 to 50. We only begin to get firm evidence from the accounts which start in 1791 with a list of 52 'Gentn Subscribers'. This hardly compares with the cricket club with a membership of 139 which a few years earlier played in White Conduit Fields near London. On paper at least, Hambledon was about the same size as the Essex Cricket Club at Navestock with 49 members but considerably larger than Coxheath Cricket Society, which promoted several great matches near Maidstone in the late 1780s, with a published list of only 35. Moreover, charging three as opposed to two guineas subscription, it commanded something like double Coxheath's annual income.

Although the fully paid up, rather than nominal, membership may never have reached let alone exceeded 50, Hambledon included a number of influential figures - several county sheriffs, a lord lieutenant and county treasurer. Many others were or subsequently became either generals or admirals while, perhaps surprisingly, several were later appointed Lord Lieutenant of Ireland. Also worth noting is the prominent part played by Richards, Jervoise, Dehany and Powlett in forming (in 1775) the anti-government Hampshire Club in Winchester, organised after the style of the cricket club under a president and two stewards and their later membership of the mildly radical Society for Constitutional Information.

In the year that the club decided on its own club-house, the Down saw two important matches, but afterwards none until 1786. This break thus pre-dated the supposed formation of the MCC in 1787, which according to conventional wisdom sent Hambledon into swift decline. Mote claims that it had fallen into a state of disintegration by 1788 and afterwards played no part in promoting great matches - a myth based partly on the fanciful notion that in 1787 Hambledon handed over its alleged role as controlling, law-giving body of cricket to the MCC, partly in the mistaken belief that the club staged no more cricket of any consequence on Windmill Down after September 1787. But the MCC was essentially, if not actually, a continuation of the White Conduit, so in this respect the date 1787 has little significance. And after the two-year hiatus at Hambledon a series of great matches was held annually from 1786 up to and including 1793. Moreover besides the home games - for instance Hampshire *v* Kent in July 1789, made by the gentlemen of the Hambledon Club and Sir Horace Mann - the club was involved in away fixtures like the one in Bourne Paddock the following September, got up by the Duke of Dorset and Lord Winchilsea for England and 'Sir Horace Mann and the Gentlemen of the Hampshire-Club' for 'Hampshire, with Aylward and Ring given' (*Daily Universal Register* 4 September 1789).

A decline in the club's fortunes only becomes really noticeable in the 1790s. One ominous sign was the falling attendance for the annual end-of-season dinners at Nyren's *George Inn*. From 1783 to 1789 the average turn out was 13 to 14, with the most (20) in 1788. But in 1790 it was down to a mere four and, despite a healthy 13 the following autumn (doubtless attracted by the presence of Lord Winchilsea and Colonel Lennox), the next three years drew only five, and the year after that (1795) just three. There was an equivalent problem with the membership. The auspicious 1791 figure of 52 included several who failed to renew or were behind with their subscriptions while that year's opening meeting received notice of nine resignations. In 1793 it was felt necessary to reduce to five the quorum required 'to ballot any future candidate' and after that season only two more members were elected before the club folded in the autumn of 1796. From this distance of time it is difficult to determine why it failed to recruit and retain sufficient new members. The only obvious factor is the outbreak of war with France in 1793 which must have been especially serious for Hambledon because of its close links with the military. In 1792 the entry 'gone abroad' is found against only one name, Captain Gower's, while in 1793, 1794 and 1795 as many as six were 'gone abroad' or 'gone to sea'. But none of this explains why, for example, someone like Edward Hale, a prominent local amateur, one of the family which owned the Windmill Down ground, chose to resign in 1791 or why the Revd Richard Richards, who attended more meetings than almost anyone else, never joined in the first place.

No big cricket was seen on Windmill Down in 1794, but a final grand match was mounted between elevens backed by two of the remaining subscribers, Richard Leigh and Lord Winchilsea, on 20-22 July 1795. Afterwards the players made their way to Stoke Down for a second game, one which remained unfinished after three days' play from the 23rd to 25th. Remarkably, it was completed on the same ground the following season, on 28 June 1796, immediately before England *v* Surrey & Kent. A week later Messrs Holder and

Mellish were proposed as members, then duly elected on 18 July. However neither, it seems, ever paid their three guineas. By then the only definitely fully paid up members were Bennett, the two Bonhams, Dehany, Jervoise, Richards, Ridge, Coles, Winchilsea, Leigh, Mill and Ricketts. Scott, who is recorded as paying twice for 1795, should perhaps be added. Four others, Powlett, Palmer, Radcliff and Saxton, attended as members but without mention of their three guineas. Nevertheless funds were still sufficiently buoyant to pay for players practising on Windmill Down on eight separate days until 15 August. On the 22nd the final match known to have been held there under the auspices of *the* Hambledon Club was advertised in the *Portsmouth Gazette*:

CRICKET
On Monday, August 29 1796, will be played, on
Windmill Down.
A MATCH at CRICKET,
The Gentlemen of Hambledon, Eastmeon and Petersfield,
against the Gentlemen of Portsmouth, with Stewart of Porchester, for 100 Guineas.
The wickets to be pitched *precisely at one o'clock.*
Accommodations, as usual, on the Down.

and on 5 September the same paper reported that it 'terminated in favour' of 'Hambledon, Petersfield and the two Smalls, and Eastmeon', and that 'the return match was played here [Portsmouth] on Friday, and, after an excellent day's sport, the Portsmouth players lost again, by 36 runs'.

Confirmation that the Windmill Down game was arranged by the club comes from the accounts which under 29 August has the entry 'Paid for the Match 5 15 6' [£5 15s 6d]. Only three subscribers were present - Bonham, Richards and Coles - and numerous non-members: R. Richards, Revd Tyner, Hale, Revd Howell, Capt Ayles, Andrews, Gretham, 'Mr Thos. Pain, author of the Rights of Man', Col Verlo, Nelham, Callaway and Hood junior. Bonham and Coles doubtless came down with the Petersfield contingent while some of the others must have been visitors from Portsmouth. Richard Richards, second son of John senior, later became vicar of Hambledon. William

Tyner, who conducted a wedding in Hambledon church the following October, was apparently the local curate (and subsequently for almost fifty years vicar of Compton with Upmarden in Sussex).[27] Hale must have been Edward, the former club member. The Revd Howell, who had previously attended as a non-subscriber in 1791, was possibly William, son of John Howell of Kingston in Hampshire, who entered Magdalen Hall, Oxford, as a fifteen-year-old in 1780 and received his BA in 1785. Hood junior seems to have been Francis Hood, then aged fourteen, son of the former club president, destined to be killed in action in France in 1814. The name of the radical propagandist Tom Paine is a conundrum which has yet to be satisfactorily solved. The views of Birley, that his appearance provoked such disapproval from more conservative members of the club that they left of their own accord or else the club was closed by the government are hardly sensible. In the middle of August Paine, who if arrested in Britain would have faced a death sentence for treason passed in his absence, was living in Paris and towards the end of the year declined to leave France for America on account of the risk of being picked up by a British warship patrolling the Channel. So it is unthinkable that he should risk a two-way crossing when liable to be arrested both on land and on sea. Still less would he have appeared in public at a cricket match in the company of military men like Lieutenant-Colonel William Verlo of the Royal Marines. The only rational explanation of his presence on Windmill Down in August 1796 would be that he was on a confidential mission, presumably on behalf of the French government, which had been officially approved by the authorities in Britain.[28] But rather than premature speculation it might be wiser to wait until the original minutes have been expertly examined in order to determine (a) who actually wrote the entry, and (b) whether it could be a later (hoax?) insertion, which admittedly seems unlikely.

Following the return match with Portsmouth on 2 September we have no further information until the intended close-of-season gathering at the *George* on the 21st. It was unattended. Even John Richards failed to put in his usual appearance. 'No gentlemen' is the final entry in the minute book. There is no doubt, therefore, despite the assertions of Underdown in *Start of Play* (2000), that the Hambledon Club ceased to exist.

1. West End - Home of John Goldsmith jnr until 1845, where he entertained William Cobbett.

2. Park House - Seat of Squire Land, the club patron, (1759-1791) and then John Foster until 1848. The families had intermarried.

3. Whitedale - Home of John Richards snr, the long serving club treasurer, (1771-1814) and jnr until 1835.

4. Hambledon House - The family home of Edward Hale who also owned Windmill Down.

5. The Bat and Ball - Richard Nyren's *Hut* from 1760 to about 1772 and after occupied by William Barber.

6. The George Inn - Richard Nyren's main residence from about 1772 until at least 1795.

7. The New Inn - John Stewart was the licensee here in the early 1800s. The third headquarters of the cricket club.

8. The Green Man - Buck Stewart was landlord here from 1784 until his death in 1796.

9. The Half Moon, Northchapel, Sussex - never owned by Noah Mann.

10. Hyde Farm, Churt - Birthplace of Thomas and Harry Walker in the 1760s.

11 Gravestone of John Small (snr) at Petersfield - the only stone still standing in the churchyard.

12. The earliest surviving scorecard - obviously a forgery.

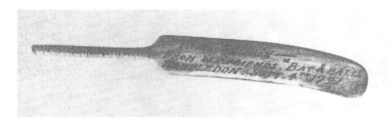

13. The bat presented to Richard Nyren - almost certainly a modern piece of cricket memorabilia. Nyren had left the Bat and Ball 20 years earlier.

In view of the performance of one Cawthe of Ryegate on September 23rd that ffour and quarter inches shall be the breadth forthwith. — this 25th Day of September 1771

Richard Nyren
T. Brett
J. Small

14. The famous document restricting the width of the bat to 4¼ inches is almost certainly a forgery.

Thomas Tueler of the Parish and Ann Merrick
Parish Likewise
Married in this Church By Licence
this Thirtieth Day of March in the Year
Hundred and seventy two by me R Phoenix
This Marriage was solemnized between Us Thomas Tueler the Mark of [...]
In the Presence of R Nyren Wm Edwith

Marriage George Leer and Martha Tueler were [...]
18 & 20th by me Wm Phoenix Vicar
George Leer of this Parish
and Martha Tueler Spin
Parish Likewise
Married in this Church by Band
this Eleventh Day of August in the Year One
Hundred and eighty by me Wm Phoenix Vic
This Marriage was solemnized between Us George Leer
Martha Taylor
In the Presence of Richd Nyren
William Hine

15. Nyren's signatures as a witness at the marriages of two Hambledon members in 1772 and 1780 bear no resemblance to the signature above.

Chapter Nine

SPECTATORS

John Nyren paints a picture of 'the multitude forming a complete and dense circle' around Broadhalfpenny 'patiently and anxiously watching every turn of fate in the game, as if the event had been the meeting of two armies to decide their liberty', adding that 'I cannot call to recollection an instance of their wilfully stopping a ball that has been hit out among them by one of their opponents. Like true Englishmen, they would give an enemy fair play'. As already noted, his description has been challenged by university historians who contend that during the 1770s and 1780s, the period covered by Nyren, matches at Hambledon were subject to frequent disruption by unruly spectators. Their 'evidence', if one may use the term, consists of nothing more substantial than extrapolation from an incident claimed to have occurred in 1778. During an alleged crowd invasion we are informed that the Duke of Dorset struck one of 'the Hampshire people' with his bat and 'the crowd backed off respectfully to a safer distance'. Needless to say, the story relates to the incident on Laleham Burway five years earlier in 1773 when the Hampshire team adopted a close-fielding tactic and one of them, standing too near the bat, was struck when the Duke played at the ball. This minor incident has been transferred from Surrey to Hampshire, the cricketers turned into spectators and the fielding ploy into a full-scale pitch invasion - from which derives the mythology of matches at Hambledon being subject to regular interruption from disorderly spectators.

So far as Hampshire teams are concerned our only genuine record of spectator trouble relates to single-wicket games in London's Artillery Ground. In 1772 'a very great concourse of people' assembled on the first day, 'which prevented the players from having a ring sufficiently spacious, and was attended with some inconveniences'. But despite 'confining the players' play seems to have continued without interruption. However three years later things got more out of hand. According to the *Morning Post* during the afternoon of the opening day (Monday 22 May 1772) 'many persons got on the wall of Bunhill-Fields Burying Ground to see the cricket match ... and pelting the crowd with brick-bats etc., a battle royal ensued in which several persons were terribly wounded'. And John Baker, who had never seen so many people together in the same place, reported that the fielders 'out of humour pretended the ring so much broke in upon ... [that they] could not play on'. At this juncture he decided to leave, spending forty-five minutes getting out of the ground, 'the passage so narrow and crowd so great'. Evidently he believed that play could have continued uninterrupted throughout the day had the cricketers been sufficiently determined. His valet stayed on and afterwards told him that, with 'the Mob gone', cricket resumed later in the evening. The following morning (23 May 1772) a report in the *Morning Chronicle* mentioned none of this:

> Yesterday the great cricket match between Kent and All England was begun to be played in the Artillery Ground. The Duke of Dorset, Lord Cholmondeley, and about twelve more noblemen and gentlemen met about half after eleven o'clock, when the wickets were pitched, and at twelve the Kent people went in, who got thirty-seven notches. At three o'clock the opposite party went in, and Small, the first man on that side, got what is almost incredible, seventy-five notches, and was at last bowled out just before eight o'clock.

While a much longer account in the *Middlesex Journal* noted the hiatus in play, but nothing more serious than that:

> Yesterday, about eleven o'clock, the great match of cricket between the Duke of Dorset and Lord Tankerville, for five hundred guineas aside, began to be played in the Artillery Ground;

Lumpey and Kent against all England.	
Kent	**Hampshire**
Lumpey, 6	Small, 74 (sic)
Bulline (sic), 7	Lear
Bookham, 8	Suter
Brazier, 13	White
Miller, 3	Brett

Kent had the first innings; and got thirty-seven notches, when Small went in for Hampshire, and got fifty-one [misprint for forty-one?] notches. The company then, who were very numerous, broke into the ground, and the players took up the stumps about half after five o'clock; but being brought into good humour returned again in about an hour, when Small continued his good play, and notwithstanding every man bowled, none could beat up the stumps, and Small got thirty-four notches more, which made seventy-five in all. It being then near eight-o'clock, it was resolved to defer the finishing of it to this day. Brett, Suter, White, and Layer (sic), of the All England side, have yet to go in for their first innings, after which the Duke's men are to go in again, and then their opponents.

Such a circumstance as one person running 75 notches at single wicket, was never known before.

The betts ran prodigiously high, Small having hurt his hand just after he went in: In short the knowing ones were, to use the Turf expression, fairly taken in.

The Duke of Dorset, and some other Noblemen and Gentlemen were there best part of the time.

The result was at last announced on Thursday 25 May 1772:

Yesterday was finally ended the great Cricket Match between Kent and All England. Tuesday night there was 24 notches to get on the side of the latter by four Wicketts; three were bowled out, and Small, who went in last, had 12 notches to get, which he did in two Hours and three Quarters.

This was the celebrated occasion when Lumpy is said to have bowled the ball three times right through Small's wicket without removing the bail, thereby prompting the introduction of the third stump. And perhaps it was these or similar press reports of proceedings in the Artillery Ground which inspired lines in the scurrilous verse-attack on Dorset and Tankerville printed as *The Noble Cricketers* in 1778 in which they, along with Small, Lumpy and other players, joined the

Scum of St. Giles's, and their Lordships Pride.
Where mob-encircl'd midst th'Artillery Ground,
Pimps, Porters, Chimney Sweepers grinning round,
Far from the Cannon's Roar, they try at Cricket,
Stead of their Country, to secure a Wicket.

Bearing in mind that several thousand matches are recorded in the 18th century, those known to have been disrupted, let alone completely abandoned because of spectator violence represent a very tiny proportion of the whole. And if we discount cricket in the metropolis they were so rare as to be almost negligible. Therefore whereas modern scholars argue that crowd disturbance was characteristic of 18th century cricket, the serious historical evidence indicates the very opposite - that crowds were pretty well behaved, remarkably so in view of the absence of policing in all but a handful of games, the prevalence of betting, plentiful supplies of liquor and the fact that so many matches were held on land with public access. In the Artillery Ground the pressure of thousands of people within a confined space must be seen as the prime cause of encroachment inside the ring with, in 1775, the situation exacerbated by outsiders climbing on top of the wall separating it from the burial ground. When there were densely packed crowds a certain criminal element was inevitable in a city like London. In 1763, for instance, a countryman in the Artillery Ground had his pockets picked of over £20 while looking on at the cricket players. But spectators, at least in and around the capital, had a traditional way of dealing with offenders. When Surrey played England in the ground in 1749 'a fellow was detected by a gentleman in picking pockets' and found himself seized and carried into the stable yard where he was 'severely ducked in the horse-pond', rolled in soot, then set free. At a cricket match on Blackheath three years later two pickpockets were taken away and 'severely ducked'. And 'at the great Cricket-Match behind Montague House' in 1764 two were conveyed to 'the Horse Pond' for the same punishment.[29]

In some parts of the country intrusion into the circle was less a human than a canine problem. Dogs were apparently running loose on Broadhalfpenny when Rover got lost in 1756 and again at the women's match on Rogate Common umpired by 'a principal of the Hambledon Club' in 1768, hence the following notice in the *Reading Mercury:*

> LOST, on Wednesday the 22nd of June Instant, during the Cricket-Match on the Common near Rogate in Sussex, A Small SPANIEL DOG, with Liver-coloured spots on his Back, and Liver-coloured Ears, other Parts white, and answers to the Name of CHANCE.

> Whoever has found him shall, on delivering him to Mr Eames at the Flying Bull at Rake, receive Five Shillings for their Trouble.

So far as we can tell, neither dog troubled the players, unlike in East Kent, where in the 1770s 'they greatly obstructed the players' and were threatened with being shot at Margate, Faversham, Canterbury and in Bourne Paddock, and in Norwich where in 1747 would-be spectators were warned that 'upon any interruption as may be caus'd by them in the game, or any other accident in regard to the sheep, all such dogs will certainly be kill'd on the spot'. Evidently they also caused problems in London: when cricket began to be played at Lord's in 1787 match notices included the caveat 'No dogs will be admitted'.

In 1777 Baker revisited the Artillery Ground to watch five of Hampshire play five selected by the Duke of Dorset. On the first day he stayed till 7 in the evening and as a 'new thing' noted '3 stumps to wicket'. On the next he spent the morning at the Guildhall hearing '3 or 4 small cases', then towards 12 o'clock he went to the ground and 'stay'd till near 4 when Aylward in who had fetched 15 and I find after fetched one more only and then bowled out when Hants was 35 ahead and after it seems the D of Dorset's 5 went in and fetched only 20 or 21'. The Artillery Ground is only five to ten minutes walk from the Guildhall - next to nothing compared with the six miles which William Pitt, in introducing an amendment to his Defence Act of 1803, declared was 'not more than the sturdy English peasantry are in the habit of going when led to a cricket match', or the fifteen miles which the yeoman farmer, Richard Hayes, rode to see Hampshire play on Sevenoaks Vine in 1776. But in his own only slightly younger days Baker was prepared to journey twenty miles to watch cricket on Broadhalfpenny Down. While living at Nursling near Southampton in 1770 the fifty-eight-year-old retired lawyer rose at 5 and at 6.30 left home on horseback accompanied by two servants. About halfway they stopped for half an hour at Upham, breakfasting at the *Red Horse* on bread, cheese and ale, and, after three and a half hours in the saddle, reached Broadhalfpenny at 10 o'clock. Baker spent eight hours watching Hambledon against Caterham, then after 6 rode by the light of the moon about seven miles to Petersfield where he had supper and slept at the *Red Lion*. Next day after dinner Baker returned to the cricket ground and later in the afternoon went with Messrs Court and Norton, 'one Cole, a brewer' [Henry, owner of the *George Inn*] and another unnamed 'into Nyren's house (the *Hut*) and dined', finally leaving for home sometime after 4 o'clock. In all he must have ridden over fifty miles in two days - lending a degree of confirmation to a report in the previous year's *Whitehall Evening Post* that 'nothing can exceed the vogue that cricket is in some parts of Surrey and Hampshire' where 'the people are so fond of it that it is common for them to ride 40 miles to be mere spectators at a cricket match'.

In 1772, soon after moving to Horsham, Baker accompanied his parson friend, the Revd Woodward of West Grinstead, to see the club play at Guildford. The Reverend called round at 6.15 and before setting out they drank chocolate. Travelling by chaise-and-four for upwards of six miles, they left their carriage in favour of continuing on horseback and arrived on the ground at a quarter to eleven. In the evening Baker rode down into Guildford, returning next morning before 10 o'clock in time for the resumption at half-past.

Baker identified several ladies watching the cricket. And around the same time their presence was also being encouraged at Hambledon. A minute for 17 August 1773 tells us that the club ordered a supply of green baize 'sufficient to cover the seats of the tent for the ladies', and another for 28 September 1784 that alterations to the booth or club-house on Windmill Down would include a *dulce Lenimen* as a convenience 'for the ladies.'[30] For Hambledon parish v Hampshire on Kilmiston Down in 1775 the *Hampshire Chronicle* for 28 August gave notice that:

> Barber from Broad Halfpenny will pitch several tents on the Down, where Wines & Provisions of all Sorts may be had at the most reasonable Rates, and the Ladies who honour him with their Company will be as much at their Ease as if they were in their own Dressing Room.

Three years later Richard Nyren travelled further still, trusting that for the Hampshire v England match 'the air of Stoke Down will, with the ladies at least, stand in the place of marbres, aspiques, blancmanges &c' and informing potential customers that 'for good appetite there will be a sufficient quantity of beef, ham, chicken and tarts'. In 1777 they were invited to Broadhalfpenny to patronise both caterers: 'Ladies and gentlemen will find an excellent cold collation every day on the Down, at Nyren and Barber's booths'. This time poor weather affected the attendance. But for the next match Richard Nyren announced:

> On Thursday July the 17th, will be played, for 100 guineas, on Broad Halfpenny-Down, near Hambledon, Hants, the most extraordinary Cricket-Match ever seen in the West of England. Eleven of the Hambledon Club against the best twenty-two that can be found within ten miles of Liphook. This will be the last match on Broadhalfpenny this year, and those ladies and gentlemen who were prevented by the rain last week from attending the match against All England, may now have an opportunity of seeing much diversion, and may be sure of finding, as at all times, the best provisions and liquors of every kind at Nyren's Booth.
>
> (*Hampshire Chronicle* 14 July 1777)[31]

For the six-a-side game on Stoke Down in 1784 - the only big event seen in Hampshire that summer - the *Salisbury Journal* (19 July) advertised 'an ordinary for the ladies at three o'clock, by order of the Stewards of the Hambledon Club'. And the club accounts attest to a continuing provision for the fair sex with sums laid out 'for Ladys Dinners, Tea &c' at all the great matches on Windmill Down from 1791 to 1795. In the latter year the *Portsmouth Gazette* also notified them that 'a cold dinner will be provided on the Down for the Ladies, by the Gentlemen of the Hambledon Club, who hope for the honour of their company as formerly'.

By the 1790s a woman had actually taken over the catering at one county venue - Perriam Down, just over the border in Wiltshire. Shortly before Hampshire met England there on 25–26 July 1791 the *Hampshire Chronicle* noted that 'an ordinary on Down [will be] provided by Mrs Mercer, of the Star and Garter, Andover'. From 1787 great matches were held annually on Perriam Down under the auspices of Hambledon member Thomas Smith of Tidworth whose son's biographer (Wilmot 1862) observed that they were 'celebrated as the most agreeable meetings in Hants (sic), for the hospitality of Tedworth (sic) was open to the players and their friends; while the fair sex had their share of the day's amusement by the festivities being closed with a dance'. We have no record before the 1820s of cricket at Hambledon being followed by dancing. But eight miles away, at Upham in 1765, the maidens beat the married women for 'a large plum-cake, a barrel of ale, and regale of tea', after which the company met for tea and concluded the evening with a ball. Also in the 1760s the gentlemen of Greenwich used to hold an annual match to decide who should pay for a ball and supper for the ladies. And in 1773 we hear of a game on similar lines at Falmouth where the married beat the young gentlemen who then 'gave a very elegant entertainment to the ladies, likewise a ball'. For the Duke of Dorset's cricket 'fete' at Sevenoaks in 1782 a grand ball, which it was anticipated 'will be one of the most splendid within the memory of man', was arranged to conclude the second day's play of the match Kent (or the Duke of Dorset's team) *v* an England side composed mostly of Hampshire men. Not to be outdone, about three weeks later Sir Horace Mann organised a ball to accompany All England *v* Hampshire in Bourne Paddock, prompting the widowed Lady Hales, residing two miles away at Howletts, to write to a lady friend:

To-morrow Sir Horace Mann begins *his* fetes by a great

cricket-match between his Grace of Dorset and himself, to which all this part of the world will be assembled ... Many out of compliment to Sir Horace, who is never so happy as when he has all the world about him, and, as he gives a very magnificent ball and supper on Friday, it would not be so polite to attend *that*, without paying a compliment to his favourite amusement.

The attendance of the county ladies was a regular feature of cricket at Bishopsbourne. For Kent *v* 'Hambledon Club' in 1787 'the ladies ... made a very splendid appearance' and the following year, when an alphabetical match preceded Kent *v* Hampshire, six a-side, among the 'very large party of ladies and gentlemen of rank and fortune' were Lady Ann Lindsay and her sister, Lady Margaret Fordyce, assisting Sir Horace as 'Mistress of the Ceremonies'.

In those days female spectators at the great matches were rarely named by the press. But John Nyren identified one of them when his work was first serialised in *The Town* in 1832. She was Nancy Parsons, the daughter of a Bond Street hatter who at one stage became mistress of the Duke of Dorset:

He kept a mistress - a beautiful woman - I think her name was Parsons, who was fond of witnessing the playing of the matches. The cricketers are not famed for being Adonises in temperament if they are so in linear conformation. To show the easy footing upon which the respectable men in the club were placed by the noblemen who associated with them, Lord Tankerville, upon Nyren's expressing a wish to see the lady above-named, told him to pass such a carriage, while he was talking with her, and he would contrive to bring her head out of it.

Reputedly 'endowed with rare powers of attraction', she had previously been kept by the Prime Minister, the Duke of Grafton, whose joint passion for Nancy and for the turf were uppermost in Horace Walpole's mind when he complained about a state of government in which 'the world should be postponed to a whore and a horse race'. After Grafton separated from his Duchess in 1765 in order to live with Nancy

Parsons it was said he thereby 'insulted the virtue and decency of mankind by the most unblushing violation of both'. Then, discarded by the Duke as a necessary preliminary to his remarriage in 1769, Nancy was taken up by the Duke of Dorset who took her on a European Grand Tour lasting until 1771. Her attendance at the grand matches must have been around 1772-73, before the arrival of Dorset's new mistress, Mrs Armistead who in turn, by 1776, had given way to the Countess of Derby. For her part, Nancy in 1776 took a younger husband in the person of Viscount Maynard, later a member of the club which played cricket in White Conduit Fields. A facetious report in the *Daily Universal Register* in 1787 (19 December) alluded to her past and present liaisons with three dukes, including the then twenty-two-year-old Duke of Bedford.

> The present Viscountess Maynard is a remarkable instance of the powerful ascendancy of female captivation. This lady has had no less than three noblemen of ducal rank to grace her chariot wheels.

> The first on the list was the Duke of Grafton, at the time he was Prime Minister, and on which account the immortal Junius is so severe upon him in elegant letters.

> The second was his Grace of Dorset, who took all diplomatic lessons from Nancy Parsons.

> After her separation from this second attachment, she had the good fortune to captivate Lord Maynard, to whom she would surrender on no other terms than those of matrimony.

> Since her Ladyship's accession to the honors of Peerage, she has had the goodness to accompany the young Duke of Bedford on his travels abroad, and Lord Maynard was polite enough to be of the party.

Bedford, who played for Hertfordshire *v* Buckinghamshire in 1785, was a member of the White Conduit Club around 1786 and in 1787 attended one of the earliest matches held at Lord's first ground - 'many persons of the first fashion were on the ground - the Duke of Bedford, Lord Derby, Lord Galloway, Mr

Fitzroy, Mr Onslow, and many other gentlemen' (*Daily Universal Register* 25 June 1787). His younger brother, Lord John Russell, was president of Hambledon in 1795.

Nancy's preference for watching cricket from her coach was shared by several ladies in John Baker's circle. He gives instances at Horsham in 1773 when Mrs Swinburne 'sent horses away and sat in chaise during cricket match against Henfield', and, for Horsham *v* Reigate, Lady Irwin stayed in her carriage while Lord Irwin 'got out of the coach and stood with the crowd'. Sometimes ladies used to travel together to matches. The diarist William Bray of Shere mentions his wife and Mrs Skurray going by post-chaise to watch cricket in Albury Park, Surrey, in 1761, while Baker's diary entries for 1773 include: 'After dinner Mrs Swinburne went with Mrs Blunt to cricket match who called on her with Phaeton or Italian chaise' (16 June); 'Mrs Swinburne went in a post chaise a quarter before 8 to Mrs Woodwards to go with her in her chaise to Cricket Match' (29 July); and 'Came Mrs Woodward and took Mrs Swinburne to cricket match' (6 August). We also know from Baker that some ladies journeyed a fair distance to watch the Hampshire players, even when it meant having to find overnight accommodation near the ground. In 1772, on the first day of the Guildford match (see page 102), he was unable to find a seat in the dining booth because it was packed with 'so many ladies and gentlemen'. Among them were Miss Molyneaux (who had the misfortune to be taken with fits while drinking tea and had to be conveyed into Guildford to be attended to by Mr Shaw the apothecary); Mrs Steer and her daughter from Rusper in Sussex; the Countess of Tankerville (in the company of the Earl) and her sister-in-law, Lady Frances Alicia Tankerville; Lady Vincent (with Sir Francis) and Mrs Cayley accompanied by Miss Swindon. The last two had taken lodgings with Mrs Dixon, a milliner near the *White Lion* in Guildford, and drove up to the ground in Mrs Cayley's carriage. A party of ladies was invited to the match and Mrs Cayley afterwards complained that all were called upon for 5/- for the ordinary and 1/- for tea 'at which surprised and offended thinking they all at free cost from the invitation'. On the second day, sitting in the stand built over the dining booth

Baker saw just one (unnamed) lady dressed, as he noted, in a brown riding habit.[32]

The following year when watching England play Hampshire at Sevenoaks he noticed among the onlookers Mrs Evelyn, Mrs Blunt and Mrs Barrett (all with their husbands), Miss Bohun and his own daughter, Martha, whom he invariably styled, with unusual formality, 'Mrs Swinburne'. That same summer, when her husband, the travel-writer Henry Swinburne, was away from home, Baker records her presence at seven matches within the space of eight weeks - on 16 June, 25 June, 28-29 June, 7 July, 29 July, 6 August and 9 August - a revealing insight into the social status and essentially civilised character of rural cricket during the 18th century.[33]

Chapter Ten

STAKES AND GAMBLING

One long disputed feature of 18th and early 19th century cricket is the question of stake money - were the sums cited in advertisements real or were they invented in order to attract bigger crowds? John Nyren observed that at Hambledon 'these grand matches were always made for £500 a-side' while the view of Birley is that great matches were held every week 'usually for £500 but occasionally for £1000'. On a similar basis Ashley-Cooper once calculated that the Hambledon Club played for stake money amounting to at least £32,527 10s, winning £22,497 10s, losing £10,030, thereby finishing with a nett profit of £12,467. But if the club was so awash with money why is there no trace of it in the carefully compiled accounts covering the period 1791-96?

On a point of detail, the contention that matches were 'always' or 'usually' played for £500 or £1000 is contradicted by the newspapers which mostly quote stakes in guineas. As for actual amounts, Hampshire games organised by the club were indeed often claimed to be for 500 guineas, or 500 guineas a-side, sometimes even for 1,000 guineas:

> On Sevenoaks Vine, on Wednesday, the 18th of June inst., will be played the first match for a thousand guineas. Hampshire (with the Rt. Hon. Earl Tankerville) against All England. The wickets to be pitched at ten o'clock, and to be played with three stumps, to shorten the game. (*Kentish Gazette* 4 June 1777)

> To be played in Bourn Paddock on Wednesday next the 31st instant, A match of cricket, Hampshire, with two given men, against All England. For one thousand guineas. The wickets to be pitched at ten o'clock, and an ordinary on the ground, by Richardson, of the Fountain, at five shillings each, and another at eighteen pence. (*Canterbury Journal* 22 August 1780)

But some matches, such as the one at Bishopsbourne in 1773 commemorated in *Surry Triumphant*, were advertised for 2,000 guineas while at the other end of the scale there were other discrepancies, as indicated by the *Hampshire Chronicle*'s notices of Hambledon's home fixtures against Kent and Surrey in 1776. On 27 June it announced 'the third great cricket-match of the year, and the last that will be played in Hampshire this season ... for 500 Guineas a side', on 22 July 'the 5th and last match that will be played this season ... for Five Hundred Guineas', and on 26 August:

> On Monday the 26th inst will be played, a Match on Broadhalfpenny, Surrey with Miller against Hambledon Club with Colchin, for one Hundred Guineas. The wickets to be pitched at ten o'clock.

The home side had won the previous match by the huge margin of 198 runs, then according to the *Salisbury Journal* of 2 September, 'offered to play All England within a fortnight for any sum exceeding £50, but the superiority of the Hampshire gentlemen was acknowledged by the Surrey and Kentish gentlemen, and the challenge refused' - all a far cry from a standard £500 a-side!

Other great matches were advertised for 100 guineas or less - for example Kent *v* Surrey in 1776 for £50 a side; Chertsey *v* London, Kent & Surrey in 1775 for 50 guineas a side; Surrey *v* Hampshire at Laleham Burway in 1774 for £100 and the one arranged by Dorset and Tankerville in 1775:

> We hear the Duke of Dorset and Lord Tankerville have made an Alphabetical Cricket-Match of eleven on a side, for one hundred guineas, which is to be played in the Artillery-ground on Monday se'nnight.
> (*Middlesex Journal* 29 May 1775)

So if a match between two of the wealthiest patrons was for only 100 guineas how is it that a game between boys, Hambledon *v* Petersfield & Buriton, held on Broadhafpenny in 1781 could be advertised for 500 guineas a-side? At the very least it suggests that not all reputed stakes of 500 guineas or more were genuine. To take another example, in 1772 the town of Guildford is said to have donated 500 guineas in order to stage England *v* Hambledon while in 1777 England met Hampshire there 'for 1000 guineas and a purse of £100 given by the town of Guildford'. However we know from the Duke of Dorset's own score-sheets preserved in the Sackville MSS that Guildford's 1777 purse was actually 50 guineas - the same as those put up that season for other Hampshire games in the Artillery Ground and on Broadhalfpenny. Therefore it looks as though the figure touted in 1772 was a tenfold exaggeration, the one in 1777 almost double the true amount (with no mention, in Dorset's score-sheet, of the additional 1,000 guineas). On this basis it is hard to resist the conclusion that stakes were normally within the 50 to 100 guineas range - in keeping with the £50 a side for Nottingham *v* Beeston in 1792 which we may accept as bona fide because it was cited in the teams' correspondence in the *Nottingham Journal*. Of course it might be reasoned that whenever rich aristocrats became involved the financial stake increased according to their rank and fortune. But this is not what we find in the private account book of Lord Winchilsea, Hambledon's president in 1787 and 1789. Under neither income nor expenditure is there a single entry for 500 or 1,000 guineas (or pounds) or anything remotely similar. When personally concerned in promoting great matches the amounts were usually well under £100. Here are a few examples from Snow:

According to Newspaper, etc.	Related Entry in Account Book
1789 Hants *v* Kent, Windmill Down, for 500 gns a side.	'to cricket expenses at Hambledon' £44.0.0 (40 gns)
1789 Winchilsea's *v* Mann's XI, 'Phenix New Ground, Uxbridge' (sic), also called England or Hambledon *v* Kent, for 1,000 guineas.	'Balance of cricket acct Uxbridge' £73.10.0 (70 gns)
1789 Kent *v* Surrey, Bishopsbourne, for 1,000 gns.	'Balance of Cricket match' £129.3.0 (123 gns)
1789 Kent *v* Hants, Bishopsbourne. £16.16.6 (16 gns)	'rec'd balance of cricket match'
1789 Hants *v* England, Sevenoaks, for 1,000 gns.	'Balance of cricket Sevenoaks' £69.16.6 (66fi gns)
1790 Hants *v* Kent, Lord's, backed by Winchilsea and Darnley	'balance of cricket match with Lord Darnley' £44.2.0 (42 gns)

1791 Hambledon *v* 22 of Middlesex, Lord's, for 1,000 gns	'cost of the 22 and 11 match' £87.3.0 (83 gns)
1793 MCC *v* Kent, Lord's depicted In *The Sporting Magazine* as 'Grand Cricket Match .... Between the Earls of Winchelsea (sic) & Darnley for 1000 Guineas'	'Balance of Kent Match at Lords' £31.10.0 (30 gns)

123 guineas is the only £100 plus entry for 1789. The following year we have £153 for a match at his own country seat, Burley-on-the-Hill, and £136 for one at Uxbridge; in 1792 £130 for 'expenses of players cricket matches at Burley' and £168 covering two matches at Brighton; and in 1793 £130 for another match at Burley.

John Nyren identifies two of the gamblers present at a match on Broadhalfpenny in 1775 as club members Charles Powlett and Philip Dehany who, he says, told his father that they had 'edged off all their money' by 'laying it pretty thickly on the England side', and were likely to lose it all. Thereupon

> The proud old yeoman [in 1775 Richard Nyren was only 41] turned short upon them, and, with that honest independence which gained him the esteem of all parties, told them to their heads that they were rightly served, and that he was glad of it. "Another time (said he) don't bet your money against such men as we are!"

Yet though hedging[34] against one's own side seems to have been viewed by some as inherently unsporting, switching bets during the course of a match (at the fall of a wicket, between innings, etc) was part of the normal tactics, indeed for many part of the game's fascination. Odds would be quoted before the start, several days before in the case of some Hampshire matches:

> The great match at Bourn, for one thousand guineas, Hampshire with Lumpy against All England will be played on Thursday next the 25th of July. The wickets to be pitched at eleven o'clock precisely. The Duke of Dorset and Sir Horace Mann against the Hampshire gentlemen. The odds are six to five in favour of Hampshire. (*Kentish Gazette* 20 July 1782)

and then shift during the various turns in the play, as at Bishopsbourne in 1772:

> The betts at pitching the wickets were two to one and six to four in favour of Hampshire; the same betts were laid that All England would not make a tie the first innings. On the second day's sport the bets were even; in the course of All England's second innings the bets were much in their favour ...
>
> (*Kentish Gazette* 22 July 1772)

and on the Vine in 1773:

> The betts before they began to play were in common five to four - nay, some curious calculators ventured eleven to eight on the Hampshire Club; but knowing as they were, the odds soon became even, and presently turned against the Club, gradually increasing till twenty to one was offered ... (*Kentish Gazette* 3 July 1773)

Newspapers tended to be vague when it came to actual amounts. Typically, 'great sums were depending' when Hambledon met Chertsey in 1771, the Duke of Dorset won 'a considerable sum of money' when England beat Hampshire on Broadhalfpenny in 1774, and 'more money was won and lost than ever known on the like occasion' when England beat Hampshire the same year on Sevenoaks Vine. But what was meant by 'considerable' or 'great'? The *St James's Chronicle* in 1765 reported that a young butcher instead of going to buy cattle in Smithfield Market went instead to the Artillery Ground, where Dartford was playing Surrey and where he 'sported away' all the money on the cricket players - though the quoted sum (£40) might seem rather large for re-stocking a butcher's shop. Four years later (1769) the *Whitehall Evening Post* claimed that near £5,000 was laid on a match between Englishmen on the downs just outside Calais. And according to John Nyren 'many thousands' rested on the result when Hambledon (or rather England) scraped home by one wicket on Windmill Down in 1786. The following year as much as £20,000 was said to have been depending when six of England, backed 'by a number of Hampshire gentlemen', lost to six of Kent supported by Sir Horace Mann. We are not informed how this figure was arrived at, but if anything like correct we may assume Sir Horace made a handsome profit. According to *The Cricket Field* he 'would often bet some hundreds'. Less credibly, Mote and Birley are agreed that his betting on cricket brought about his financial ruin. He was so hooked on the game, we are told, that he went bankrupt and was forced to give up his estate at Bishopsbourne along with his private cricket ground. But this is a myth, not history. He did not own Bourne Place - he relinquished his tenancy a few years after inheriting the family seat at Linton Park from his uncle and namesake who died in Florence in 1786. And his bankruptcy occurred about fifteen years after leaving Bishopsbourne and ten after giving up patronage of big cricket. More plausibly, his money troubles may have had to do with his subsequent passion for whist.

With respect to Mann's rival patron of the late 1780s and 1790s, on the day he won 123 guineas backing Surrey against Kent in 1789 the *Daily Universal Register* observed: 'Cricket has this year been rather favourable to Lord Winchilsea. Let the men of the turf, my Lord, laugh at your game if they please - it will, we trust, enable your Lordship to laugh, when they are beneath the turf'. But his winnings only brought his season's income from cricket up to £241 15s 6d - as against expenses of over £300. Most of his bets that summer were relatively small. His accounts include such entries as 'won at cricket' 4 guineas; 'of Sir Horace Mann at cricket' 7 guineas; 'of Mr Pawlett' £11 18s; 'lost at cricket' 15 guineas; and 'lost at cricket' 4^1/2 guineas. And later, for games on Windmill Down, we have 'Lost at Hambledon match' £6 16s in 1791, and 'won at cricket Hambledon' £33 12s in 1792. All this is small beer set beside his play at hazard at which he once won 800 guineas at Boodles and often ended an evening with a profit or loss around £200. And even Winchilsea in no way approached the reputed expenditure of a gambler like the Duke of Dorset's nephew, Lord Thanet - a cricket spectator, player and patron between 1786 and 1794 - who was said to have won £40,000 and lost £120,000 during the course of two sittings at the Paris Salon. Thus, despite the undeniable fact that betting was an integral feature of early cricket, and despite the extravagant claims made by certain historians, our only really reliable evidence suggests that even among the very wealthy it tended to involve comparatively small sums and rarely if ever reached the excessive levels of many other forms of organised gaming.[35]

Chapter Eleven

SOME LATER PLAYERS

JAMES AYLWARD, according to Haygarth (*S&B* Vol I p 8), was born about 1741 at Peak Farm in Warnford parish, a few miles north of Hambledon, and worked on his father's farm in nearby Corhampton. *The Sporting Magazine* (December 1796, p. 135) claimed that in 1771 he 'fetched 160 runs' on Laleham Burway while batting for Middlesex & Hampshire *v* Kent & Surrey. But this has never been verified from contemporary sources. And if he really scored so many in a single match in 1771 it is strange that his name is missing from the Hampshire team of 1772 and from the Hambledon cricket song of about the same date. His known association with Hambledon began in 1773 and his long career ended with the most impressive figures of any Hampshire-born batsman of the under-arm era - almost 4,000 runs, average about 19. Nonetheless John Nyren tends to be dismissive, preferring to dwell less on his merits than on his supposed faults and foibles:

> His father was a farmer. After he had played for the club for a few years, Sir Horace got him away from us, and made him his bailiff, I think, or some such officer; I remember, however, he was but ill qualified for his post. Aylward was a left-handed batter, and one of the safest hitters I ever knew in the club. He once staid in two whole days, and upon the occasion got the highest number of runs that had ever been gained by any member; one hundred and sixty seven. Jemmy was not a good fieldsman, neither was he remarkably active. After he left us, to go down to live with Sir Horace, he played against us, but never to my recollection to any advantage to his new associates - the Hambledonians were almost always too strong for their opponents ... Aylward was a stout, well-made man, standing about five feet nine inches; not very light about the limbs, indeed he was rather clumsy. He would sometimes

affect a little grandeur of manner, and once got laughed at by the whole ground for calling for a lemon to be brought to him when he had been in but a little while. It was thought a piece of finnikiness by those simple and homely yeomen.

Some social historians claim that he was engaged by Sir Horace after making his record 167 for Hampshire *v* England on the Vine in 1777. One, in a passage of purest historical fiction, makes out that 'when the game ended Sir Horace Mann was seen in deep conversation with him' - all most unlikely bearing in mind that Mann was over five hundred miles away at the time, living on the Continent. He did not return to this country until after the close of the 1778 season and evidently had not taken Aylward into his employ by early June 1779 when Aylward played in a single-wicket game for the Duke of Dorset *against* Sir Horace. The same month he twice represented Hampshire *v* England, and in early August took part in two matches with his county colleague, Richard Veck, described as 'Kent, with two men out of Hampshire, against Surry (sic)'. Then in late August he scored 51 as given-man for England *v* Hampshire on Broadhalfpenny and on 13–16 September played for England seemingly as a qualified man. Therefore it looks as though he finally moved into Kent to work for Sir Horace Mann sometime in August or September 1779. He had certainly settled there by April 1780 when his name began to appear in the Bridge parish register. The parish of Bridge is close to Sir Horace's seat at Bishopsbourne, near Canterbury.

John Nyren's memory was at fault when he claimed that Aylward never played 'to any advantage to his new associates'. He often returned to Hampshire, on Stoke Down hitting 25 (top score of the innings) & 73 in 1781 and 75 in 1782; and on Windmill Down 21 & 27 (highest score in an innings of 91) when Kent won by one run in 1783; 53 in 1786; 31 (top score of the innings) & 65 in 1787; and 15 out of 34 in 1789 when Hampshire's two innings amounted to just 49 & 27.

From 1784 to 1794 he was registered as licensee of the *White Horse* at Bridge and on 16 June 1784, for Bridge *v* Sittingbourne & surrounding parishes on Bridge Hill, advertised 'a good ordinary at one o'clock' and 'a booth and good accommodation'. From 1786 to 1790 he also provided the ordinary during the great matches in Bourne Paddock - in 1789 and 1790 serving 'tea, coffee, etc' - prompting *The World* to comment in 1787 that 'Aylward lives at Bridge, a little place near Barham Downs. He is one of the Duke of Dorset [error for Horace Mann]'s men; and the Duke (sic) gives him the booth on the Cricket Ground and all their profit. In consequence of this, at home Aylward is a very inferior player'. He had eight children christened at Bridge between 1780 and 1792. One, Horace James, received the name of his employer while the eldest, Frances Augusta, was named after the Hambledon patron, Thomas Ridge's daughter born five years earlier at Kilmiston, a parish neighbouring both Warnford and Corhampton. According to Nyren, Aylward was 'introduced' to the Hambledon Club by the much younger player, Tom Taylor. This is an obvious error, perhaps confusing Taylor with Thomas (Tom?) Ridge.

Although Mann left Bishopsbourne in the early 1790s Aylward continued to combine innkeeping with cricket until at least 1793. His absence from the 1794 and 1795 scores suggests that this was when, as Haygarth says, 'he went abroad with Sir Horace'. Mann had returned by July 1795 when seen by Frederick Reynolds at a match on Stoke Down. Aylward evidently settled in London where in August 1796 he hit 98 for the combined Montpelier & Kennington *v* Thursday club. In 1797 he made 82 and 57 at Lord's and played his last match of note, between twenty-twos of Middlesex and Surrey, in 1802 when apparently in his early sixties. He died in Edward Street, Marylebone, in December 1827 - age given as eighty-six - and was buried in St John's Wood churchyard.

RICHARD PURCHASE first played for Hampshire in 1773 at the age of sixteen but after 1774, for reasons so far unexplained (unless there were two different players of the same surname), not again until 1781. The minute for 10 May 1774 instructed 'that Purchase be allowed Two Shillings and Sixpence for the hire of his horse whenever he attends Broady. meeting'. This represented a journey of some ten miles from his home at Liss where he was born on 24 September 1756 and always resided:

By trade he was a blacksmith in his native village, where he lived all his life, but was very poor latterly, giving up his business to his sons, who supported him. He used to be called "Old Doctor Purchase", which name he obtained because he used occasionally "to bleed the villagers". (*Scores and Biographies* Vol I p 13)

Like several cricketers of the period he worked part-time as a game-keeper, in his case after being appointed to the manors of Priors Dean, Colemere and Hawkley in 1780. According to John Nyren:

He was a slowish bowler - rather faster than Lord Beauclerk. His balls got up uncommonly well, and they were generally to a length. But he had no cunning about him; nor was he up to the tricks of the game - In playing as in all other actions in life, he was the same strait-forward honest fellow. Purchase was a fair hitter, and a tolerably good field. He was a slightly made man, and of a dark complexion.

Haygarth also reports that Purchase and William Harding of Frensham once went in first, chasing a target of 228, and put on 200 only to see their team-mates dismissed for another 20 and thus lose the match. For Hampshire his principal scores were 59 *v* Kent in Bourne Paddock in 1789 and 61 *v* England (Kent barred) in Burley Park in 1792. But his biggest innings in the first-class game were 73 for Lord Darnley's *v* Lord Winchilsea's XI on Windmill Down in 1790 and 73 for T.A. Smith's *v* Lord Winchilsea's XI on Perriam Down in 1796. He died at Liss on 1 April 1837. In 1858 a son was a blacksmith there, another kept the *White Horse* at St Cross near Winchester. The last was perhaps the Purchase who with Freemantle (son of Andrew - See page 144) and Windebank, all of Winchester, played the brothers John, Thomas and Henry Beagley of Alton on Twyford Down in 1833, when *The Sporting Magazine* reported that 'so animated a scene has not been exhibited on Twyford Downs since the grand match between All England and the Winchester Club, when the latter was victorious after three days admirable play'. Purchase top-scored with 39 in his only innings (Compare *Scores and Biographies* Vol. II p. 210).

DAVIS features in *Scores and Biographies* as Davis esq who scored 11 & 0 for Hambledon Town and 0 & 4 for 'Hambledon Club', both against Surrey, in 1773 but as plain 'Davis' who made 1 for the club *v* England in 1776. He was also simply 'Davis' in the scores of the second Surrey match given by Waghorn (1899 p. 108) and in the advertised list for Hambledon Club *v* Sussex in 1773. On the other hand in *The Hambledon Cricket Chronicle*'s additional scores 'Mr T. Davis' is credited with 6 & 3 *v* Surrey in 1773 and 40 & 13 *v* England in 1776. Since Ashley-Cooper fails to give his sources not a great deal may be deduced about this player. There is no record of a Davis subscribing to the club, so all that can be said is that if his initial really was T, and the 'esq' and 'Mr' subsequent embellishments, then the only obvious person living in Hambledon itself was the Thomas Daves (sic) who witnessed a marriage there in 1775 and, as Davis, married the twenty-five-year-old Mary Newell (signed x) on 8 November 1778.

JAMES BAILEY was mentioned in the minute for 17 August 1773 - 'Ordered that James Bayley be allowed the expence (sic) of his horse hire when he comes to practice of a Tuesday meeting on Broadhalfpenny and that he may hereafter be looked on as one of the Club' - and drafted into the team a month later, making 4 & 19 against Surrey at Laleham Burway and 24 (innings top score) & 1 in the return on Broadhalfpenny - matches described as being 'between Surrey and Hampshire, with two men given to each - viz., Miller and Minshull to Surrey, Frame and Bayley to Hampshire' (Waghorn 1899 p. 114). Although advertised to play *v* Kent in 1774 he never again played for the county, unless he was the Bayley who ten years later, against Kent in 1783, scored 2 & 12 on Windmill Down and 25 & 0 in Bourne Paddock. One thing is certain: he did not come from as far afield as Mitcham in Surrey as claimed by Ashley-Cooper. Bailey, or Bayley, was a Sussex man, one of three bearing the same surname - 'Jo', 'W' and 'Ja' (sic) Bailey - therefore probably brothers, selected for Sussex in the abortive match with Hambledon Club in 1773. Doubtless he was also one of 'the Bailys' who, with 'Parson Ellis', belonged to a team from West Sussex which according to John Baker met Henfield on 27 July 1774.

RICHARD FRANCIS after batting with some success for Surrey in 1773 - 30 & 36 *v* Kent and 35 *v* Hambledon Town - represented Hampshire as a qualified player from 1774 to 1784. John Nyren relates that he was a Surrey man and that

> One day I met him in the street of Hambledon and ran to tell our General [Richard Nyren, his father] that the famous Francis had come to live among us; he could scarcely believe me - perhaps for joy. This was the luckiest thing that could have happened to us, for Brett had just about the same time left off playing. Francis was a fast *jerker*; but though his delivery was allowed to be fair bowling, still it was a jerk. We enlisted him immediately, for we all knew what he could do, having seen him play on the Surrey side! against us. At that time he was a young man, and he remained many years in the club. He was a game-keeper; a closely made, firm little man, and active. His batting did not deserve any marked praise, still we always set him down for a few runs. He was both a better batter, however, and field too, than Brett; but as a bowler he ranked many degrees below that fine player.

The 'street' could mean the short High Street leading from almost opposite the *George* up the little hill towards the church. However with reference to '*we* enlisted him', etc., John Nyren was only nine at the time and he is wrong insofar as Francis began playing for Hampshire long *before* Brett retired. Also it is hard to believe that Richard Nyren knew nothing about him moving into the neighbourhood until after he had actually arrived. As a gamekeeper Francis presumably received the deputation of a nearby manor, perhaps from a landowning member of the Hambledon Club. The Surrey IGI contains two mid-18th century baptisms of a Richard Francis, at Thursley and at Haslemere, both in 1740. But if he was still 'a young man' in 1773, as stated by John Nyren, it is unlikely that either could relate to the cricketer. Francis hit 18 & 32 for Hambledon *v* Petworth in 1784 but soon afterwards must have moved away because in 1786 we find him on the Kent side against the White Conduit. He appeared again for Kent two years later and is next heard of in 1793 playing for Essex teams - Hornchurch, Essex and the twenty-two of Hertfordshire & Essex which met England first on Stoke Down then at Lord's. A second man named Francis (or Frances), perhaps Richard's brother, played once for Hampshire *v* Kent in 1775.

THOMAS TAYLOR made many good scores for Hampshire, including 62 *v* England at Guildford in 1777, 80 *v* England at Moulsey Hurst in 1779, 51 *v* Kent on Windmill Down in 1783 and 66 *v* Kent at Bishopsbourne, again in 1783. But his highest was 117 as given-man for the White Conduit against Kent at Bishopsbourne in 1786, when the *Kentish Gazette* (11 August 1786) remarked that 'it is extremely singular that after Walker had two such hands [95 & 102] that he should lose the lottery - a subscription purse - which at present Taylor bids fair to carry off, as having got the most runs in one innings'. Despite the fact that he only began to take part in the great matches in 1775 John Nyren treats him as one of the elite 'old eleven', ahead of Aylward:

> Tom was an admirable field - certainly one of the very finest I ever saw. His station was between the point of the bat and the middle wicket to save the two runs, but Tom had a lucky knack of gathering into the wicket, for Tom had a licence from our old General; so that, if the ball was hit to him he had so quick a way of meeting it, and with such a rapid return (for no sooner was it in his hand, than with the quickness of thought it was returned to the top of the wicket) that I have seen many put out by this manoeuvre in a single run, and when the hit might be safely calculated upon for a prosperous one. He had an excellent general knowledge of the game, but of fielding in particular he was perfect both in judgment and practice. Tom was also a most brilliant hitter, but his great fault lay in not sufficiently guarding his wicket; he was too fond of cutting, at the point of the bat, balls that were delivered strait; although, therefore, he would frequently earn many runs, yet, from this habit, he could not be securely depended on, and indeed it was commonly the cause of his being out ... Taylor was a short, well

made man, strong, and as watchful and active as a cat ... he was without guile, and was an attached friend.

According to Beldham, as retold by Pycroft in *The Cricket Field*, the lbw law was not introduced 'till Ring, one of our best hitters, was shabby enough to put his leg in the way, and take advantage of the bowlers; and when Tom Taylor, another first-rate hitter, did the same, the bowlers found themselves beaten, and the law was passed to make leg-before-wicket Out'. An lbw law had in fact been part of the laws of cricket since 1744. But in the 1774 revision it was stated that the striker would be out if there was 'a design to stop the ball'. Clearly, on this basis, provided a batsman stepped in front of the wicket and made just a token attempt at a stroke he could not be dismissed. And as no one is known to have been out lbw under this law it presumably proved unworkable. Ring and Taylor seem to have taken advantage of this loophole by stepping before the wicket as they played their strokes, so that whenever they missed the ball they avoided being bowled out. It was presumably to stop this practice that the lbw law was altered on 30 May 1788 with the 'design to stop the ball' clause omitted. This may be why in thirty completed innings during the two seasons 1788 and 1789 Taylor could average only 5, and why, despite making a few useful scores, he never again became a really top-class bat.

Taylor was baptised at Ropley on 18 October 1753 but spent most of his life at Alresford where we find him helping to promote cricket in 1780:

> NOTICE is hereby given, that on Tuesday, July 11, 1780, A MATCH at CRICKET will be played on the New Ground (the NYTHE) near Alresford, between the gentlemen of Farnham, Alton, Odiham and Yately, against the gentlemen of Alresford, for a SILVER CUP, value 10 *l.* to be given gratis by Mr. Thomas Taylor, and also for Eleven Guineas a side. The wickets to be pitched precisely at ten o'clock. A good cold collation will be provided. Tea, coffee, &c.
>
> *(Reading Mercury* 3 July 1780)

and four years later catering on nearby Stoke Down for 'the

long-expected MATCH between the Gentlemen of the HAMBLEDON CLUB and Sir H. MANN, six of a side at single wicket; Lumpey with five Hampshire men against any six in England':

> Tom Taylor has laid in a stock of the best wines, with tea, coffee, &c. Cold provisions of all kinds, such as beef, mutton, ham, chicken, tarts, jellies, &c. &c. will be found at any hour, and in any quantity, at his booth and marquees on the Down. He humbly begs leave to solicit the protection of the public in this his first essay, and he flatters himself that his behaviour on the 26th will entitle him to the future favours of all those who shall be pleased to honour him with their company.
>
> *(Salisbury Journal* 19 July 1784)

Besides working as an innkeeper he was also a gamekeeper. At the Quarter Sessions on 5 October 1784 Charles Powlett's cousin, the Duke of Bolton, appointed him to the deputation for Itchen Stoke and on 6 October 1789, when styled a victualler of Alresford, gamekeeper to the manors of Itchen Stoke and Itchen Abbas. In its 1806 May edition *The Sporting Magazine* reported: 'Lately died Mr Thomas Taylor, master of the Globe Inn, at Alresford. He was well known as an excellent cricketer for some years'. He was buried in Old Alresford churchyard.

RICHARD AUBREY VECK, unaccountably overlooked by John Nyren, from 1776 to 1784 hit 1,095 runs in the great matches for an average, 17.66, second only to Aylward among Hampshire batsmen of his era. His runs included five half-centuries within the space of three seasons - for Hampshire *v* England 79 in the Artillery Ground and 54 on Broadhalfpenny in 1777; 53 not out at Sevenoaks in 1778; and 79 also at Sevenoaks in 1779; and 55 as given-man for Kent *v* Surrey at Laleham Burway in 1779. A 'well grown man', 5' 9 1/4" tall, he was a native of New Alresford and doubtless one of 'the victorious Alresford boys' said to be playing for Hampshire against the parish of Hambledon in 1774. One of his local matches was advertised in 1780:

> On Monday the 24th instant, A Third Match between

the gentlemen of Alton and Odiham, with Noah Man (sic), against the gentlemen of Alresford, with Veck and Taylor, will be played on Alton Butts. The wickets will be pitched at nine o'clock, that the lovers of this noble game may expect to see it concluded in one day. A cold collation, tea, coffee, &c. will be provided on the green.

(Reading Mercury 24 July 1780)

In 1783 Veck moved to Bishops Waltham:

BISHOP'S WALTHAM, HANTS.

Richard Aubrey Veck begs leave to inform the public that he hath taken the house, shop and premises, lately occupied by Mr. Thomas Hart, Hosier and Draper, at Bishop's Waltham, wherein he intends to carry on the LINEN and WOOLLEN DRAPERY, HOSIERY, and HABERDASHERY BUSINESS on the most reasonable terms, and hopes for a continuance of the favours of Mr. Hart's customers to the same shop, as well as those of his own friends, whose encouragement and preference he shall uniformly endeavour to deserve and acknowledge.   Funerals Furnished.

(Hampshire Chronicle 7 July 1783)

and on 22 April 1784 he married Elizabeth Bulpett at Old Alresford. A few months later he played his last important match, six a side Hambledon *v* England on Stoke Down towards the end of July, though he was presumably the Veck who after an eight-year absence made 3 & 17 not out for a Hampshire team *v* Brighton on Windmill Down in 1792. He is buried in a vault in Old Alresford churchyard, marked by an inscription reading:

IN MEMORY OF
RICHARD AUBERY VECK,
who died at Bishops Waltham,
on the 18th day of November, 1823,
AGED 67 YEARS.

His son, Henry was baptised at Bishops Waltham on 16 April 1785 and at the age of thirty-two, in 1818, went to Magdalen Hall, Cambridge, as son of Richard Veck, gentleman of Bishops Waltham, and after taking holy orders became a chaplain to the Royal Marines and, in 1831, perpetual curate of Forton St John, Alverstoke, where he remained until his death in 1866.

NOAH MANN, perhaps the most brilliant all-rounder connected with the club, began to play for Hampshire in the late summer of 1777 while in his early twenties. In a few early games he only once made more than 11, a top-score of 23. But he must have created a big impression because early next season, on 25 May 1778, the *Hampshire Chronicle* hailed him as 'the famous Noah Man (sic)' when given to Hambledon parish in a match against the rest of the county. Then, in 1784, before he faced Richard Lawrence of Windsor at single-wicket in the Old Field near Maidenhead for £50 a side, the *Reading Mercury* (21 June) announced that 'as Noah Mann is thought to be the best single wicket player in England great sums of money are depending.' John Nyren was one of his greatest admirers:

> He was a fellow of extraordinary activity, and could perform clever feats of agility on horseback. For instance, when he has been seen in the distance coming up the ground, one or more of his companions would throw down handkerchiefs, and these he would collect, stooping from his horse while it was going at full speed. He was a fine batter, a fine field, and the swiftest runner I ever remember; indeed such was his fame for speed, that whenever there was a match going forward, we were sure to hear of one being made for Mann to run against some noted competitor; and such would come from the whole country round. Upon these occasions he used to tell his friends, "If, when we are half-way, you see me alongside of my man, you may always bet your money upon me, for I am sure to win." And I never saw him beaten. He was a most valuable fellow in the field; for besides being very sure of the ball, his activity was so extraordinary, that he would dart all over the ground like lightning. In those days of fast bowling, they would put a man behind the long-stop, that he might cover both long-stop and slip: the man always selected for this post was Noah ... Mann would, upon occasion, be employed as a change-bowler, and in this department he was very

extraordinary. He was left-handed, both as bowler and batter. In the former quality his merit consisted in giving a curve to the ball the whole way. In itself it was not the first-rate style of bowling, but so very deceptive, that the chief end was frequently attained ... Sometimes when a batter had got into his hitting, and was scoring more runs than pleased our general, he would put Mann in to give him eight or twelve balls, and he almost always did so with good effect. Noah ... was a good batsman, and a most severe hitter ... short (in stature) and, when stripped, as swarthy as a gipsey. He was all muscle, with no incumbrance whatever of flesh; remarkably broad in the chest, with large hips and spider legs; he had not an ounce of flesh about him, but it was where it ought to be. He always played without his hat (the sun could not affect *his* complexion) ...

John Nyren also recalled a match against England when, chasing victory in the final innings, the general of the side, Richard Nyren, put him in last:

Mann kept on worrying old Nyren to let him go in, and although he became quite indignant at his constant refusal, our General knew what he was about in keeping him back. At length, when the last but one was out, he sent Mann in, and there were then ten runs to get. The sensation now all over the ground was greater than anything of the kind I ever witnessed before or since. All knew the state of the game, and many thousands were hanging upon this narrow point ... After Noah had had one or two balls, Lumpy tossed one a little too far, when our fellow got in, and hit it out in his grand style. Six of the ten were gained. Never shall I forget the roar that followed this hit. Then there was a dead stand for some time, and no runs were made; ultimately, however, he gained them all, and won the game. After he was out he upbraided Nyren for not putting him in earlier. 'If you had let me go in an hour ago (said he), I would have served them in the same way'. But the old tactician was right, for he knew

Noah to be a man of such nerve and self-possession, that the thought of so much depending upon him, would not have the paralysing effect that it would upon many others. He was sure of him; and Noah afterwards felt the compliment.

This seems to be a slightly inaccurate recollection of the match played on Windmill Down from 13 to 15 July 1786 - Kent *v* Hambledon Club according to *Scores and Biographies* but at the time also described as Kent *v* All England. The home side scraped home by one wicket with Mann (entered, on the basis of the first innings, at number ten in the order) 15 not out. Lumpy did not play, nor did Richard Nyren, though the latter presumably acted as captain by directing affairs from the boundary.

Mann's father, Noah senior, a shoemaker, married Sarah Boxall in 1749 at Northchapel in Sussex where the cricketer was born, according to *Scores and Biographies* on 15 November 1756 - though elsewhere his baptism is given as 14 August. His own marriage, to Ann Paddick, is recorded at Northchapel in 1777. The same year be bought a small ale-house, the *Seven Stars*, more commonly known as the *Stars*, at the northern end of the village and spent the rest of his life there, at the same time following his father's trade. By 1779 he (or Noah senior?) was also a tollhouse keeper at the old Toll House across the road not far from the *Stars*. His career in the great matches - 1,384 runs, average 15, top-score 73 England *v* Kent on Stoke Down in 1781- came to a premature end with his death in December 1789 at the early age of thirty-three. Nyren relates how he spent a day shooting with some friends, and the evening in 'a free carouse':

he could not be persuaded to go to bed, but persisted in sleeping all night in his chair in the chimney-corner. It was ... the custom in that part of the country, to heap together all the ashes on the hearth for the purpose of keeping the fire in till the next day. During the night my poor playmate fell upon the embers, and being unable to help himself, burned his side so severely, that he did not survive twenty-four hours.

All this happened at the *Half Moon Inn* near thc centre of Northchapel, kept by Mrs Bookham from 1785 to 1792, where an inquest was convened two days later:

> On Wednesday the 10th ult., an inquest was taken by Mr. Johnson of Petworth, at the House of Mrs. Brookham, (sic) the Half Moon in Northchapel in this county, on the body of Noah Mann, the famous cricketer, who, on the preceding Monday was burnt to death; being very much intoxicated, he could not be prevailed on either to leave the house or go to bed; in consequence he laid down in the middle of the kitchen, and as there was very little fire, he was thought quite safe; however, in the night Mrs. Brookham's (sic) son, hearing a noise, went to see the cause, and found this unfortunate man all in flame. The young man, in endeavouring to extinguish the flames, was so terribly burnt, that he now lies dangerously ill. Verdict, accidental death.   (*Hampshire Chronicle* 4 January 1790)

More acerbically, *Sarah Farley's Bristol Journal* commented:

> Noah Mann who was burnt to death whilst sleeping before an ale-house fire at North Chapel, was undoubtedly the first cricketer in England at all points of the game; and had his integrity been equal to his dexterity, he might have acquired an independency from the patronage of amateurs of the game; this unhappily was not the case, and he fell a victim to his own intemperance.

To judge by the *Hampshire Chronicle* Noah died on 8 December. But one account says 17th, and he was buried, as Noah junior, on the 18th. His children included Horace, named after Sir Horace Mann who according to John Nyren stood godfather; Noah, a practice bowler at Lord's for some sixteen seasons who was one of the umpires when John Willes was no-balled for bowling round-arm in 1822, and John who died at Northchapel around 1858 after umpiring country matches for forty-seven years.[36]

DAVID HARRIS though born at Elvetham about 1754 moved while 'quite a child' to Crookham where he worked as a potter until his death in 1803. Haygarth gleaned this information from a nephew, Timothy Hill of Ewshot near Farnham, who also said he died at the age of forty-eight. But apparently the age has never been verified from contemporary records. So far as we know he did not play for the teams fielded by nearby Alton, Farnham & Odiham *v* Alresford in 1779 or 1780, but was advertised for 'the gentlemen of the Alresford and Odiham Clubs' against 'the Gentlemen of the County of Hants' in May 1782. Two months later he made his debut in the great matches, when apparently already in his mid to late twenties. Yet even at this mature age, according to John Nyren, he was still very inaccurate and prone to bowl too many full tosses:

> When he first joined the Hambledon club, he was quite a raw countryman at cricket, and had very little to recommend him but his noble delivery. He was also very apt to give tosses. I have seen old Nyren scratch his head and say "Harris would make the best bowler in England if he did not toss." By continual practice, however, and following the advice of the old Hambledon players, he became as steady as could be wished; and in the prime of his playing very rarely indeed gave a toss, although his balls were pitched the full length.

Haygarth (*S&B* Vol I p 51) notes that he developed his skill by regular practice in a barn during the winter or in wet weather, while in *The Cricket Field* we read that:

> in a kind of skittle-alley formed between hurdles, he used to practise by bowling four different balls from one end, and then picking them up he would bowl them back again. His bowling cost him a great deal of practice; but it proved well worth his while, for no man ever bowled like David, and he was always first chosen of all the men in England.

John Nyren has left the following description of his bowling:

> It would be difficult, perhaps impossible, to convey in writing an accurate idea of the grand effect of Harris's bowling; they only who have played against can fully appreciate it. His attitude when preparing for

131

his run previously to delivering the ball, would have made a beautiful study for the sculptor. Phidias would certainly have taken him for a model. First of all he stood erect like a soldier at drill; then with a graceful curve of his arm, he raised the ball to his forehead, and drawing back his right foot, started off with his left. The calm look, and general air of the man were uncommonly striking, and from this series of preparations he never deviated … His mode of delivering the ball was very singular. He would bring it from under the arm by a twist and nearly as high as his arm-pit, and with this action push it, as it were, from him. How it was that the balls acquired the velocity they did by this mode of delivery I never could comprehend … In bowling, he never stooped in the least in his delivery, but kept himself upright all the time. His balls were very little beholden to the ground when pitched; it was but a touch, and up again; and woe be to the man who did not get in to block them; for they had such a peculiar curl that they would grind his fingers against the bat …

He goes on to say that he often walked with him 'to Windmill-down at six o'clock in the morning of a day that a match was to be played' and noticed the trouble he took 'in choosing the ground for his fellow-bowler as well as himself'. But this can only have been for practice games. Under the then laws the visiting team had choice of ground for pitching the wickets. We are also told by Nyren that

He was a muscular, bony man, standing about five feet 9 ½ inches. His features were not regularly handsome, but a remarkably kind and gentle expression amply compensated the defect of mere linear beauty. The fair qualities of his heart shone through his honest face, and I call to mind no worthier, or, in the active sense of the word, not a more 'good man' than David Harris … He was a man of so strict a principle, and such high honour, that I believe his moral character was never impeached. I never heard even a suspicion breathed against his integrity, and I knew him long and intimately.

Harris missed several matches in 1791, doubtless owing to the early effects of the illness which clouded his later career. According to Haygarth he 'suffered much from the gout, and latterly, in fact, was quite a cripple. He often walked to the ground on crutches to play, when, after delivering a few balls, and getting warm, would still perform splendidly'. Likewise Nyren - who 'passed a very pleasant time with Harris' when he stayed at his father's *George Inn* 'by invitation, after an illness' - testifies that 'Lord Frederick has been heard to say that Harris's bowling was one of the grandest things of the kind he had ever seen; but his lordship could not have known him in his prime; he never saw him play until after he had many fits of the gout, and had become slow and feeble'. And in *The Gentleman's Magazine* in 1833 the Revd John Mitford relates that 'Harris was terribly affected with the gout; it was at length difficult for him to stand; a great armchair was therefore always brought into the field, and after the delivery of a ball, the hero sat down in his own calm and simple grandeur, and reposed. A fine tribute this, to his superiority, even amid the tortures of disease'. One of his last matches before succumbing to ill-health was R. Leigh's XI *v* Lord Winchilsea's Xl on Stoke Down in 1795 when the playwright Frederick Reynolds was drafted in as a late substitute, to be dismissed 'b Harris 3' and 'run out 0'. Reynolds recorded the occasion:

> I, for the first and last time, played against the celebrated, formidable Harris. In taking my place at the wicket I almost felt as if taking my ground at a duel ... and my terrors were so much increased by the mock pity and sympathy of Hammond, Beldham, and others round the wicket, that when this mighty bowler - this *Jupiter tonans* - hurled his bolt at me, I shut my eyes in the intensity of my panic and mechanically gave a random desperate blow which, to my utter astonishment, was followed by a cry all over the ring of "Run, Run!" I did run, and with all my force ... getting *three* notches ... I could not *stop* the next ball. To my great joy up went my stumps and out I walked ...

Harris died, still a comparatively young man, in May 1803. He was buried on the 19th in the churchyard at Crondall between Odiham and Farnham.

JOHN FREEMANTLE who played a few times in the early 1780s was elder brother of the more famous Andrew (see page 143), described by Nyren as 'a stoutly-made man', about 5' 10" tall, who 'delivered his ball high and well, and tolerably fast; yet he could not be ranked among the *fast* bowlers'. Furthermore

> As a batter, John Freemantle would have been reckoned a good hand in any club. He would now and then get many runs; yet, withal, he could by no means be pronounced a fine batter. As a man, he bore a high character for straight-forward manly integrity; in short he was a hearty John Bull, and flinched no more from his duty, than he did from a ball in the field, and this he never did, however hard it might hit him.

He came from Bishops Sutton but later lived in Alresford as a master-builder. His memorial stone in New Alresford churchyard bore the legend:

IN MEMORY OF
JOHN FREEMANTLE
Who Died August 3, 1831,
AGED 73 YEARS.

JAMES WELLS was one of those who in 1785 were to be considered as belonging to the club and paid when they came to play at Hambledon (minute 26 July). Haygarth says he was brother of the more famous John (see page 139) and was presumably the Wells who assisted Alton, Farnham & Odiham *v* Alresford in 1780, Farnham in the 1780s and Hampshire *v* England on Windmill Down in 1783. In 1789 he hit 80 for Surrey *v* Hampshire at Moulsey Hurst.

JOHN SMALL junior, son of a famous father (see pages 41-48), was born at Petersfield in 1765 and played in the great matches from 1784 to 1811, scoring 3,641 runs for an average of 13.58. His biggest innings were 95 for R. Leigh's XI *v* Sir H. Mann's XI at Margate in 1795 and 88 for Lord Yarmouth's XI *v* R. Whitehead's XI at Lord's in 1799. In the words of John Nyren, 'Young Small was a very handsomely made man. For perfect symmetry of form, and well-knit, compact limbs and frame, his father was one of the finest models of a man I ever beheld; and the son was little inferior to him in any respect'. Then, switching to the second person, Nyren adds: 'your judgment of the game was equal to that of any man. Your style of hitting, to my mind, was of the very first quality; and I can name no one who possessed a more accurate judgment of a short run ... I am not sure that your middle-wicket (the post that your father occupied) was not as good as his - though, I dare say, you would not allow this'. And finally, reverting back to the third person, notes that

> he was as complete a chap as I ever knew - a genuine chip of the old block - an admirable player, and a highly honourable man. The legs at Marylebone never produced the least change in him; but, on the contrary, he was thoroughly disgusted at some of the manoeuvres that took place there from time to time.

As a mercer of Petersfield, age given as twenty-eight, he was licensed on 24 December 1794 to marry Mary Lever, spinster. She died on 3 July 1809 aged forty-five. His monumental inscription in Petersfield churchyard read: 'Sacred to the memory of JOHN SMALL, who departed this life the 21st of January 1836 aged 70 years'. In 1860 his son, another John, continued the drapery business at Petersfield in the same premises previously occupied by John senior and junior.

GEORGE BELDHAM, 'a finer player; a good batter, and generally competent to fill the different posts in the game' (Nyren), was baptised at Farnham on 17 May 1758 and married Sarah Butt there on 17 February 1789. He must have been the Beldham playing for Alton, Farnham & Odiham in 1780 and for Farnham from 1782. He was engaged by Hambledon at the age of twenty-seven when the minute for 1785 ordered that he along with his younger brother William 'be considered as players belonging to this club'.

HARRY WALKER first played for six of Hambledon or Hampshire *v* the same of England in 1784. Born at Hyde Farm at Churt in Frensham parish c1760, 5' 11" tall and weighing 13 stone, he was an aggressive left-hand bat, the opposite of his brother Tom - 'his half hour at the wicket was better than Tom's whole afternoon' (*The Cricket Field*). William Beldham remarked that 'Harry Walker was the first, I believe, who brought cutting to perfection ... [he] would wait for the ball till all but past the wicket, and then cut with great force' (*The Cricket Field*). According to John Nyren he was not a very active but effective field. In the great (double-wicket) matches his career lasted from 1786 to 1802 with 2,767 runs, average 14.87 and a highest score of 115 not out for Surrey *v* England at Lord's in 1794. His family were farmers with land near the Devil's Punchbowl. But around 1794 he moved to Brook near Witley where he worked as a maltster until his death at forty-five. He was buried at Witley on 22 July 1805.

THOMAS WALKER, younger brother of Harry, but right-handed, established himself as the greatest run-getter of the day in 1786, his first season in big cricket, making

17 & 13 White Conduit Club *v* Kent, White Conduit Fields
43 & 10 England (?) *v* Kent, Sevenoaks Vine
55 & 26 England (?) *v* Kent, Windmill Down
56 & 6 Alphabetical Match, Moulsey Hurst
95 not out & 102 White Conduit Club *v* Kent, Bishopsbourne

During the course of the last match the *Kentish Gazette* of 11 August remarked that 'the game of cricket seems now to have arrived at its meridian for it was universally allowed that the batting in this match exceeded any that had ever been played before'. And a month later, on 12 September, the *Whitehall Evening Post* noted that 'a new player is sprung up in Hampshire (sic) far superior to all of the old or new school of Cricket; his name is Walker: he plays the whole game with admirable skill, and is so dextrous a batsman as frequently this summer to have gone in first and run [seen] the other ten of his party out'.

As unathletic and awkward a player ever to make a major mark in cricket, John Nyren spoke of his 'hard, ungain, scrag-of-mutton frame; wilted, apple-john face, (he always looked twenty years older than he really was), his long spider legs, as thick at the ankles as the hips, and perfectly strait all the way down'. In William Beldham's opinion 'Tom Walker was the most tedious fellow to bowl to, and the slowest runner between the wickets I ever saw'. To John Nyren 'he moved like the rude machinery of a steam engine in the infancy of construction, and when he ran, every member seemed ready to fly to the four winds. He toiled like a tar on horseback'.

He amassed runs laboriously, regardless of time and effort, hence his nickname 'Old Everlasting'. His initial season closed in September 1786 with a six a side game in which he top-scored in each innings with 26 & 12 - 38 runs from 703 balls, three times slower than the other side's best bat: 68 from 404. Yet even this was brisk compared to his 5 in 230 balls (at one stage 1 in 189) in a similar match, Hampshire *v* England, at Lord's in 1788, or the occasion mentioned by the *Maidstone Journal* in 1790: 'Cricket was formerly an exertion of strength: it is now an application of skill. One of the Walkers some time ago continued his innings four hours and got but 9 notches'. But according to *The World* (1788) he was 'the first bat in the kingdom. His caution (though a very young man) is superior to any veteran in the field; and the instances are very rare of his raising a ball'. The playwright Frederick Reynolds believed 'no man could equal Harris in bowling, or surpass Tom Walker in batting ...' And this is John Nyren:

> I have very frequently known Tom go in first and remain to the very last man. He was the coolest, the most imperturbable fellow in existence: it used to be said of him that he had no nerves at all. Whether he were only practising, or whether he knew that the game was in a critical state, and that much depended upon his play, he was the same phlegmatic, unmoved man - he was the Washington of cricketers ... I remember Tom going in first, and Lord Frederick Beauclerk giving him the first four balls, all of an excellent length. First four or last four made no difference to Tom - he was always the same cool, collected fellow. Every ball he dropped down just before his bat. Off went his lordship's white hat - dash upon the ground (his constant action when disappointed), calling him at the same time "a confounded old beast". "I doant care what ee zays", said Tom, when one close by asked if he had heard Lord Frederick call him "an old beast". No, no; Tom was not the man to be flustered.

Though never quite repeating his early run-getting heroics, from 1786 to 1812 Walker accumulated 6,429 runs, average 18.90, and ground out five more centuries - highest 138 for Surrey & Sussex *v* England in 1793. Some two years after joining the club he began (about 1788?) to experiment with a form of round-arm bowling, deprecated by John Nyren as 'the system of throwing instead of bowling, now so much the fashion' - 'it was esteemed foul play, and so it was decided by a council of the Hambledon club, which was called for the purpose.' In the words of Haygarth (*S&B* Vol I p.64), 'he then took to underhand lobs of the tedious slow school, which was very successful'. Indeed, for Surrey *v* England at Lord's in 1794 he bowled 9 wickets. In this connection John Nyren further observed:

> I never thought much of Tom's bowling; indeed the bowling of that time was so super eminent, that he was not looked upon as a bowler - even for a change. He afterwards, however, greatly improved; and what with his thorough knowledge of the game, his crafty manner, (for he was one of the most fox-headed fellows I ever saw), and his quickness in seizing every advantage, he was of considerable service to his party, but he never was a first-rate bowler.

Haygarth states that like Harry he was born at Hyde Farm, close to the Hampshire border, on 16 November 1762.[37] On 1 December 1795 he married Sarah Hone at Thursley and about that time is said to have moved into his wife's parish to work as a farmer. He was still there when his son, Henry, was baptised in 1797, but by 1802 had moved to Chiddingfold where he kept a grocer's shop and where he died in 1831. The inscription over his grave read:

IN MEMORY OF
THOMAS WALKER,
Who died March 1, 1831,
AGED 68.

His widow survived him by about thirty years. In 1859 she was in Chiddingfold 'still alive and hearty' at eighty-four.

JOHN WELLS of Farnham - presumably either Wells or J. Wells of the 1782 Farnham team - was engaged by the club in 1785 and began to play first-class cricket in 1787, seemingly at the rather advanced age of twenty-eight.[38] From John Nyren we learn that

> He was a short, thick, well-set man; in make like a cob-horse, proportionately strong, active and laborious. As a bowler he had a very good delivery; he was also a good general field, and a steady batter - in short, an excellent "servant of all work" ... John Wells possessed all the requisites for making a thoroughly useful cricketer; and in his general deportment he was endowed with those qualities which render man useful to society as well as happy in himself. He was a creature of transparent and unflawed integrity - plain, simple, and candid; uncompromising, yet courteous; civil and deferential, yet no cringer. He always went by the title of "Honest John Wells", and as long as I knew him he never forfeited the character he had gained ... in addition to his level merits as a general cricketer, he was esteemed to possess an excellent judgment of the game, and in questions that were frequently mooted, his opinion would be appealed to.

while according to *The Cricket Field*

> John Wells was a most dangerous man in a single-wicket match, being so dead a shot at a wicket. In one celebrated match, Lord Frederick warned the Honorable H. Tufton to beware of John; but John Wells found an opportunity of maintaining his character by shying down, from the side, little more than the single stump.

His top scores were 93 for Surrey *v* England at Lord's in 1799; 75 when given to Hampshire *v* Kent & Surrey on Stoke Down in 1794 and 63 for MCC with five of Hambledon *v* England at Lord's in 1792.

Wells followed the trade of baker in his native parish where on 9 October 1791 he married William Beldham's sister, Hannah (born 1768), and had several cricketing sons. In 1813

The Sporting Magazine reported how three of them, with their father, 'Mr Wells of Farnham', lost to four brothers from Winchester named Holloway by 17 (or 16) runs on Twyford Downs after 5-1 had been offered on the Holloways at the start: 'the parties being the most celebrated players of the present day, great interest was excited, and bets to a large amount depending'. The Wells family won the return at Farnham on 29 June. Seven years later Farnham fielded an eleven against Godalming which included J. Wells senior and junior, George (who top-scored with 43) and James Wells. The younger John was born at Farnham in 1801; George, 'believed' to have died in 1845 aged fifty-four, took part in a few great matches 1814-21, while James, the fourth son, was keeping a public-house at Bourne near Farnham in 1862. John Wells himself was buried at Farnham where his gravestone carried the inscription: 'JOHN WELLS Who died December 15, 1835, AGED 76'. Haygarth records that in Wrecclesham, an outlying hamlet of Farnham parish, there was (in 1861) a tavern with the sign 'The Rendezvous of the Celebrated Cricketers Beldham and Wells'.

WILLIAM BELDHAM, one of the boys coached by 'a gingerbread baker at Farnham of the name of Harry Hall' [Henry born 1750], was playing for Farnham, his native parish, by the age of sixteen and joined the club with his elder brother, George, in 1785. In *The Cricket Field* he is quoted as saying

> I was a lad of eighteen at this Hampshire (sic) village, and Lord Winchilsea had seen us play, and watched the match with the Hambledon Club on Broadhalfpenny, when I scored forty-three runs against David Harris, and ever so many of the runs against David's bowling, and no one could manage David before. So, next year, in the month of March, I was down in the meadows, when a gentleman came across the fields with Farmer Hilton ... I was to play Hampshire against England, at London, in White Conduit Fields ground, in the month of June. For three months I did nothing but think about the match. Tom Walker was to travel up from the country, and I agreed to go with Tom; and found myself, at last, with a merry company of cricketers. All the men whose names I had

ever heard as foremost in the game, met together, drinking, card-playing, betting, and singing, at the Green Man (that was the great cricketers' house) in Oxford Street ...

This passage requires a few comments. Firstly, he was eighteen by the summer of 1784 but the match at Hambledon apparently took place a year later, most likely being the one recorded on 19 September 1785. Secondly, great matches ended in White Conduit Fields after 1786, so Hampshire *v* England can be identified as White Conduit Club (also styled Star and Garter Club) with six picked players of Hampshire and Surrey *v* five gentlemen and six picked men of Kent on 22-24 June 1786. And thirdly, although Tom Walker took part Beldham did not - implying he was either unfit to play or else travelled as a reserve. Surprisingly, for by this time he was already twenty, Beldham took part in none of the great matches of the 1786 season. Yet in June 1787 he went to Lord's and scored 17 & 63 run out, as well as taking 4 wickets, prompting the *Daily Universal Register* to declare that 'Beldam (sic) was by far the best player on the ground'. And four years later, after hitting 36 & 59 for MCC with five of the Hambledon Club *v* Kent, the *Kentish Post* observed that 'Beldham in batting and fielding maintains his superiority as the first player in the kingdom'.

His long career in major cricket, stretching from 1787 to 1821, yielded 7,810 runs, average 21.87, with three centuries and forty-one fifties, among them 144 for MCC *v* Middlesex in 1792 and 77 & 102 for Surrey *v* England in 1794, both at Lord's. To John Nyren he was 'the finest batter of his own, or perhaps of any age'. He relates that

> William Beldam (sic) was a close-set, active man, standing about five feet eight inches and a half. He had light-coloured hair, a fair complexion, and handsome as well as intelligent features. We used to call him "Silver Billy". No one within my recollection could stop a ball better, or make more brilliant hits all over the ground. Wherever the ball was bowled, there she was hit away, and in the most severe, venomous style. Besides this, he was so remarkably safe a player; he was safer than the Bank, for no mortal ever thought of

doubting Beldam's (sic) stability ... Beldam (sic) was quite a young man when he joined the Hambledon Club; and even in that stage of his playing I hardly ever saw a man with a finer command of his bat; but, with the instruction and advice of the old heads superadded he rapidly attained to the extraordinary accomplishment of being the finest player that has appeared within the latitude of more than half a century. There can be no exception against his batting, or the severity of his hitting. He would get in at the balls, and hit them away in a gallant style; yet, in this single feat, I think I have known him excelled; but when he could cut them at the point of the bat, he was in his glory; and, upon my life, their speed was as the speed of thought. One of the most beautiful sights that can be imagined, and which would have delighted an artist, was to see him make himself up to hit a ball ... It was the beau ideal of grace, animation, and concentrated energy.

Moreover he was 'one of the best judges of a short-run' and 'possessed a generally good knowledge of the game'. Also 'as a general fieldsman there were few better; he could take any post in the field, and do himself credit in it', and 'was a good change-bowler too; he delivered his balls high, and they got up well. His pace was a moderate one, yet bordering upon the quick ... he would very quickly discover what a hitter could do and what he could not do, and arrange his bowling accordingly.'

The son of George Beldham senior of Farnham who married Ann Benfill in 1756, he was born at Wrecclesham on 5 February and baptised in Farnham parish church on 21 March 1766. One still repeated myth is that he fathered almost forty children by two wives. The more mundane fact is that he married Ann Smith at Farnham on 24 May 1797 and had eight baptised over a period of about twenty years - Ann 1800, Frederick 1806, William 1809, Henry 1809, Louisa 1812, Emily 1815, George 1817 and Robert 1819. The parish register describes him as a yeoman. But at one time he kept a public house at Tilford, another hamlet in the same parish, where the Revd John

Mitford visited him in or shortly before 1833 when he wrote in *The Gentleman's Magazine* that

> Beldham still survives. He lives near Farnham; and in his kitchen, black with age, but like himself, still untouched with worms, hangs the trophy of his victories; the delight of his youth, the exercise of his manhood, and the glory of his age - his BAT. Reader! believe me, when I tell you I trembled when I touched it; it seemed an act of profaneness, of violation. I pressed it to my lips, and returned it to its sanctuary.

A few years later, according to the 1841 census, he worked in the area of Tilford known as Sheephatch as a batmaker, his occupation touched upon by Pycroft when in *The Cricket Field* he recorded that 'Beldham related to us in 1838, and that with no little nimbleness of hand and vivacity of eye, while he suited the act to the word with a bat of his own manufacture, how he had drawn forth the plaudits of Lord's as he hit round and helped on the bowling of Browne (sic) of Brighton ...' Others living in his cottage were his son Henry, an agricultural labourer, his married daughter Louisa, her husband William Cæsar, a blacksmith, her son William aged two and one Mary Lovell, ten. Louisa married William at Farnham on 23 August 1834 and had her child while living at Thursley. Her husband, born at Frensham in 1809, the son of James and Mary, was perhaps a distant cousin of Benjamin Cæsar from Peperharow (father of the celebrated Julius) who played cricket for Godalming and Surrey in the 1820s and 1830s. In the 1851 census Beldham appears as a retired victualler, this time with his wife Anne, aged seventy-three, as well as the three other family members: son Henry, daughter Louisa, son-in-law William Cæsar and his by now twelve-year-old grandson. Seven years later, in April 1858, Haygarth went to Farnham and 'found him at work in his garden before 8 o'clock in the morning. He was then well and hearty, very little deaf, only slightly blind with one eye, did not stoop in the least, or require a stick to walk with'. Beldham died at Tilford on 20 February 1862.

ANDREW FREEMANTLE, younger brother of John, was baptised at Bishops Sutton on 22 October 1768, the son of

Nicholas and Sarah Freemantle, and played his early cricket for Alresford in the 1780s. According to John Nyren:

> Andrew was a shortish, well-set man, and a left-handed player. He was an uncommonly safe, as well as good hitter; and few wickets that I could name were more secure than Andrew's. He would often get long hands, and against the best bowling too; and when he had once warmed into his hitting, it was deuced hard matter to get him out - an accident would frequently do the business … He usually played the long field, and was remarkably steady and safe in this department. But Andrew Freemantle could be depended upon, whatever he might undertake, whether in cricket or in his worldly dealings.

His biggest 'hands' were made on the two principal Hampshire grounds - 58 on Windmill Down for Hampshire *v* Surrey in 1792, and 57 not out on Stoke Down for England *v* Surrey in 1796. John Nyren mentions seeing him batting for the Players *v* Gentlemen at Lord's in 1806. A carpenter by trade, in about 1800 he moved to Easton where he became landlord of the *Bat & Ball Inn* (subsequently run by his son Henry) and died there on 19 January 1837. Another son, George, born at Easton in 1806, was a famous cricketer in the 1820s and 1830s.

JOHN NYREN's career, especially his authorship of *The Young Cricketer's Tutor*, has been written about many times (*Dictionary of National Biography*, etc). Nonetheless a few points concerning his own account of his early life perhaps deserve further comment. His accepted date of birth is 15 December 1764 and he writes: 'I was born at Hambledon, in Hampshire - the Attica of the scientific art I am celebrating'. However, the family home was *The Hut* at Broadhalfpenny (now *Bat and Ball*) so unless his mother moved to another house for the confinement he must have been born just over the parish boundary in Catherington. Shortly before the introduction of the third stump, that is to say in 1775 or 1776, he claims that 'the Hampshire gentlemen did me the honour of taking my opinion upon this point'. Since he was then only ten or eleven 'I' presumably denotes the unidentified author of the 'small manuscript, written some years since by an old cricketer',

144

which forms the basis of this section of the 'Young Cricketer's Tutor'. In 1784 at the age of nineteen he scored 12 & 0 while batting number 11 in the order for Hambledon parish *v* Petworth. So in his late teens he was evidently still not considered a particularly outstanding player, even in village cricket. Yet he states: 'the first match of any importance in which I played was when the Hambledon Club challenged all England. I was then between 17 and 18 years old and played for England ... I had the good fortune in the course of the match to put out two of the Hambledon Club and received in consequence the thanks of Sir Horace Mann'. In fact the match was held on Windmill Down in September 1787, when Nyren was twenty-two and drafted into the England team as a late substitute. As he is not credited with a catch we may assume he was responsible for two of the home side's seven run-outs. The following year he represented Hampshire *v* Surrey at Moulsey Hurst, and was bowled out in each innings by the redoubtable 'Lumpy' Stevens, for 3 and 9.

NOTE. John Nyren goes into some detail about a cricketer whom he calls Lambert but whose real name was Lamborn (or Lambourn, etc). Several books feature him as one of Hambledon's regular and leading bowlers throughout his career in the great matches from 1777 to 1781. This is quite wrong. Lamborn had no connection with the club. He played mostly for England XIs and only four times for Hampshire, on each occasion as a given-man. Dr McLean's assertion that the bowler appearing for Hambledon (sic) from 1777 to 1781 was actually Tom Boxall - who played for Kent during the 1790s - is frankly ridiculous.

Chapter Twelve

HAMBLEDON CLUB
MEMBERS 1772-1796

e = elected r = resigned

The Hambledon Cricket Club's minutes were published by F.S. Ashley-Cooper in *The Hambledon Cricket Chronicle 1772-1796* in 1924 (pp. 40-97) and a later chapter, is headed The Membership Roll where biographical details of the members appear. The following expands and revises that information although it should be noted that in some cases the identity of the Hambledon member remains speculative. The decline of the club can be assessed by the reduction to the numbers of elected members and by those recorded as 'gone to sea'.

ABERDEEN - e 1776.

WILLIAM CHARLES KEPPEL, Earl of ALBERMARLE - attended as non-subscriber in 1787 and 1788; e 1789 (when his mother was said to be residing in Hambledon); withdrew 1793. He was a grandson of the Lord Albermarle who with the Duke of Richmond and others 'diverted themselves at cricket in Hyde park' in 1730, and nephew of G.C. Garnier (see page 161). He was born in London on 14 May 1772 and succeeded to his father's titles at five months. Master of the Buckhounds 1806-7, Privy Councillor 1830, Master of the Horse 1830-34, 1835-41. While his father was one of fifteen children he too had fifteen by his first wife who died in 1817. Possibly the last surviving Hambledon member, he died at Quidenham, Norfolk on 30 October 1849.

ALLEN - e 1787, steward 1791. Perhaps he was the 'Allen' present as a non-subscriber in 1783. Ashley-Cooper calls him L.R. Allen of Lymington, on the basis of the initials L.R.A. entered against nine names in the 1791 accounts when collecting subscriptions. If a misreading of 'L.B.A.' he was probably Launcelot Baugh Allen, patron of the church at

Boldre (adjoining Lymington) in the early 1800s.

HENRY HERVEY 'HARVEY' ASTON - proposed 24 September 1792 but not elected till 15 July 1793 when he attended the club meeting. Although appearing in the membership lists for 1794 and 1795 (and despite a reputed income of £5,000 a year from estates in Cheshire and Derbyshire) there is no record of his paying a subscription. Descended from the Herveys, Earls of Bristol, his grandfather married Catherine Aston, the heiress of Aston Hall, Cheshire, and adopted her surname. Harvey, born c1759, entered the army, becoming a captain in the 1st Regiment of Foot in 1784, and during a period on half-pay figured as a patron of the ring and played cricket for White Conduit Club v Gentlemen of Kent in 1785 and was advertised for an alphabetical match at Moulsey Hurst in 1786. Following a dispute at Ranelagh Gardens with Lieutenant Fitzgerald he fought a duel at Chalk Lodge Farm near Hampstead on 25 June 1790. Receiving the first shot from ten yards, the ball (bullet) glanced off Harvey's wrist and passed under his right cheek bone. He declined his own right to fire and was assisted from the field into his carriage. However by 27 August he had recovered sufficiently to turn out for Brighton v Wadhurst & Lamberhurst on Brighton Level, then twice, home and away, v Tunbridge Wells in September. Between 1791 and 1793 he appeared for Middlesex, Brighton, MCC, Hampshire, England and Horsham, including matches which he made with Sir John Shelley and Lord Winchilsea. In December 1793 Harvey obtained a lieutenant-colonelcy in the 12th Foot and afterwards went to Madras where in 1798 he fought a duel with Major Picton. Both fired into the air. Next day, in his third duel, he was wounded by a new adversary, Major Allen, and after languishing about a week died on 23 December 1798.

Revd JOHN BALLARD - e 1777, r 1779. Born c1741, a son of John, doctor of Steeple Langford, Wiltshire, he entered Trinity, Oxford, 1759 aged 18 (BCL New College 1768, DCL 1783) and was vicar of Portsea and rector of Twineham until his death in 1787.

T. BARKER - e 1783, r 1787. Perhaps Thomas, born c1750, son of Thomas sen of Titchfield, who enrolled at Balliol, Oxford, aged 18 in 1768.

THOMAS BARTLETT - e 1780. Possibly connected with the Major Bartlett who made a match, South Hants *v* Sussex Militias, with the Duke of Richmond in Goodwood Park in 1803 in which both played.

RICHARD BARWELL - e 1782. A son of William, Governor of Bengal, born in Calcutta on 8 October 1741, he became a writer in the East India Company 1757, transferred to Bengal the following year, took seat as 12th member of Council in Bengal 1770 (4th by 1774) and reportedly amassed £20,000 a year illicit profit from salt contracts. Resigning in 1780 he arrived home with one of the largest fortunes (one estimate £400,000 plus) ever brought back to England and in 1781 bought the estate of Stansted, Sussex, from the trustees of Lord Halifax for over £100,000, enlarging the house at great expense and employing Capability Brown to lay out the grounds. According to William Hickey, once in residence he closed all the gates and public paths in the park, 'preventing the poor from supplying themselves with water from a spring they had long been used to frequent', with the result that 'men, women and children hissed and hooted at him as he passed, with all his oriental state, through the villages'. And after insulting the Corporation of Chichester by failing to turn up for a dinner arranged in his honour 'not a single gentleman visited or took the least notice of him'.

In 1776 Barwell married Elizabeth Jane Sanderson who died in India three years later when his notorious private life prompted the appearance of a pamphlet titled *The Intrigues of a Nabob; or Bengal the Fittest Ground for Lust* (1780). On 24 June 1785 at Stoughton, Sussex, he took as his second wife Catherine, the 15-year-old daughter of Nathaniel Coffin of Bristol, a former cashier of customs in Boston, America. A lady visiting in the neighbourhood wrote:

> While I was at Uppark a marriage took place near there that surprized most people. Mr Barwell, the great East Indian of Stanstead, to Miss Coffin, a very pretty little girl not 16, of American extraction. Till a fortnight before this event he kept a very beautiful mistress close to his park, by whom he has several children, and till very lately he declaimed most strongly against

149

matrimony. He seems a good-natured man, but the Mogul prevails strongly, I think, in his way of life and conversation.

He lost the contest at Wallingford in 1780, but was elected MP for Helston in 1781, St Ives in 1784 and Winchelsea in 1790 and 1796, resigning his seat in December 1796. Barwell died at Stansted on 2 September 1804 (see *DNB*).

FRANCIS LOVE BECKFORD - e 1788, r 1794. A cousin of the notorious William Beckford of Fonthill, he was born in 1764, son of Francis and Susannah née Love, heiress of Basing Park, and he married in 1788 Johanne (died 1814), daughter and co-heiress of John Leigh of Northcourt House, Isle of Wight. He resided at Southampton, Basing Park (which he sold) and Mitcham, Surrey, where he died on 24 February 1838.

Sir WILLIAM BENETT, or BENNETT - first mentioned 14 October 1777 when appointed a steward for the 1778 season; president 1786. Born 13 December 1733, he resided at Fareham where this inscription can be seen in the parish church:

> WILLIAM BENETT of Fareham, Esq. High Sheriff of the County, AD 1761 who, on presenting an address of congratulations from Hampshire on the accession of HM King George 3rd, to the throne, received the honour of Knighthood. He was the only son of William Benett, Esq. of Fareham by Anne, daughter of the renowned Seaman, Admiral Sir Thomas Hopsonne, died 25 November 1813 aged 80. Elizabeth Benett, daughter of John Hammond of Blackbrook, Esq, died 8 April 1823 aged 82, their remains with those of their only Son and six daughters are deposited with a long succession of their ancestors in this chancel.

His daughter, Caroline Matilda (born 1764), married Alexander Radcliffe (see page 179). Sir William's portrait, when aged 12, is superbly printed in colour in David Frith's *Pageant of Cricket* (1987 p 19) and shows him standing by a wicket.

JOSEPH BETTESWORTH - e 1780, r 1782. Baptised at St Mary, Portsea on 19 February 1745, son of Henry, he was a lawyer and JP of Portsmouth and belonged to the club while residing nearby at Clanfield where his daughters, Sarah Cumming and Eliza Mary, were christened in 1779 and 1781. Two other daughters, by his wife Ann - Caroline 1783 and Augusta 1787 - were baptised at St Mary's, Portsea. In 1789 he purchased the manor of Ashey in Newchurch, Isle of Wight, devised to his wife in 1805. The non-subscriber Bettesworth who attended a meeting on 5 June 1781 was probably his brother, William Augustus (1736-1805), judge-advocate of H.M. Fleet and a founder-member of the Hampshire Club. (see page 92)

BINSTED - e 1773, r 1785. Most likely Thomas Binstead, gentleman of Portsmouth, who witnessed the sale of the *Hut* at Broadhalfpenny to Lord Clanricarde in 1772 and the will of John Ridge, father-in-law of Thomas (see page 184), in 1774. With £50 he was one of the main legatees, with William Cooley (see page 155), under the will of Dame Mary Ridge (PCC 1776–77).

JOHN BLAGROVE - e 1785; attended as 'Blackgrave', a non-subscriber, 1785. Although no first name is given he can be identified as John, brother-in-law of club members Shakespear and Oliver (e 1784 and 1786), and son of Thomas Blagrove of Jamaica. He entered Eton in 1761 and Trinity College, Cambridge, aged 17, in 1769 and married Ann, daughter of John Shakespear, alderman of London, in 1777. His horses ran at Winchester races in the 1780s. Resided at Cardiff Hall Estates, Jamaica; Ankerwyke House, Wraysbury, Buckinghamshire; and Abshot House, Hampshire, where he died on 9 April 1824.

EDWARD BLIGH - e 1790. Brother of Lord Darnley (see page 156), born 19 September 1769, died Ditton House near Kingston, Surrey, 2 November 1840; buried at Thames Ditton. No Hampshire associations.

HENRY BONHAM - with Charles Powlett he was elected a steward for the following season on 1 October 1773; again steward with Powlett 1783, 1784, 1789 and 1795. Presumably he was the Bonham who assisted Petersfield & Catherington *v* Alresford in 1776 and scored 4 & 9 for Hampshire *v* Surrey on Laleham Burway in 1778. Either he or his brother was the Bonham on the MCC committee named in the Hambledon

151

minute of 16 July 1791. Said to have been born in 1749, though a Henry, son of John Bonham of Havant, matriculated from Magdalen College, Oxford, 16 May 1770 aged 19. Attended Cotton's Hyde Abbey School at Winchester in the 1760s, and in 1778 was a trustee of Cotton's daughter's marriage contract and executor of his will. Served as a steward at Winchester races in the 1780s; Deputy Lieutenant, Hampshire, 1788; High Sheriff in 1794 when he called a county meeting at Winchester for augmenting the militia. Resided at Petersfield until buying Mapledurham in Buriton from Lord Stawel (see page 191) on 19 April 1798 and died unmarried in 1800, leaving his estate to his brother Thomas (see below).

THOMAS BONHAM - e 1778, steward 1793. He is supposed to have succeeded his brother Henry as club secretary. He was a member of the new Hambledon club in 1804 and for some years maintained his own pack of harriers. Born in 1754, he inherited Mapledurham in 1800 and on his death in 1826 left the property to his cousin, John Carter (died 1838), who assumed the surname Bonham-Carter. Thus neither he nor Henry was an ancestor of the Bonham-Carters as sometimes claimed.

GEORGE T. BOULT - e 1786, r 1791. A heavy-scoring batsman from the Maidenhead area credited with 54 for Maidenhead *v* Chertsey 1780, 53 not out & 55 for Berks Club *v* Hornchurch Club 1785, 108 & 67 for Windsor Forest *v* a Surrey XI 1788 and 89 in 1791 and 76 in 1795 for Middlesex *v* MCC. His initial T. appears in the *Reading Mercury* for 27 May 1782: 'Odiham Down, a match at cricket, for fifty pounds; the gentlemen of the Alresford and Odiham Club, with Noah Mann and G.T. Bolt [sic], against the Gentlemen of the County of Hants; - whose names are authentic as under ... G.T. Bolt [sic] ...' Regarding the Kent match at Sevenoaks in 1786 *The Daily Universal Register* stated: 'Hampshire are reinforced with Mr. Bolt [sic], who hits with more safety and severity in all parts of the field than any man ever yet seen. His runs are laid very high against Aylward and Ring'. In the event he did not play but in the return on Windmill Down he made 3 & 11. Lord Winchilsea's and Mr Boult's club played Hornchurch in 1789. In 1783 the Boults beat the Bray Club by 26 runs, the umpire and scorer also having the name Boult. Boults were still playing for Maidenhead in 1836.

JOHN BRADBURN - e 1781, r 1783.

BRETON - e 1777.

RICHARD BRICKENDEN - e 1774, r 1777. A steward and president (1788) of the Hampshire Club; Sheriff of Hampshire 1790. In 1792 he married in France, Sarah, daughter of Mary Lewis, widow of Essex, and resided at Malshangar, an estate between Basingstoke and Overton, but also owned a house in Park Street, Grosvenor Square, London. Died 'near Basingstoke' 4 January 1793 after making a long will, with later codicils dated 14 March 1792 (proved PCC 29 January 1793).

Capt. BROWNE - e 1784, r 1785.

Capt. BUCK - e 1786.

BUNBURY - e 1777; a Bunbury attended as a non-subscriber in 1792. Probably Matthew of Droxford, Lord of the Manor of East Hoe, elected to the Hampshire Club in 1782; he was perhaps related to Humphrey Minchin (see page 169) of nearby Soberton, whose mother was one of the Anglo-Irish Bunburys, and connected with Matthew who died on 11 August 1786, and has a long memorial inscription at Ballyroughtera (?), Castle Martyn Demesne, Co Cork.

Capt. ROBERT CALDER - e 1783 as Captain Calder of Southwick, steward 1785, 'gone to sea' 1794. Born 1745, 4th son of Sir James, Bart, of Kent and Alice, daughter of Admiral Robert Hughes, he entered the navy in 1759 and in 1762 took part in the capture of the Spanish ship *Hermione*, 'probably the richest prize on record, even a midshipman's share amounting to 1,800 (pounds)'. Promoted to Lieutenant in 1762, Commander in 1779, Post Captain in 1780, then paid off following the peace with America and no longer employed until the outbreak of the French War in 1793. Captain of the Fleet at the Battle of Cape St Vincent, after which he was knighted on 3 March 1797 and created baronet on 22 August 1798. His active service ended when he was court-martialled in 1804 for failure to bring home the attack against enemy fleets that July. He became Rear Admiral of the Blue in 1799 and continued to advance by seniority until finishing as Admiral of the White in 1813. KCB in 1815. He was married in 1779 to Amelia, daughter of John Michell of Bayfield, Norfolk, and he died on 31 August (or 1 September) 1818 leaving no issue. He is the only Hambledon member mentioned in the will of Revd Charles Powlett. His brother, Sir Henry, 4th Bart, attended a club meeting as a non-subscriber in 1786. (See *DNB*)

Capt. CARTER - e 1781.

JAMES BRYDGES, Duke of CHANDOS - at the last meeting of 1776 he was elected president for 1777, r 1784. Born on 16 December 1731, and educated at Cambridge; Grand Master of Freemasons 1754-57; MP Winchester 1754-61 and co. Radnor 1761-68; Lord Lieutenant of Hampshire 1763-64 and 1771-80; High Steward of Winchester; Privy Councillor 1775; Lord Steward of the Household 1783 until his death on 29 September 1789 at Tunbridge Wells.

CLARKE - see Jervoise, T.C.

CHARLES COLES - e 1775, steward 1777 and 1794. Member of the committee which famously met at the *Star and Garter,* Pall Mall, to revise the laws of cricket in 1774; Sheriff of Hampshire 1779. Resided at Buriton.

Capt. HUGH SEYMOUR CONWAY - e 1791, president 1792, 'gone to sea' 1793. He was a younger son of the 1st Earl (later Marquess) of Hertford. Conway was born on 29 April 1759, entered the navy (Lieutenant 1776, Captain 1779) and sat in Parliament for Newport, Isle of Wight, 1784-86, Tregony 1788-90, Wendover 1790-96 and Portsmouth 1796-1801. He was said to have been a 'principal favourite' of the Prince of Wales, and to Horace Walpole he was 'one of the most amiable men in England, and of a character the most universally esteemed'. He married Lady Anne Horatia, daughter and co-heiress of the 2nd Earl Waldegrave, in 1786 and in the early 1790s resided at Bury Lodge, half a mile south of Hambledon village. In 1792, the year he was charged at the local Court Leet and Court Baron with encroaching onto the highway and onto manorial land, he purchased the manor of Butvellins in Hambledon from Mr and Mrs John Richards (see page 178) and Mrs Richards' sister, Mrs Haverkam. Presumably he was the 'Mr H.Conway' listed c1786 as a member of the cricket club which met at the *Star and Garter* and played in White Conduit Fields.[39] He died, as Admiral Conway, on board ship off Jamaica 11 September 1801.

Revd WILLIAM COOLEY - e 1781; 'gone to sea' 1793, but paid his subscription for 1794 and though his membership then lapsed he was presumably the Cooley who attended as a non-subscriber on 15 August 1796. He was baptised at St Thomas', Portsmouth, 9 December 1757, son of William senior, a local merchant and executor of Dame Mary Ridge (compare George Ridge see page 181) whose will, proved PCC 1777, left William junior £100. After attending school at Holybourne, Hants, he entered Trinity, Cambridge, in 1776 (BA 1780, MA 1785) and as William of Portsmouth he married in Hambledon church on 17 July 1786 Catherine Palmer whose father and brother were Hambledon members. Though a resident of Hambledon according to a 1793 directory, his children, Catherine Elizabeth (1790), William Roddam (1792) and Georgina Maria (1799), were all baptised at St Thomas', Portsmouth. He died in Plymouth on 27 January 1809 from wounds received while attached to Lord Paget's Horse Brigade in Spain.

Revd REYNELL COTTON - see Chapter Three.

JOHN CUSSANS - proposed McQueen, one of his wife's relatives, on 4 May 1773; presumably 'Cozens' who represented Gentlemen of Hampshire *v* those of Sussex in 1771. Of Harmsworth, Jamaica, he was born in 1742, and attended Westminster School according to 'Burke's Landed Gentry', but the school register only mentions his elder brother, Thomas. He matriculated from Trinity, Oxford, in 1759 and after gaining his MA in 1765 returned to the West Indies where in May 1767 he married Euphemia, daughter of Daniel McQueen of Kingston, Jamaica. A year later, on 1 May 1768, their daughter Euphemia Jane was baptised at Kilmiston, Hampshire. He had three sons - Thomas, John and William - and a second daughter, Jemima, baptised at St Mary's, Marylebone, on 14 May 1775. He died at sea on 8 March 1777. His brother married Catherine, sister of another club member, Francis Holburn.

Revd JOHN DAMPIER - e 1779, r 1783. Born c1750, he attended Eton College, and entered Merton, Oxford, in 1769 aged 19 (BA 1773, MA 1776) and succeeded his father as rector of Wylye, Wilts, as well as holding the rectorship of Westmeon from 1776-1826. Also a prebendary of Ely from 1812 until his death at Ely on 18 August 1826.

JOHN BLIGH, Earl of DARNLEY - e 1790, president 1793. Born in Ireland on 30 June 1767, and died at Cobham Hall, Kent, 17 March 1831. He played cricket at various levels over a period of at least forty years, but he was a late subscriber with no genuine connection with Hampshire.

JOHN THOMAS DE BURGH (Burke till 1752) - was first mentioned in the minutes in June 1773, president 1784, r 1785; attended as non-subscriber 'De Burgh' 4 July 1786 and 'Col De Burgh' 28 August 1787. Brother of Lord Dunkellin (see page 158) and son of Hester Amelia (died Corhampton 1803) whose brother, Sir Francis Vincent, Bart, of Stoke d'Abernon, Surrey, was seen by John Baker watching Hambledon play at Guildford in 1772. De Burgh's cousin, Francis Vincent (1747-91), formed one of the *Star and Garter* committee which revised the laws of cricket in 1774. De Burgh was born on 22 September 1744, attended Eton from 1754 and entered the army in 1762. He played for Hampshire gentlemen v those of Sussex in 1771; as given-man for Surrey v Kent at Laleham Burway in 1773 (failing to score) and for Petersfield v boys of Alresford in 1775. With his brother he was co-owner of the Broadhalfpenny *Hut* 1782-88 when his residence was given as Droxford. Lieutenant-Colonel of the 68th Foot; Major-General 1793; Lieutenant-General 1798 and full General in 1803. He succeeded his brother as Earl of Clanricarde in 1797 and died at Dublin on 27 July 1808.[40]

GEORGE DEHANY - e 1789, 'withdrawn' 1791. Only son of George of Jamaica, he was born on 17 October 1760, and from Westminster School was admitted to Lincolns Inn in 1779 and called to the bar in 1784. He died in 1807. Presumably he was the Dehany who attended at Hambledon as a non-subscriber in 1784, and he took part in several important matches in the early 1790s: for Gentlemen of England, MCC, Old Westminsters, Hampshire and Surrey & Sussex. It is not clear whether he or Philip (see below) was the 'Dehaney' who belonged to the club at the *Star & Garter* c1786; whose chaise was robbed by footpads on Shooters Hill when returning from a cricket match at Bishopsbourne in 1786; who with the Duke of Dorset, made the Hampshire *v* England match on Sevenoaks Vine in 1790. Nor is it clear whom Budd had in mind when he told Pycroft that in the old Lord's pavilion which burnt down in 1825 'here many a time have I looked over the old papers of Dehany and Sir H. Mann; but the room was burnt, and the old scores perished in the flames'.

PHILIP DEHANY – His membership was first recorded in 1773 and he remained with the club until 1796. He was one of the *Star and Garter* committee which revised the laws of cricket in 1774. Born in 1733, son of David, merchant and planter of Jamaica, he was at Westminster School 1743-52 and matriculated from Cambridge 1753, apparently leaving without a degree. By 1759 he was residing at Hungerford Park, Berkshire, and by the late 1760s at Farleigh Wallop. Soon after 1770 he bought the nearby estate of Kempshott, pulling down the old manor house and replacing it with a large brick mansion, which he sold in 1787 to a rich East India merchant. The only reason some historians identify Dehany as a founder of the Hambledon Club seems to be John Nyren's anecdote concerning a match on Broadhalfpenny in 1775 in which he and Powlett were 'the backers of the Hambledon men'. After the loss of early wickets in the second innings they 'began to shake, and edged off all their money, laying it pretty thickly on the England [actually Surrey] side'. And when Richard Nyren was out for 98, having made a big stand with Small (who scored a century) 'the backers came up to Nyren and said "You will win the match and we will lose our money".' A leading light of the Hampshire Club (steward 1776), he had a brief career in Parliament as MP for St Ives (1778-1780). Dehany moved to Hayes Place in Kent where he died in 1809. At her death in 1832 his daughter left the property to Miss Traill who afterwards promoted annual cricket matches on Hayes Common. Her nephew, J.C. Traill (West Kent CC, Gentlemen of Kent, etc) seems to have inherited Dehany's pictures since his sale in 1880 included a family portrait of Mr and Mrs

'Dehaney' and daughter painted by Gainsborough during his Bath period (1759-74) - reproduced in the J.B. Robinson sale catalogue (no. 5), 6 July 1923.

Revd HENRY ROGER DRUMMOND - e 1791. Born c1761, he went to Christ Church, Oxford, 1779 aged 18 (BA 1783, MA 1788) and resided in Hambledon during the early 1790s. He became rector of Fawley and died on 27 July 1806.

HENRY DE BURGH (Burke till 1752), Lord DUNKELLIN - r 1779. Born 8 January 1743, he was baptised at Kensington, son of John, 11th Earl of Clanricarde (1720-82), who resided at Warnford Park, five miles north of Hambledon, and he bought Broadhalfpenny *Hut* 1772. Dunkellin was MP for co. Galway 1768-69, succeeded his father in 1782 and created Marquess of Clanricarde in 1789. He married Urania Anne, daughter of George Paulet, 12th Marquess of Winchester, and died at Portumma Castle, Ireland on 8 December 1797.

JEREMIAH DYSON - e 1781, r 1784. He was baptised at St Martin-in-the-Fields on 24 May 1751, and he attended Eton and Christ Church, Oxford. He was admitted to Lincolns Inn 1777 and served as Clerk Assistant (1797-1814) and Deputy Clerk (1814-20) of House of Commons. As Jeremiah esq, bachelor of Compton, 23, he was licensed to marry Elizabeth Collins, spinster, 19, of Winchester, in 1781. He later married Mary Newbolt and after selling his family seat at Stoke near Guildford, he died at New Grove, Petworth, on 14 September 1835.

JOHN EDWARDS - e 1776. Born in India 10 July 1759, the only son of Captain John, late of the East India Company, he first attended St Paul's School but soon transferred to Charterhouse where he remained at least nine years. From there he went up to Oriel, Oxford, without obtaining a degree, and entered Lincolns Inn, but was not called to the Bar. A wealthy young man, he resided as a country gentleman in Hampshire, at one time at Worting House near Basingstoke, and became a captain in the Hampshire Yeomanry. According to one account he kept his own pack of hounds, and joined Hambledon when only 17. A close friend of the Prince of Wales, he squandered his fortune, and after running out of funds retired to Epping

Forest where he was a JP and in 1810 gained the appointment as headmaster of Chigwell School - a post for which, as a non-graduate, he was ineligible. Unsurprisingly, he was described as 'the worst headmaster in the history of the school morally and otherwise'. He continued as head for three years, for much of the time absent and part of the time in prison for debt. During his absences his sons took over the school and were reputedly notorious for 'immoral conversation, swearing and blasphemous behaviour'. One was accused of sleeping with one of the maids and getting her with child. Nevertheless instead of being dismissed Edwards was allowed to resign in April 1813. He died at Lee, Kent, 6 November 1823 but was buried at Worting where there is a memorial tablet in the parish church.

Capt. CHARLES HOLMES EVERITT - e 1780, steward 1788, r 1791. A naval officer, he rose from Lieutenant in 1772 and Captain in 1777 to Rear Admiral of the Blue in 1794 and finally Admiral of the Blue in 1804. He married Pollexfen Calmady at St Nicholas Cole Abbey, London, on 8 September 1783 and assumed the name Calmady in 1788. He died 'suddenly' in March 1807 at Longdon Hall near Winbury, Devon.

Capt. THOMAS COOPER EVERITT - e 1779, r 1784. On 24 June 1783 he was 'requested to send for a Mess Tent belonging to the Prince of Wales's Regt. of Dragoon Guards the Expence of wch is to be paid by private Subscription of the Members of the Club', but on 8 July it was reported that 'The Mess Tent order'd to be purchased by Captain Everett (sic) for the use of the Club is sold'. He was probably the Captain Everett of the Odiham & Alton XI 1784 and the Captain Everitt who attended a club meeting on 5 September 1786 as a non-subscriber. A captain in the 3rd Dragoons (Prince of Wales's Regiment) and in 1795 Colonel of the Hampshire Fencible Cavalry, he married Mary Bruckner at St Nicholas Cole Abbey on 15 September 1783. Brother of Admiral Calmady (see above).

FITZHERBERT - e 1775, steward 1779 and 1782, r 1783. Probably Thomas, born c1747, who at about the age of 21 was reputedly 'measuring coals to the labourers in the dock-yard at Portsmouth at thirteen pence a bushel'. During the 1774 election his energetic support for the Admiraty candidate attracted the attention and patronage of the First Lord, Lord Sandwich, which led to lucrative contracts for supplying waggons for the Army in America, ironwork for gun-carriages, musket stocks, small arms, etc, as well as hire of horses for fortifications of Portsmouth. He was MP for the corrupt borough of Arundel 1780-90; and in 1782 stated in Parliament that he knew Portsmouth 'because he lived in the neighbourhood and had more frequent occasion to visit its dockyard than any other', arguing that Britain's weaknesses at sea were 'owing to the want of shipwrights' and that 'sufficient encouragement (was) not given to old and deserving shipwrights'. His contract for supplying horses expired in 1783 and was not renewed. He married Anna, daughter of Revd Robert Pye, in 1789 and resided at Stubbington Lodge, Portsea, and later at Pitt Place, Epsom, dying at Chichester on 30 January 1822 aged 75. By a codicil he left £10,000 in stock or annuities for 5 poor widows and 5 poor spinsters of Portsea aged 50 or more.

JOHN FLEMING - e 1773, r 1783. The second son of Thomas Willis, said to have been born in 1743, he assumed the name Fleming when he succeeded his brother as owner of the Fleming estate at Stoneham in 1767. Sheriff of Hampshire 1774; MP for Southampton 1774-80 and 1784-90; captain South Hants Militia. Resided at Stoneham Park until his death on 29 January 1802 according to his MI at North Stoneham. (Another account says 28 February).

FORBES - e 1773.

Capt. THOMAS LENNOX FREDERICK - e 1792. Born 25 March 1750, a son of Sir Charles, Surveyor-General of Ordnance, and Lucy, daughter of Hugh, 1st Viscount Falmouth, he became Lieutenant RN 1770, Captain 1779, Rear Admiral of the Blue 1797, Rear Admiral of the White 1799, and died 7 November 1799.

Maj. HENRY GAGE - e 1789, r 1793. He was presumably the Gage who attended meetings as a non-subscriber in 1786. Born in Montreal on 4 March 1761, son of General Gage, Commander-in-Chief, North America, he was a major in the 93rd Foot, and Major-General 1805. In the year he joined the club he married Susan Maria, eldest daughter and heir of Lieutenant-General William Skinner of Westbury, East Meon. Succeeded an uncle as Viscount Gage on 11 October 1791 and died in London on 29 January 1808. His nephews, William and Thomas Gage Blake, were prominent players with the Bury St Edmunds club in the 1820s.

GAMBIER - e 1774.

GEORGE CHARLES GARNIER - was first mentioned in the minute book on 14 October 1777 when he was appointed steward for the following season, and he was president in 1781. Born 19 October 1739, educated Eton and Trinity, Cambridge, he was described as 'a man of scholarly mind and attainment' whose house, according to Dr Halifax, physician to the Prince of Wales, was the very best in London at which to meet the celebrities of the day. The latter included his friend David Garrick who used to submit plays to him for advice and criticism. In the country he resided four miles from Hambledon, at Rookesbury Park in Wickham. After his father's death in 1763 he succeeded him as Apothecary-General to the Army and served as High Sheriff of Hampshire. He married in 1766 Margaret, daughter of Sir John Miller, Bart, and died on 2 November 1819; buried with his wife (died 1807 aged 65) at Wickham where an inscription refers to him as one 'who by strict integrity & invariable practice of every Christian Virtue, endeared himself to the inhabitants of the parish among whom he resided for 60 years'. His nephew, Lord Albermarle (son of his wife's sister), joined the club in 1789. 'Mr Garniers Sons' who attended a club meeting in 1781 must have included the eldest, George (1769-96), also present as 'G' 1784 and 'Capt' Garnier 1791. A non-subscriber, T. Garnier, in 1792 was his son Thomas (1776-1873), later Dean of Winchester, who according to A.E. Garnier's *The Chronicles of the Garniers of Hampshire* (1900), 'would occasionally ride over to Twyford School where his grandson was being educated, and where he would bowl left-handed "sneaks" all along the ground, as he had done years before at the Hambledon Club'. The above Dr Halifax attended a club meeting along with Garnier and Garnier junior on 29 July 1788.

CAREW GAUNTLETT - e 1785 having previously attended as

a non-subscriber on 4 May 1784; he was one of three Winchester wine merchants in the club's 1773 wine ballot. He died at Winchester in 1796: 'On Monday evening died, after a short illness, Carew Gauntlett, Esq., a respectable wine-merchant, of Southgate St., and Treasurer of this County' (*Portsmouth Gazette* 20 June). The club accounts include entries for £36 19s 6d 'paid Mr. Gauntlett for Wine' 1793; £37 9s 1d paid to his executors for wine 1791 and 1792, and subscriptions for 1794, 1795 and 1796 received from his executors. He and his brothers attended Cotton's Hyde Abbey School. One of them, Peter (1748-1807), supplied wine to the club in 1773 but was not recorded as a member as claimed by Ashley-Cooper. A prominent member of the Hampshire Club, he went to Winchester and New College, Oxford, and for many years served as Clerk of the County of Hampshire. Presumably there was a connection with Hannah Gauntlett of Hambledon who married James Willson of Midhurst on 9 March 1785.

GIBBS - e 1772.

Capt. ERASMUS GOWER - e 1784 as 'Gore'. Eldest son of Abel Gower of Glandoven, Pembrokeshire, he entered the Navy in 1755, advancing to Lieutenant 1762, Captain 1780 and Rear Admiral of the White 1799. 'Gone abroad' in club accounts for 1792, when he commanded the *Lion* 1792-94 taking Lord MaCartney on his embassy to China and he was afterwards knighted. He saw no further service after 1799 but rose through seniority to the rank of Admiral of the White in 1810. He resided at the Hermitage, Hambledon, where he died on 21 June 1814 (see *DNB*). He has an inscription in Hambledon church.

GRIERSON - e 1790, r 1793.

PHILIP GRIFFIN - r 1780. Baptised Holy Trinity, Gosport, 30 January 1740, son of Admiral Griffin, he entered St Edmund Hall, Oxford, 1759 (BCL 1766, DCL 1785) and was sometime vicar of Warnford. When licensed to marry Elizabeth Barfoot, spinster of Droxford, at Droxford, in 1789 he was described as Philip, bachelor, clerk of Hadnock in Dixton parish, Monmouthshire. He died at Hadnock House in July 1802.

EDWARD HALE - e 1789, r 1791. For Hambledon he scored 7

& 2 *v* Petworth in 1784 and 4 & 22 *v* West Sussex in 1791; and for Hampshire 2 & 9 *v* Surrey in 1789, 2 & 8 *v* Surrey in 1792, 17 & 11 and 0 & 6 *v* Brighton in 1792 and 2 & 0 *v* MCC in 1797. He attended, and probably played in, the last match arranged by the old Hambledon club on Windmill Down in 1796. Son of Edward senior (c1719-1806), 'many years an eminent surgeon in this parish', who married Hannah Barlow in 1761, he was baptised at Hambledon on 1 September 1764. One Edward witnessed Land's 1791 codicil and Edward junior, with Edward Aburrow, was one of the executors of Henry Coles, owner of the *George Inn*, in 1793. A captain in the Hambledon Volunteer Infantry in 1798, he was presumably the Major Hale who hit 24 for Hambledon *v* Meonstoke & East Meon in 1800; he was also perhaps H. Hale (sic) who represented Hambledon *v* Portsmouth in 1807. The family resided at Hambledon House in the centre of the village, close to Richard Nyren's *George Inn*, and owned Windmill Down, rented to farmer Edward Garrett who sub-let it to the cricket club. Edward junior was noted for his pack of harriers, kept until his death on 16 November 1823. His son, another Edward (c1806-70), married Caroline, daughter of Admiral Downman (see Thomas Palmer page 171).

Capt. CHARLES POWELL HAMILTON - e 1783, 'gone to sea' 1794 and 1795. Elected President of the newly formed Hambledon Club in 1800. A son of Lord Anne Hamilton (youngest son of the 4th Duke of Hamilton), born c1747, he became Lieutenant RN 1769, Captain 1779 and Rear Admiral of the Blue 1797. Married Lucretia Prosser at St Mary's, Portsea, 1777 and died at his seat, Fir Hill near Droxford, 12 March 1825. For his naval career see *The Gentleman's Magazine*'s 1825 obituary.

Col. WILLIAM HAMMOND - e 1779 as Major Hammond, r 1791. Promoted from Major to Lieutenant-Colonel North Hants Militia 1780.

WILLIAM HARRIS - e 1772. Of New Place, Alresford, a JP and member of Kilmiston Hunt; according to an inscription at New Alresford he died on 30 May 1817 aged 68, and his wife Jenny on 28 May 1833 aged 85.

HARRISON - e 1782.

Sir FRANCIS HOLBURN Bart - e 1774. Son of Rear Admiral Francis, he succeeded a cousin to the baronetcy in 1772 and died at Southampton on 13 September 1820. His sister Catherine married Thomas Cussans, brother of John (see page 155).

HOLDER - e 1796.

HENRY HOOD - e 1778, steward 1780, president 1788. Born on 25 August 1753 and baptised at Portsmouth on 17 April 1754, he was the son of the famous Admiral Hood of Catherington House, Horndean, and Susannah, daughter of Edward Linzee, Mayor of Portsmouth. He succeeded his mother (created Baroness Hood of Catherington 1795) as Lord Hood in 1806 and his father as Viscount Hood in 1816. He was Chamberlain of Household 1820-21 to Queen Caroline whom he accompanied when she demanded entry to the Coronation of George IV. He married in 1774 Jane Wheler of Whitley Abbey, Warwickshire, and died at Whitley on 25 January 1836.

Capt. SAMUEL HOUGH - e 1778. As Captain Samuel of the Hermitage, he married at Hambledon 5 September 1777 Robina Turner of Hambledon (witnesses John Richards and her uncle, Robert Turner, both club members) and on 9 July 1778 Robert Hunter, son of Samuel and Robina, was baptised 'at a house call'd the Hermitage' (parish register). Samuel died two months later on 19 September - 'At the seat of Robert Turner, Esq; in Hermitage, near Petersfield, Samuel Hough, Esq;' (The *Gentleman's Magazine*) - and was buried in Hambledon on the 21st as Captain Samuel of the Hermitage. His widow, Robina Hough, married James Kerr on 20 June 1781 at St Martin-in-the-Fields.

HOUNSOM - e 1793 (as Hounsome), steward 1794; on 8 September 1794 he proposed Mr Woods of Chilgrove, Sussex, but the latter declined membership for the present and the entry was erased. In Hambledon church there is a plaque to a Timothy Rhodes Hounsom (baptised at Woolwich on 9 January 1766) who died 11 November 1768 aged 22 months (buried 20 November). He was presumably a son or grandson of Henry 'Houndsom' named in the Hambledon court book on 11 October 1771 as a customary tenant of the manor who had died since the previous court leaving his son Henry, aged about 24, next heir. The elder Henry Hounsom, gentleman of Hambledon but formerly of Woolwich, owned property in the parish occupied by Henry Kennett as well as lands in the manor of Bosham and elsewhere in Sussex. By 1769 he held the manor of Todham in Easebourne which he left in trust for his wife, Sarah (living 1805), with reversion to Henry junior, and it was sold after 1805 to George Mullins. There was also a daughter, Ann, and a younger son, John. The Hambledon member could have been either Henry or John, though the former went bankrupt in 1775. The name of Edmund Woods Hounsom, baptised at Woolwich in 1775 together with the land holdings in West Sussex, suggests a family connection with the above Mr Woods. Doubtless the Hambledon member was also related to the cricketer named Hounsam who played for Woolwich for several seasons around 1800.

Revd THOMAS JEANS - e 1779, r 1780. Son of Thomas of Christchurch, born c1749, who went to Merton, Oxford, 1767 aged 18 (BA 1773, MA 1776, DD 1816); fellow of New College, and rector of Witchingham, Norfolk, and vicar of St John's Maddermarket, Norwich, 1785 until his death in 1835. A 'Jeans' attended as a non-subscriber on 15 August 1796.

JERVOISE CLARKE JERVOISE (formerly Clarke) - president 1782. The minute for 17 September 1782 reads: 'Mr Jervoise be fined a buck for his omitting to send venison this day according to custom, he being President of the Club'. He was born c1733, son of Samuel Clarke of West Bromwich and Mary Elizabeth, daughter of Thomas Jervoise of Herriard, Hampshire, and sister of Richard Jervoise (1704-62) who married Anne Huddlestone of Croydon in 1733 and two years later chose eleven 'out of Croydon and that neighbourhood in Surrey' to play London on Kennington Common; he entered Emmanuel, Cambridge, in 1751 aged 18; and married at Bedhampton on 12 July 1763 Kitty, daughter and heiress of Robert Warner of that place; and assumed the name Jervoise in compliance with the will of his maternal grandfather in 1777. In 1776 he was a steward of the Hampshire Club at Winchester and became its president in 1779. His estates brought in a reputed income of £20,000 a year and he sat as MP for his pocket-borough of Yarmouth, Isle of Wight, (where he held over half the landed property, etc), 1768-69, 1774-79 and 1791-1808, and for Hampshire 1779-90. He resided at Idsworth Park and died in 1808 when *The Gentleman's Magazine* remarked that 'in public spirit, personal honour, and gentleman-like liberality, Mr J. was equalled by few, and surpassed by none'. His youngest son and principal heir, Samuel of Idsworth (1770-1852), attended a club meeting on 9 August 1793, and possibly on other occasions as C. Jervoise, Clarke, etc.

THOMAS CLARKE JERVOISE (formerly Clarke) - steward 1787. Eldest son of the above, born 1764, there is no record of his election under the name of Jervoise. However he was possibly the Clarke jun who attended as a non-subscriber in August 1783 and doubtless the Clarke elected two years later. The names for the 28 June 1785 meeting were erased, reappearing on 5 July with the only difference 'C. Jervoise' becoming 'Clarke jun'. 'Mr Clarke' was proposed at that meeting and elected on 12 July. The name T. Jervoise first occurs on the following 30 August. He was High Sheriff for Hampshire, 1786-87, a steward of the Hampshire Club 1788 and MP for Yarmouth, Isle of Wight, 1787-90, relinquishing his seat to his father when he lost the Hampshire contest. He was a lunatic by the time of his death on 30 December 1809.

THOMAS SAMUEL JOLLIFFE - r 1778. Born 22 June 1746, educated at Winchester and MP for Petersfield 1780-87. Resided at Trotton Park, Sussex, but married the heiress of Kilmersdon, Somerset, in 1778. After his mother-in-law's death in 1788 he settled in that county, acquiring considerable property and serving as High Sheriff from 1792-93 'with a degree of splendour which has seldom been equalled'. He died on 6 June 1824 when the *Bath Herald* noted that 'of late years he resided almost entirely in the country; but he formerly mingled in the brilliant circles of the Metropolis, and sat in several parliaments during the government of Lord North, and the first portion of Mr Pitt's administration' and 'sustained the character of a high minded and scrupulously honourable gentleman'.

WILLIAM JOLLIFFE - r 1780. Elder brother of the above, he was born on 16 April 1745, attended Winchester and Brasenose College, Oxford, and sat as MP for Petersfield 1768-1802 (a Lord of Trade 1772-79, and the Admiralty 1783). In 1769 he married Eleanor, daughter and heiress of Sir Richard Hylton, Bart, of Hayton Castle, Cumberland, and at one time had seats at Petersfield House, Hayton and Chester-le-Street, later purchasing the Merstham estate near Gatton, Surrey. After his 1776 bill for a tax on dogs was thrown out of the Commons someone remarked that 'Jolliffe was most violently attacked last night by nine young ladies at once, for his inhuman intention; these ladies so *worried* him that he had not a word to say and they fairly barked him off'. (Hampden p. 261) Edward Gibbon , author of *The decline and fall of the Roman Empire,* once noted that 'his extravagant behaviour was much worse than anything you saw in the papers'. A quarrelsome man, he infuriated his relatives, his superior officers in the Hampshire Militia and his neighbours in Petersfield, where he had his father's fine house pulled down and where, acccording to his own autobiographical memoranda:

> They asked more than I could grant; alleging that my house was undertaxed, I made bread at home, bought groceries in London, in short, was not so devoted as they expected ... Every trifling object of mine was opposed, I was not suffered to plant some trees in the churchyard, and I was opposed in building a wall near my own garden.

He died on 20 (or 27) February 1802.

DAVID RAMSAY KARR - attended club meetings 1779-80, r 1787. Born in 1730, he was recorded as a surgeon at H.M. Dockyard, Portsmouth 1777-82 and as a naval surgeon and physician at Kippilaw, Roxburghshire, 1794. In his will, signed 19 March 1790 (apparently in London, the address of two of the witnesses) and proved PCC 14 January 1795, he describes himself as resident of Kippilaw but late of H.M. Dockyard, Portsmouth, and mentions his uncle John Karr of Kippilaw, brother Andrew Ramsay Karr of Hatchford, Surrey, sister Jean Seton and adopted daughter Martha Maria Adams, 'who is and always is in the care of Mrs Berrysford of Wood Street, Cheapside, London', to whom he bequeathed £1,000 payable at 21 with the interest until then to be paid for her education and support.

LAWRENCE - e 1772, r 1777. He played for Gentlemen of Hampshire *v* those of Sussex 1771, scored 0 & 6 for Hambledon Town *v* Surrey 1773 and assisted the boys of Alresford *v* Petersfield 1775. He was presumably the Mr Lawrence who won the Hunter's Sweepstakes on his horse *Carabon* at Basingstoke races in 1774, and on his horse *Garland,* came second in a sweepstakes there in 1775.

SAMUEL LEEKE - steward 1780 and 1782, r 1790. He was son of Samuel senior, merchant of Portsmouth, who married Mary Bingham at Warblington on 21 October 1748 and made his will 29 September 1770 (proved PCC 9 May 1775). He was christened at St Thomas', Portsmouth, on 29 June 1754 and first appears in the club minutes in 1779. As there is no record of his election and as he was still only 17 in June 1772 he probably joined the club during one of the periods (in 1775, 1776 or 1778) for which minutes are missing. Called Mr Leeke in 1782, but 'Capt Leeke' in 1783, so he was possibly an officer in the militia. A Portsmouth JP, as Samuel esq, bachelor of St Helens, he was licensed to marry Sophia Bargus, spinster of Fareham, in 1788; his son William was baptised at Havant in 1799. His mother (baptised Havant 1730) was a sister of Ann (1731) whose son, Richard Bingham Newland, became a member in 1780.

RICHARD LEIGH - e 1793. A prominent cricket patron, though without genuine Hampshire connections, who backed one of the sides in the last great match held at Hambledon. For an account see 'Some Local Sportsmen', *Dartford Historical and Antiquarian Society News-Letter* No. 11 (1974) pp. 31-9.

CHARLES LENNOX - e 1789, president 1791. A celebrated cricketer and supporter of the game, but without other Hampshire associations and not, as claimed, one of the old Westminsters who allegedly founded the club in the 1760s. He was born in 1764, succeeded as 4th Duke of Richmond in 1806 and died in 1819. There is no record of his name in the Westminster School register and he is believed to have been educated privately.

LINDERGREEN - e 1779, r 1785.

Capt ROBERT LINZEE - e 1785, r 1791. Baptised at St Thomas',

Portsmouth, 13 February 1739, son of Edward (several times mayor of Portsmouth) and Ann, his aunt, Susannah Linzee (1726-1806), married the future Admiral Lord Hood in 1749 so Lord Hood, club president 1788, was his cousin. He married Elizabeth Loby at Portsmouth on 30 January 1762 and, as widower of Portsmouth, Mary Grant, spinster, in 1792. A naval officer, he advanced to the rank of Lieutenant in 1761, Captain 1770, Rear Admiral of the White 1794, of the Red 1794, Vice-Admiral of the White 1795, Admiral of the Blue 1801. For a while he lived in Hambledon where his house was advertised for letting by the *Portsmouth Gazette* on 1 May 1797; he died on 1 October 1804. The name Linzee occurs as a non-subscriber at meetings in 1781, 1791, 1794 and 1796. These could refer to Robert or one of several naval relatives such as Lieutenant Richard (d 1782), Captain John, Lieutenant Edward (d 1792) and Captain, later Rear Admiral, Samuel Hood (d 1820).

McQUEEN - e 1773, r 1774. Brother or other relative of the wife of John Cussans (see page 155).

MAIDMAN - appointed steward for 1779 season on 18 September 1778, r 1783. Probably Richard, JP of Wickham, Sheriff of Hampshire 1776.

MARTIN - e 1786, r 1792.

MELLISH - e 1796. Probably Thomas who played for MCC, Surrey, Middlesex, Old Etonians, various England XIs and Homerton Club, and died at Uxbridge on 29 July 1837 aged 64.

Sir CHARLES MILL Bart - e 1792. Born in 1765, he succeeded his father as baronet in 1792 and married Selina Morshead of Trenant Park, Cornwall, in 1800. Of Mottisfont, he died on 26 February 1835.

MILLS - e 1787, r 1790. Possibly William, born 10 November 1750, who acquired property at Bisterne 1792, sat as MP for Coventry 1808-12 and died 20 March 1820. His son John (1789-1871) was a prominent amateur cricketer in the last years of the Regency.

MINCHIN - e 1773. He was probably Humphrey Minchin, who was baptised at Ballinakilly, co. Tipperary, c1728 and

169

admitted to Trinity, Dublin, in 1742 aged 14. After his father's death in 1764 he sold his Irish estate and bought Holywell in Soberton, 3 miles west of Hambledon. He was MP for Okehampton 1778-84 and 1785-90 and Bossiney and Tintagel 1790-96; Clerk of the Ordnance 1783 when according to Lady Spencer, wife of his patron, 'he is really, I believe an honest man, and is very intelligent and diligent in business, but is apt to think a little too highly of his own importance'. Captain, later Lieutenant-Colonel, North Hants Militia, he died 26 March 1796 at his house in Great George Street, Westminster. The end 'was very sudden' - 'He was on the point of sitting down to dinner, apparently in perfect health, and reaching to hang up his hat, he fell in a fit, and died almost instantly'. The only other feasible identification is his son, Henry, baptised Ballinakilly c1757, Lieutenant in the North Hants Militia, whose son Henry James Bunbury was baptised (according to the IGI) both at Ballinakilly 1797 and Droxford 1799.

MUDGE - e 1779.

Col. FREDERICK GEORGE MULCASTER - e 1793. He married Mary Juliana Auchmuty at St Mary's, Marylebone, on 1 March 1780 and died on 30 September 1797 as Colonel of Engineers and Major-General in the Army; will proved, as Major-General Mulcaster of Portchester, 1797 (PCC).

RICHARD BINGHAM NEWLAND - e 1780, r 1782. Baptised at Havant on 6 February 1758, son of James Newland who married Ann Bingham on 29 November 1753 at Bedhampton; he matriculated from Queen's, Oxford, 1775. His wife Selina (d 1786) has a memorial at Havant where he sold the manor of Flood in 1812; resided latterly at Rotherfield. A cousin of Samuel Leeke (see page 168).

HUGH NORRIS - proposed August 1772, e 1773. The Hugh of Romsey, born 1705, cited in Ashley-Cooper's 'Membership Roll' was dead by 1768 (will proved PCC). His son Hugh, a naval officer, only became a Lieutenant in 1779 - suggesting someone rather young for election in 1773. Hugh senior had a nephew of the same name born in 1737, but it is not known that he ever lived in Hampshire.

ROBERT HENLEY, Earl of NORTHINGTON - president 1778. Born London 3 January 1747, educated at Westminster and Oxford, he was styled Lord Henley from 1764 until succeeding as second Earl in 1772. In 1768 he took part in the Old Westminsters *v* Old Etonians match on Moulsey Hurst. Short and stout in build - 'his shape so bulky - yet his stature low' (*Daily Universal Register* 22 August 1785) - he was said to have borne a striking likeness to Louis XVI. MP for Hampshire 1768-72, PC 1783, Lord Lieutenant of Ireland 1783-84. He was taken ill in Rome in December 1785 and died of a lingering illness in Paris on 5 July 1786; he was buried in the family vault at Northington.

LAVER OLIVER - e 1786, r 1791. Born 10 December 1740, the second son of Laver senior, baker of Blackfriars, London, he went out to India as an East India Company cadet in 1770 and though promoted to ensign resigned his commission soon after his arrival, in November 1771, in order to turn to trade. For a time he held the appointment of accountant and auditor at the Court of Oudh; then paymaster to the New Brigade at Fatehgarh 1777 and at Lucknow 1780-81 before returning to England with a fortune in about 1784. On 21 October 1785 he married Mary, sister of his old Indian colleague, John Shakespear (see page 188), and in 1786 the couple settled down at Kimpton. It must have been soon afterwards that *The Huntsman's Lamentation in a Frost* was penned, describing Oliver as 'our newly-married squire' who 'sits moping o'er the fire' (*Baily's Magazine* vol. 35). He and his brother-in-law resigned from the club through a joint letter. Sometime after 1800 he moved to Brill House where 'a true benevolence of heart, and the manner of a gentleman, he adorned with the piety of a Christian', and died there on 10 December 1813, his 73rd birthday.

THOMAS PALMER - e 1783, steward 1785 (?), r 1786. From 1784 he was often styled Thomas senior, so presumably was the father of T.M. Palmer (see below). He married Elizabeth Tribe at Portsmouth in 1747 and had daughters Anna Maria on 20 July 1749, Betey on 31 March 1752 and Dorothy Maria on 24 June 1771 baptised there, along with Thomas on 14 June 1763 and Catherine who was born at Hambledon on 16 March 1765.

At Hambledon in 1765 Thomas and Elizabeth witnessed the marriage of John Goldsmith and Mary Row and in 1787 the eldest daughter married George Gayton of Portsmouth there, with 'Betsey' a witness. The groom, who attended club meetings as non-subscriber G. or Revd Gayton 1783-94, was apparently George Clark Gayton, son of Clark Gayton, gent of Fareham, who matriculated from St Mary Hall, Oxford, 1768 aged 17 (BA Magdalen College 1772, MA 1775). Also at Hambledon, Catherine married William Cooley (see page 155) in 1786, with Anna Maria a witness, and Dorothy (Dorothea) married Hugh, later Admiral, Downman in 1803. Their daughter Caroline Downman (baptised Hambledon in 1808) became the wife (1827) of Edward Hale (c1806-70) of Hambledon House, and *their* son, Edward (1828-94), author and science master at Eton College, played cricket with the Hambledon Club in 1844.

THOMAS MARTIN PALMER - e 1784 as Mr Palmer junior, steward 1788 and possibly 1785. After a note on 17 May that T.M. Palmer had withdrawn by letter there is no further record in 1790. But a 'Mr T. Palmer' is in the 1791 subscription list, appearing as a member on 6 June, etc. Later his name is entered as T.M. Palmer, so there can be little doubt that he was the one who resigned in 1790, even though we have no record of his re-election. Against his name in 1793 is written 'gone to sea'. Presumably he was the 'Thomas', son of the above Thomas Palmer senior, baptised at St Thomas' Portsmouth, in 1763. At Hambledon he and his wife Catherine had Constantine John baptised on 7 September 1784; Thomas James on 30 October 1785; Elizabeth Maria 12 January 1787; Catherine 7 July 1796 and Anna 7 July 1799. There is a monumental inscription at Hambledon to Catherine, wife of 'Thomas Martin Palmer of Hambledon', who died on 22 November 1800 aged 34. In 1798 he was a major in the Hambledon Volunteer Infantry and on 21 February 1800 was appointed Colonel of the Hambledon & Wickham Volunteers. His daughters Millicent and Anna (died 1827 aged 27) wove the volunteers' flags which were carried in procession and subsequently displayed in the south aisle of the parish church.

HENRY TEMPLE, Viscount PALMERSTON - e 1772, r 1781. Born 4 December 1739, succeeded as 2nd Viscount 1757, MP East Looe 1762-68, Southampton 1768-74, Hastings 1774-84, Boroughbridge 1784-90, Newport, Isle of Wight, 1790-96, Winchester 1796-1802, Lord of Trade 1765-66, of the Admiralty 1766-77, of the Treasury 1777-82; he died at Hanover Square, London, on 16 April 1802 and was buried at Romsey. His son, the future Prime Minister, Lord Palmerston (1784-1865), scored 0 & 2 as 'Hon Mr Temple' for Lord Duncannon's v Hon. Mr Ponsonby's XI at Roehampton in 1799.

Sir HYDE PARKER - e 1784. Born in 1739, son of Vice Admiral Hyde Parker, he entered the Navy and received a knighthood in 1779. He advanced to the rank of Rear Admiral of the White in 1793, commanded the expedition to the Baltic including bombardment of Copenhagen in 1801 and died on 16 March 1807 (see *DNB*).

JAMES PARLBY - e 1779.

PAWLETT - e 1774. He could have been Percy Powlett RN who resided in Winchester during the 1760s, younger brother of Charles (see page 175). On the other hand if this was the Mr George Poulett whose proposal by Henry Bonham on 19 July 1774 was erased (because he had already been elected?) he was very likely George, born 7 June 1722 and baptised at St James, Westminster, son of Norton Pawlet or Powlett of Amport, Hampshire. He became Gentleman Usher to the Prince of Wales in 1750, MP for Winchester 1765-74, and 1st Commissioner of Lieutenancy for Hampshire 1793-98, and succeeded a distant cousin as Marquess of Winchester in 1794. He died at Amport House on 22 April 1800.

POORE - e 1786, steward 1791, r 1794. He attended a meeting in 1792 with Poore jun, presumably his son, as a non-subscriber. Possibly they were Robert Poore, gentleman of Redbridge, and John, his son who entered Oxford University in 1793 aged 15.

Revd EDMUND POULTER - e 1788. He was born c1756 as Edmund, son of Joseph Edmund Sayer, sergeant-at-law of Clare, Suffolk; educated at Harrow and Trinity, Cambridge (matriculated 1772 aged 16, MA 1780); admitted to Lincolns

Inn 1777 and called to the Bar 1780, having adopted the name Poulter in 1778. Whilst a lawyer in the Middle Temple he belonged to the cricket club which played in White Conduit Fields c1786. On 21 August 1780 he married Ann Banister at St Mary's, Marylebone, and because his new brother-in-law held the patronage of Crawley, Hampshire, Poulter gave up the law and instead took holy orders for the purpose of becoming its rector in 1788. He remained at Crawley until 1790 and in 1791 received from the same patron the rectorship of Meonstoke. In 1815 he was appointed vicar of Barton Stacey, a living which he exchanged the following year for the vicarage of Alton. He also became rector of Soberton and prebendary of Winchester. He played cricket for East Meon & Meonstoke *v* Hambledon on Windmill Down in 1800, evidently going in last though entered at the head of the score-sheet and took part in a gentlemen's match at Cheltenham in 1805. He had joined the new Hambledon Club by 1804 when he seconded a motion proposed by General Clavering. Poulter 'was a politician of high Tory principles, and on the several occasions of Fasts and Thanksgivings during the [Napoleonic] war, he preached and published several energetic discourses against the democratic party, by which he incurred much abuse.' In particular his views, especially as expressed in a manifesto on poor relief and related topics written in his capacity as chairman of the Bench in Winchester, much annoyed William Cobbett who, in his section of *Rural Rides* penned at John Goldsmith's house at Hambledon on 18 November 1822, noted: 'Parson Poulter lives at Meon-Stoke ... so that this valley has something in it besides picturesque views! I asked some countrymen how Poulter and Baines did; but their answer contained too much of irreverence for me to give it here'. Baines was presumably the Revd John Baynes from the adjoining parish of Exton, friend and mentor of John Mitford whose review of John Nyren's book appeared in *The Gentleman's Magazine* in 1833. Poulter died on 9 January 1832 after having fallen 'from his seat in a fit during one of the trials under the Special Commission at Winchester'. His son Brownlow (born 1789), rector of Buriton, became a member of the new Hambledon Club which flourished in the first quarter of the 19th century while another son, John, a barrister, played with the club from 1810 to 1822. His daughter Sophia in 1810 married the Revd John Haygarth (1786-1854), rector of Upham, and uncle of Arthur (1825-1903), compiler of *Cricket Scores and Biographies*. Sophia's son, John Sayer Haygarth, was father of the Oxford cricket blue, John William (1842-1923), and Edward Brownlow (1854-1915), also a first-class cricketer.

Maj. ARMAND POWLETT - e 1778 , r 1780. Younger brother of Charles, he became a major in the 46th foot 1777. Possibly resigned on being assigned to the forces in America.

Revd CHARLES POWLETT - steward 1774, 1783, 1784, 1789, 1795. Born on 28 December 1728, he was the eldest of three illegitimate sons of the 3rd Duke of Bolton by an actress, Lavinia Fenton. Had his father's first wife died early enough to enable his parents to marry by 1728 Charles would have succeeded in 1754 as the 4th Duke. As it was he went to Westminster School and from there proceeded to Trinity, Cambridge, gaining an MA in 1755 and taking holy orders by the time of his marriage at Greenwich on 23 March 1755 to Elizabeth Gunman. On her death in 1760 Duchess Lavinia bequeathed Charles her lands in Westcombe near Greenwich, the sum of £1,000 plus half the money, invested by the late Duke in South Sea Securities for the benefit of their three sons. As owner of the perpetual advowson of the Hampshire churches of Sherfield upon Loddon and Itchen Abbas, she also left instructions for her executor to appoint him to the living the first time one fell vacant. Thus he was duly installed at Itchen Abbas in 1763 (most authorities say as curate, but according to 'Burke's Peerage' as rector) and remained there almost thirty years until 1792. He also produced a certificate to qualify as rector of Bigbury, Devon, 1777, served as rector of Winslade, Hants, 1782-89, of St. Martin by Looe 1785-90 and of Ludgavar, both in Cornwall, and from 1782 as chaplain to his cousin, the Duke of Bolton. These duties were somehow combined with that of a JP, his activities as a founder-member of the Hampshire Club and a lively career as a sporting parson - a keen member of the Hampshire Hunt and writer of hunting songs, one of the committee which revised the laws of cricket 1774, a subscriber to the cricket club which played in White Conduit Fields in the mid-1780s, and an influential member of the Hambledon Club. Perhaps he was also the 'Paulet' whose XI played East's XI at Lord's in 1788.

John Nyren referred to Powlett and Dehany as Hambledon's backers in a match known to have been played on Broadhalfpenny in 1775. But the main reason for him being constantly touted as chief founder of the club, variously between 1750 and 1767, is a remark attributed to William Beldham by James Pycroft in *The Cricket Field*: 'when we [Farnham] beat them [Hambledon] in 1780 I heard Mr Powlett say: "here have I been thirty years raising our club, and we are to be beaten by a single parish?"' But as a 14-year-old in 1780 Beldham is unlikely to have been privy to a conversation between two or more gentlemen - and thirty years would take us back to 1750, six years before the time when we know Hambledon was still playing as a parish and fourteen before the first mention of a club - and then under the auspices of the local landowner Esquire Land. Attempts have been made to rationalise Pycroft's evidence by surmising that Beldham misunderstood what was being said and took 'thirteen' to be 'thirty', meaning Powlett first supported the club in 1767 - or, since there is no record of Farnham meeting Hambledon before 1785, that Beldham actually heard, or rather misheard, Powlett five years later thereby producing a date of 1772. Both these versions are more feasible. But however much one juggles the figures and dates they only tell us what we may in any case reasonably infer, that he had been a subscriber to the club since sometime in the late 1760s or early 1770s. A recent assertion that Powlett formed the club after being 'rusticated' from London to Hampshire in 1763 may be disregarded: he had already been elected a freeman of Winchester by 1756 and by 1760 was already residing at Chilland, just outside the village of Itchen Abbas. Also it should be obvious that anyone starting his own cricket club in that part of the county would base it much closer to home than a distant parish such as Hambledon - most obviously on nearby Itchen Down where the manor was owned by Powlett's cousin, the Duke of Bolton. Indeed it may be suspected that it was through Powlett and his fellow Old Westminster and close family friend, Lord Northington, living about a mile away at the Grange, that the Down became the club's second home from 1778. Furthermore Altham's assertion that Powlett 'piloted' the club 'through at least one crisis, and, when the end came, was the last to abandon the sinking ship' should be treated with caution. There is no record of his subscription for the final season (1796), nor of his attendance at the final meetings of the club.

Powlett's 'faithfull & affectionate wife', Elizabeth, died on 13 January 1792 aged 66. Three months later on 25 April, at 66, he married 32-year-old Anne Mariet at St Pancras Old Church, London. He died in Upper Titchfield Street, Marylebone, on 29 January 1809. His will, which tells us that he owned the farm of Nevills or Burleigh in Itchen Abbas, mentions only one fellow Hambledon member - Admiral Sir Robert Calder. His widow died on 12 January 1815 aged 55 and was buried along with her late husband and his first wife at Itchen Abbas.

Revd CHARLES POWLETT jun - e 1791, r 1793; attended as a non-subscriber on 3 July 1787. Born at Winchester on 17 June 1761, he was the son of Percy, brother of Charles sen, who married Elizabeth Packham at Dover in 1758. He was educated at Westminster, Charterhouse and Trinity, Cambridge, and ordained in 1787 to the curacy of Winslade where he served as rector 1789-94 and 1796-1811. Also rector of St Martin by Looe 1790-1807 and Blackford, Somerset, 1794-96; vicar of Kingsclere 1796; rector of Itchen Stoke 1796-1817 and of High Roding, Essex, 1817-34 and perpetual curate of Swingfield, Kent, 1817-26, as well as a RN chaplain from 1794 and chaplain to the Prince of Wales. In spite of the considerable income from these livings he was evading his creditors when he died in Brussels in June 1834.

WILLIAM POWLETT POWLETT (formerly Smythe) - e 1780; after 1787 failed to pay his subscriptions until paid eight years (£25 4s) in one instalment in 1795 and then resigned. A leading figure in Hampshire hunting circles, he was nicknamed Pontius Pilate, and in 1795 was appointed Perpetual President of the Hampshire Hunt, though so lame he was unable to mount his horse unaided. Sheriff of Hampshire 1783, he resided at different times at Little Somborne, Lainston House near Winchester, etc, and died aged 62 at Bath in 1821.

PYE - e 1774, r 1776. The 7 May 1776 minute runs: 'Mr Pye desires to withdraw his name on leaving the County'. Ashley-Cooper says that he may have been Henry James Pye who was made Poet Laureate in 1790.

Revd ALEXANDER RADCLIFFE - e 1792, steward 1793; attended as non-subscriber 30 May 1791. Born c1759, son of Thomas of Ormskirk, Lancashire, he entered Oriel, Oxford, in 1776 aged 17 (BA All Souls 1781, MA 1785) and served as vicar of Hullavington, Wilts, rector of St Clement, Sandwich, and incumbent of Titchfield from 1791 until his death at Titchfield on 24 December 1825 aged 67. A son-in-law of Sir William Benett (see page 150).

Rev JONATHAN RASHLEIGH - e 1772, r 1777. Son of Jonathan senior of Wickham, he was born on 17 October 1740 and went to Eton. He was then admitted to Merton, Oxford, 1758 (BA University College 1763, MA All Souls 1767) and became rector of Gedney, Lincs, 1773 and of Wickham and Silverton, Devon, 1784 until his death in November 1806.

JOHN RICHARDS - steward 1787. His long association with the village and consequently with the cricket club apparently came about through his marriage to Maria Martin (c1746-1826), one of the four co-heiresses of the local manor of Butvellins, who with her sister Anna Catherine sold the manor, or their share of it, to Hugh Seymour Conway, the Hambledon Club's president, in 1792. Born about 1737, Richards had settled in the parish by 1766, the year of his daughter Dorothy's baptism in the church on 17 August. She was followed by John (see page 180) in 1767; Maria on 11 December 1770; Richard George (see later) in 1772; Ann Elizabeth on 23 May 1774 and Frances on 1 January 1776. He made his only known appearance as a cricketer at the age of about 34, in a gentlemen's match between Hampshire and Sussex on Broadhalfpenny in 1771. Right from the beginning until the club's demise in 1796 his main duties seem to have been those of club treasurer. In 1773 the members asked him to find out the expense of a machine to convey the cricketers to distant parts and later that summer to purchase the same out of surplus funds. In 1780 the Veranes tobacco was ordered to be kept in his custody. Four years after that he and two others were authorised to supervise alterations to the 'booth' on Windmill Down. And in 1787 he had to provide six spitting troughs and to send to the wine merchant in Winchester 'for a hogshead of the best port in bottle to drink immediately'.

By 1771 his residence was Whitedale, a large house just outside the village, not far from Thomas Land at Park House. On 2 April that year he was charged at the Court Leet and Court Baron 'for making an encroachment upon the Lord of the Manor's waste land at his property Wided Dell (sic) by jutting his wall and pales several roods into the highways leading from his dwelling to the Town of Hambledon'. According to the Cambridge University registers he kept a school, though this is not mentioned in directories published in 1784 and 1793. A man of many parts, in 1772 he was one of three nominees to become the next sheriff of Hampshire, and in 1775, along with fellow Hambledon members, helped found the Hampshire Club - 'established for the support of public liberty' - acting as a steward at its meeting at the *George Inn*, Winchester, in 1777 and chairing the meeting in 1780 at which the Club formally adopted a petition against Lord North's administration promoted by Philip Dehany (see page 92). During the 1770s he filled the posts of surveyor of highways in Hambledon and hayward of the Chase, and though not a farmer himself took a keen interest in agricultural matters (as noted in a letter of 5 January 1775, compare Knight vol. 27, p. 46), designing an improved plough described and illustrated in volume 1 of *The Hampshire Repository* (1799) while volume 2 (1801) alluded to him as 'a worthy and able gentleman' who has 'invented several useful ploughs and several implements of the drag and harrow, and roller kind, especially a machine to weigh draft'. Richards was also fond of shooting, and according to one account he was fit enough to walk for six hours at a stretch with a gun slung over his shoulder.

Latterly, until his death in his early eighties, he lived at North House, past the *Bat & Ball* towards Clanfield, in Catherington parish. By his will dated January 1814 (proved PCC) he left £1,000 to his younger son, Richard George; £2,000 and all his pictures to his eldest son, John; and £2,000 apiece to his four unmarried daughters. Curiously, the will mentions his claim to a tract of land in Upper Mississippi in the U.S.A. and, less surprisingly, his right to 17$^1/_2$ acres in the Forest of East Beer (sic) in Hampshire. Besides Richard George and daughters

Ann Elizabeth and Frances, he appointed the Revds Charles Richards sen and jun of Hyde Abbey School as joint-executors. John Richards died on 27 July 1819 and is buried in Hambledon churchyard under a large chest-tomb now bearing further inscriptions to his wife, who survived him by seven years, and his four daughters - including Maria, spinster of North House, whose will was proved in 1838. The Richards tomb also has inscriptions to the Rev Richard George and his wife, Susan, who died 3 November 1822 aged 43. Baptised at Hambledon on 16 December 1772 and educated under Charles Richards at Hyde Abbey and at Cambridge, as an 8-year-old Richard George was one of the '2 Mr Richards' present at a meeting on Broadhalfpenny on 19 June 1781 and though never a member, frequently attended club meetings during the 1790s. He married Susan, daughter of Henry, Viscount Hood, president of the Hambledon Club in 1788, at Catherington on 8 October 1797, and secondly, at Hambledon on 1 November 1825, Catherine Elizabeth Whyte by whom he had further children. He served Hambledon as its vicar from 1800 till his death on 15 June 1841.

JOHN RICHARDS jun - e 1788, steward 1792. Born at Hambledon on 9 May 1767, eldest son of the above, he attended school in Winchester and entered Trinity, Cambridge, in 1784 (BA 1789, MA 1793). From 1792 he appears in club records as Revd Richards while against his name in 1793 is written 'gone to sea' and in 1795 'gone abroad'. At some stage he went to America where he married and received a generous sum settled on him by his father, who later left him £2,000 and all his pictures. It is not clear whether he was the John Richards, rector of Ovington in 1801. But he is definitely recorded in 1815-16, as the Revd Richards of North House, Catherington, Master of the Hambledon Hunt, hunting the eastern side of the county at the time of its famous run of some 14 to 15 miles on 4 December 1815, starting in Stoke Woods and finishing on Tryford Down in Sussex. By his wife Susan he had a daughter, Maria Downman, baptised at St Thomas', Winchester, on 31 July 1811, while a mural tablet in Hambledon church reads:

JOHN RICHARDS ESQ.
Born at Hambledon 9 May 1768
Died in London 26 March 1835
and of GEORGE his second son
and of Susan his wife
lost at sea at the early age
of 22 years.

On 25 March 1835, as John Richards esq of North House in Catherington, 'now residing in Chapel Street, Belgrave Square', he drew up a will, witnessed by A.E., Francis (Frances?) and Maria D. Richards, apparently his sisters and daughter, which appointed his 'dear wife Susan Coffin Richards' sole legatee and executor. It reveals that he owned considerable property in Devon - a farm called Pubbaven (?) in North Bovey, one in Belstone, Marsh Mill Farm in Newton St Cyres and a house on St David's Hill, Exeter, which his uncle, Hugh Downman MD, devised to his mother Maria. Hugh (1740-1809) physician and poet (see *DNB*), was a son of Hugh senior who married Anne Richards at Exeter in 1738, and through the Downmans (one of whom appeared at Hambledon, as a non-subscriber on 18 June and 9 July 1792) the Richards were related to fellow club members Thomas Palmer, senior and junior, and Edward Hale. It may be noted that Ashley-Cooper confuses the above with John Richards, sometime rector of Nassau in the Bahamas, who married Mary Silvester of Froxfield in 1792 and whose will, dated 1827 with a codicil of 1829, was proved 2 April 1837.

GEORGE WILLIAM RICKETTS - e 1784. Bachelor of Bishops Sutton when licensed to marry Letitia Mildmay, spinster of Twyford, daughter of Carew Mildmay of Shawford House, 1791. He died at Nascot House near Watford in 1842 at the age of 82, when described as 'late Receiver General for Hants'.

GEORGE RIDGE is named once in the minutes, as 'Mr G. Ridge' proposing a candidate for election in 1774. That year a 'George Ridge jun. esq' was elected a burgess of Winchester (*Hampshire Chronicle* 3 October), but the Hambledon member seems to have been the father of Thomas (see page 184), called Ridge junior in 1771, and the one who in 1772 went to watch Hambledon play England at Guildford where the diarist John

Baker records seeing 'Mr Ridge father and son'. George was himself the son of Thomas Ridge of Portsmouth who in 1719 purchased the estate of Langrish in East Meon, immediately north of Hambledon, and in 1723 the manor of Rogate in Sussex, and died in 1730. By his wife Elizabeth he left four sons, all christened at St Thomas' in Portsmouth. The eldest, Humphrey, was admitted to Trinity Hall, Cambridge, in 1721 and Trinity College in 1730. The second, Thomas, a Portsmouth brewer, distiller and wine merchant, knighted in 1746, was declared bankrupt in 1764 and died a year later in Portsmouth. The assignee of his estate, his cousin John Ridge, sold Langrish to Hambledon member William Jolliffe of Petersfield in 1771. The two younger sons, George and Richard, were evidently the members recorded in the 1770s:

Thomas Ridge of Portsmouth d 1730; married Elizabeth
        (will proved PCC 1750?)
  —— Humphrey 1699-1732 (?); married 1730 Elizabeth,
        daughter of the scholar Richard Bentley (DNB)
        and sister of Joanna, mother of Richard
        Cumberland (below); held Rogate Manor from
        1730 to 1732 when it passed to brother Thomas.
  —— Sir Thomas 1701-1765
  —— Richard 1718-1801 (see below).
George, baptised Dec 1715; married Elizabeth Brooke.
  —— Elizabeth, married at Kilmiston 19 Feb 1759
        Richard Cumberland. (1732-1811)
  —— Thomas c1737-1801 (see below).
William c1738-72; Captain 17th Regiment of Foot; 'one
        of the best and bravest young officers of his
        time' who 'served the whole war in America
        with distinguished reputation' (Richard Cumberland)
        died 2 Dec 1772 aged 34 (inscription Kilmiston
        church) while visiting island of Grenada where
        according to his will, dated 12 Dec 1771, proved
        PCC 3 Feb 1773, he was entitled to £1,000 out of a
        sum of £9,000 secured by mortgage of several
        habitations, plantations, slaves, cattle, horses, etc.

George was admitted to the Inner Temple in 1732 as 3rd son of Thomas deceased, and bought the manor of Kilmiston

Gymming in 1739. He was mentioned in the wills of his brother Thomas (1765) and son William (1771), when described as George esq late of Kilmiston but now of Bishops Waltham. According to the memoirs of his son-in-law, the playwright Richard Cumberland *(DNB)*, 'George Ridge Esq., of Kilmiston, in the county of Hampshire, had two sons and one daughter by Miss Brooke, niece to my grandfather Bentley; with this family we had lived as friends and relations in habits of the greatest intimacy ... our families had kept up an interchange of annual visits for a course of time. From these meetings I had been for several years excluded by my avocations to college or London, till upon Mr Ridge's coming to town accompanied by his wife and daughter, and taking lodgings in the near neighbourhood of Mount-Street ... I was kindly entertained by them, and found so many real charms in the modest manner and blooming looks of the amiable daughter'. He proposed on a subsequent visit by the Ridges to Fulham and they were married by Cumberland's father at Kilmiston with George providing £3,000 for Elizabeth's marriage settlement. Cumberland, who promoted cricket at Tunbridge Wells, attended Hambledon meetings as a non-subscriber 24 July 1787 - with Cumberland jun, doubtless George's grandson, Charles (1760-1835), the bowler sketched by George Shepheard along with Beldham, Walker, Harris, etc - and 31 August 1789, on these occasions probably staying at Holt, between Kilmiston and Upham and about seven miles from Hambledon, where he was 'in the practice of interchanging an annual visit with Mrs Bludworth of Holt near Winchester, the dearest friend of my wife'.

RICHARD RIDGE - e 1772. Brother of George and uncle of Thomas, baptised at St Thomas', Portsmouth, 24 July 1718, his marriage is recorded by *The Gentleman's Magazine* for 1755: 'Rd Ridge, Esq; of Milland, Sussex, - to Miss Mary Foy'. The Manor of Fyning in Rogate parish, bought by his brother Thomas through trustees in 1757, passed to Richard, who was recorded as owner by 1783. In 1776 he also purchased the Manor of Terwick in Sussex. He died as Richard esq of Fyning in 1801 (will proved PCC), leaving an invalid widow, Mary Ann Ridge. His Fyning and Terwick estates were later held by his great-nephew, Thomas Roger Ridge, son of Thomas (see below), who in 1811 as Thomas Roger esq, widower of Rogate, married Louisa-James Waight, a 30-year-old spinster of Bishops Sutton. After his death in 1828 the properties passed to his son Thomas John Ridge (see the *Victoria County History of Sussex* vol. IV pp. 23-29).

THOMAS RIDGE of Kilmiston, a Hampshire JP, formed one of the Hambledon eleven against Caterham in 1769 and first appears in the minutes as 'Mr T. Ridge' in 1772. The son of George (see page 181), he was born c1737, attended Cotton's school in Winchester (see *Hampshire Chronicle* 26 September 1774), entered Westminster School 1750-51 aged 14 and was admitted to Trinty, Cambridge in 1754, when aged 17 (BA 1758, MA 1761, fellow 1759). He remained on close terms with his headmaster at Winchester and fellow Hambledon member who in 1778 appointed 'my friend Thomas Ridge of Kilmeston' a trustee of his daughter's marriage settlement and of his will. On 15 April 1767 he married his 17-year-old (second?) cousin, Mary (baptised Portsea 2 October 1749), daughter of John and Mary Ridge. It was his father-in-law who witnessed the sale of Broadhalfpenny *Hut* to Lord Clanricarde on 2 April 1772, and Thomas inherited the lease of Stubbington Farm in Portsea under his 1774 will, of which he was sole executor. By Mary he fathered, according to one account, twenty-one children, of whom the following can be traced in the Kilmiston registers:

Thomas Roger 1768/Elizabeth Ann 1770/Mary Sophia 1771
Margaret Henrietta 1772, married James Baynes 1805 at
    Cheriton
William 1773/Frances Augusta 1775/Charles John 1777
Henry 1778/Jane 1779/Edward Jervoise 1780
Mary Stawell 1782-82/James Brook 1783
Lucy Matilda 1784, married William Gunner 1811 at Fareham
Amelia Isabella 1785/Edwina 1789/George Richard 1790
Louisa Catherine 1786, married James Ainge 1814 at Fareham
Emma Sophia 1791, married Thomas Wolridge 1819 at
    Fareham
Caroline Susan 1793

One or more of the sons attended Hambledon meetings several times as 'Ridge jun' while the above Edward Jervoise, as Capt. E.J. Ridge, subscribed to the new Hambledon Club around

1810. In 1774 Thomas must have been responsible for raising the Hampshire team since the *Public Ledger* noted that 'a great cricket match was played on Seven Oaks Vine, for one thousand guineas, between the Duke of Dorset and ten men on the side of Kent and —— Ridge Esq and ten men on the side of Hampshire' while for the return on Broadhalfpenny, when Barber was injured, 'the Duke', reported the *Salisbury Journal*, 'generously gave Mr Ridge Hogsflesh to play in his room'. Doubtless he also had a principal hand in those fixtures arranged for Kilmiston Down - Hambledon parish *v* Hampshire 1775 and Hampshire *v* England 1777 (for which Lord Tankerville paid forfeit). On the field itself he represented Hampshire gentlemen *v* those of Sussex in 1771 and Hampshire five times between 1772 and 1775 (when already in his mid to late thirties), making 52 runs in 10 completed innings, only once getting into double figures - 24 against England on Broadhalfpenny in 1773.

By the age of forty he had evidently given up all notion of top-class cricket because his name was not advertised for the proposed Kilmiston match in 1777. However he continued to figure prominently in the county's horse races, both as rider and owner, and at his own expense maintained the Kilmiston Hunt, whose most famous run, in 1770, reputedly covered upwards of fifty miles, starting near Tichborne and ending at Rotherfield. In 1784 it changed its name to the Hampshire Hunt and was subsequently supported as a subscription pack, which was said to hunt the country from Farnham to Romsey. In 1795 he gave his hunting country over to William Powlett Powlett (see page 177). He was eulogised as follows in one of Charles Powlett's hunting songs:

> A sportsman came next, who in plain English style,
> French manners and foppery defies,
> His countenance spoke him the man without guile,
> The truth you might read in his eyes.
> When he points out the way,
> We will with pleasure obey,
> And cheerfully follow his call,
> O'er the fences we bound,
> But if some reach the ground,
> We laugh at the Cockneys who fall.

A few days after his death on 3 February 1801 the *Hampshire Chronicle* noted tersely: 'Tuesday morning died suddenly, T. Ridge, Esq of Kimpston'. His widow survived him for fifteen years, until 1816 when *The Gentleman's Magazine* recorded the death at Fareham of Mrs Ridge, relict of T. esq 'many years distributor of stamps for the Eastern division of Hants'. His monumental inscription in Kilmiston church describes him as 'Lord of the Manor'. But the estate had passed out of the family within less than a generation. When William Cobbett passed that way he noted in his *Rural Rides*, under 18 November 1822:

> A bridle road over some fields and through a coppice took me to Kilmston (sic), formerly a large village, but now mouldered into two farms, and a few miserable-tumble-down houses for the labourers. Here is a house that was formerly the residence of the landlord of the place, but is now occupied by one of the farmers. This is a fine country for fox-hunting, and Kilmston belonged to a Mr. Ridge who was a famous fox-hunter, and who is accused of having spent his fortune in that way. But what do people mean? He had a right to spend his income, as his fathers had done before him. It was the Pitt-system, and not the fox-hounds, that took away the principal. The place now belongs to a Mr Long, whose origin I cannot find out.

and again, writing from Petersfield on 11 November 1825:

> A little to our right as we came along, we left the village of Kimston (sic), where ... lived Squire Ridge, a famous fox-hunter, at a great mansion, now used as a farm-house; and it is curious enough that this squire's son-in-law, one Gunner, an attorney at Bishop's Waltham, is steward to the man who now owns the estate.

MARK ROBINSON senior - e 1783 as 'of Corhampton'. A naval officer - Lieutenant 1746, Commander 1758, Captain 1760 - who lost a leg in the action off Cape Henry 5 September 1781; owner of Corhampton Manor 1782-92. As Rear Admiral Robinson of Bath he died on 23 November 1799, leaving two sons, Mark (see below) and Charles (baptised Portsmouth 10 May 1753), both naval captains.

MARK ROBINSON - e 1776. Son of Mark senior, he was baptised at St Thomas', Portsmouth, 27 May 1754. During the 1780s resided in Hambledon where he and his wife Margaretta had several children baptised and/or buried, some with headstones still to be seen in the churchyard - Elizabeth Catherine 28 November 1783, Maria 26 April 1785 (died 20, buried 23 November 1787 aged 2), Mark 30 June 1788 (buried 5 February 1789 aged 8 months) and Mark (buried 1791). The only children mentioned in Mark senior's will (1795) were Elizabeth (presumably Elizabeth Catherine) and Thomas Pitt, christened, as son of Mark and Mary, at Bishops Waltham on 25 July 1792. He became a Lieutenant RN 1776, Commander 1751, Captain 1790, Rear Admiral of the Blue 1808 and finally Admiral of the White 1830. In 1804 he accompanied Nelson to the West Indies in pursuit of the French and Spanish fleets; further details on the career of this 'gallant officer' can be found in *The Gentleman's Magazine* for 1834. In 1799 he married Miss Shirley of Pulteney Street, Bath, who died in 1811. Mark died at Freshford, Somerset, on 21 February 1834.

Lord JOHN RUSSELL - e 1790, president 1795. Born on 6 July 1766, probably in London; MP Tavistock 1788-90 and 1790-1802; succeeded brother as Duke of Bedford 1802; Privy Councillor 1806; Lord Lieutenant of Ireland 1806-7. In 1812 ten of his servants with Lord William Russell beat eleven of Woburn (chiefly tradesmen to the Duke) in a match attended by the Duke and Duchess (see long account in *The Sporting Magazine*). According to the 'Greville Memoirs' (published 1875-87) 'a more uninteresting weak minded selfish character does not exist … He is a good natured plausible man without enemies, and really (though he does not think so) without friends … He is affable, bland, and of easy intercourse, making rather a favourable impression on superficial observers'. Died at Doune of Rothiemurchus, Perthshire, 20 October 1839.

CHARLES SAXTON – was mentioned in the club minutes in 1774. He was the youngest son of a London merchant, born 1732, and he entered the navy in 1745 as 'captain's servant', advancing to Lieutenant 1757, Commander 1760, Captain 1762 and Commissioner of Portsmouth Dockyard 1791; described by Nelson, who knew him for thirty years, as a 'rough sailor'

(1801). He remained at Portsmouth until he retired on a pension of £750 p.a. in 1806, having been created Baronet on 19 July 1794. He married Mary Bush of Burcott, Oxon, 1771 and died at Gloucester on 11 November 1808 (see *DNB*).

HENRY SCOTT - e 1779. Presumably Henry whose son John was baptised at Hambledon on 18 March 1779 and daughter Henrietta Robinson on 22 July 1784.

SCOTT - e 1793. Perhaps related to General Scott who attended as a non-subscriber in 1792.

JOHN SHAKESPEAR - e 1784, r 1791. Born 12 March 1749 and baptised in St Dunstan's church, London, the son of John senior, alderman, he left England for India 1766 and returned fifteen years later with a fortune. In 1782 he married Mary Davenport, an heiress to the Lacock Abbey estate; in 1784 he bought Brookwood House, 'consorted with wealthy folk and hunted', and towards the end of his life also kept two yachts at Cowes. After selling Brookwood in 1789 he moved to Twyford Lodge, but following his wife's death in 1793 resided at Singleton near Goodwood where he regularly hunted with the Duke of Richmond's hounds. He lived latterly at Cheltenham and died there on 10 January 1825.

BYSSHE SHELLEY - as 'Mr Shelley' he proposed Richard Ridge for membership in the earliest surviving club minute of 30 June 1772, and as 'Mr B. Shelley' his brother John Ridge the following 4 August. In 1771 he represented Hampshire gentlemen *v* those of Sussex and in 1772 Baker saw him at Guildford watching Hambledon play England. 'Handsome, enterprising, and not over scrupulous, dignified in appearance and manner, but addicted to inferior company', he was born at Christchurch, Newark, in America on 21 June 1731 and when still young came to England where he made his fortune through two 'runaway marriages': in 1752 to Mary Catherine (died 1760), only child of Revd Theobald Michell of Horsham; on 17 August 1769 to Mrs Elizabeth Jane Perry, daughter and heiress of Thomas Sidney and his brother, the Earl of Leicester of Penshurst Park who died without issue in 1743 - reported by *The Gentleman's Magazine* as 'Bysshe Shelley, Esq; of Hambledon, Hants - to Hon. Miss Sidney (sic) of

Penshurst-place, Kent, 80,000 *l.*' He resided in Hambledon until at least 1778 and had three children baptised in the church - John (later a baronet and father of the first Lord De Lisle of Penshurst) on 18 December 1771, Percy John Borlase on 23 July 1773 and Phillip on 20 February 1778. His second wife was buried at Hambledon on 17 May 1781. He later moved to Castle Goring near Arundel, became a baronet in 1806 and died on 6 January 1815. The 'Shelley jun' who assisted the Gentlemen of Hampshire in 1771 must have been his son Timothy (born 7 September 1753, died 24 April 1844), then only 17, 'a kindly, pompous, capricious, well-meaning, ill-doing, wrong-headed man', who succeeded his father as 2nd Baronet and was father of the poet Percy Bysshe Shelley, born in 1792, who described his grandfather as 'a bad man ... a curse upon society.'

JOHN SHELLEY - e 1772. Brother of Bysshe (see above), he resided at Field Place near Horsham, about forty miles from Hambledon, and was seen at several cricket matches by Baker - on Broadbridge Common on 28 May 1772, at Guildford, accompanied by his brother, watching Hambledon against England in July, umpiring at Horsham on 18 September and, the following year, as a spectator there on 16 June. He died on 4 October 1790.

Col. WILLIAM SHIRREFF - e 1782, steward 1786, r 1791. Of Upton house, Old Alresford, he rose to the rank of Colonel on 20 November 1782, Major-General 1793 and Lieutenant-General 1798. According to one of Charles Powlett's hunting songs (1782) he served under Wolfe in 1759:

> A soldier accomplished appears in our front,
> Whose valour no danger can check;
> With the same eager spirit he leads on the hunt,
> As Wolfe led him on at Quebec.

Col. WILLIAM SKINNER - in 1778 the minutes refer to a letter received from the Colonel asking for his name to be withdrawn but on 5 May 1779 it was ordered that his resignation be expunged at his own request. He was William, late of the 85th Regiment of Foot (Lieutenant Colonel 1763, full Colonel 1777), perhaps a son or some other relative of

Lieutenant-General William Skinner, born c1699, died 25 December 1780 aged 81. The General is stated to have married Susanna, daughter and co-heiress of Admiral Warren of Westbury in East Meon, in 1767 (when almost 70) and to have acquired complete ownership of the estate in 1772. His daughter, Susanna, married Lord Gage (see page 161) in 1789 and died at Westbury House in 1821 aged 51.

NICHOLAS PURDUE SMITH - e 1774. Born 1722, he was sometime County Treasurer and alderman of Winchester, and a wine merchant supplying the Hambledon Club. In the wine ballot of 11 May 1773 he received 5 votes to Peter Gauntlett's 8, but on the 25th it was 'ordered that a pipe of wine be sent for to Mr Smith of Winton for the use of the club', and the following year, when he was proposed on 24 May, it was ordered 'that the stewards procure 3 Doz: of Madeira at 40/- from Mr. Smith'. He owned several houses in Winchester and a copyhold farm at Droxford, three miles from Hambledon. His will dated 23 June 1779, with codicil, was proved (PCC) 25 August 1780. The probate papers include an inventory of his properties, taken on 1 July 1779, amounting to £14,946.

THOMAS ASSHETON SMITH- e 1786, president 1789. Son of Thomas Assheton of Ashley, Cheshire, he was born c1752, attended Eton and assumed the name Smith as heir to a wealthy uncle. By succeeding his father in 1774 and through marriage to the heiress Elizabeth Wynn he became a very rich man in his early twenties, with extensive landed property in North Wales as well as in England. He was MP 1774-80, Sheriff 1783-84 and Lord Lieutenant 1822-28 of Cærnarvonshire and MP 1797-1821 for Andover, but best known on the turf and in the hunting and cricket field. He only took up the game seriously in his mid-thirties when associated with the Hambledon, White Conduit and Moulsey Hurst clubs from 1786, playing for MCC 1790-93, with a top-score of 30 not out v Middlesex in 1790, and in several great matches for Hampshire and England XIs 1789-92. From 1787 to 1796 he also promoted a series of matches, Hampshire v Surrey, Hampshire v England, etc, on Perriam Downs near his seat at Tidworth. In 1801 he subscribed to Boxall's cricket manual. Following his death at Tidworth House on 12 May 1828 *The*

Gentleman's Magazine commented that 'he was distinguished by unbounded kindness of heart, spotless integrity, the firmest friendship, and the most unaffected sincerity'. His son, T.A. Smith junior (1776-1858), became a noted cricketer and all-round sportsman.

SNELL - e 1774, r 1785.

HENRY BILSON-LEGGE, Lord STAWEL - e 1778, president 1779, r 1791. Born at Westminster 22 February 1757, educated at Eton and Cambridge, he married Mary, daughter of lst Viscount Curzon, 1779 and succeeded as Baron Stawel on the death of his mother, Baroness Stawel (created 1760), in 1780. He was advertised to play for Farnham *v* Odiham & Alton in 1784 and engaged William Beldham to lay out the cricket ground at Holt Pound near Farnham. A correspondent to *The Sporting Magazine*, February 1850, wrote: 'I think in the year 1783 I was at school at Andover, and recollect that during the two years I was there, Lord Stawell brought a clever pack of fox-hounds to the *Star Inn*, kept by Mercer ... Lord Stawell, I believe, lived at Marelands, near Farnham, and hunted about that country. I presume there were not many foxes at that time; in consequence, his pack was shifted about a great deal. For instance, he had a kennel at the public house, a mile out of Basingstoke, on the Preston Candover-road: his own quarters very frequently at Hackwood, in the late Duke of Bolton's time'. For some years he also lived at Mapledurham in Buriton which he bought from Edward Gibbon for £16,000 in 1789 and sold to Henry Bonham (see page 151) in 1798. He died at Grosvenor Place, London, 25 August 1820.

STEEL - e 1776.

Capt SHERBORNE STEWART - e 1779, steward 1780. Originally entered as Mr or Stewart esq, but as Captain Steward (sic) in membership lists 1791-93. The son of John and Amelia Stewart, he was baptised at St Olave's, Hârt Street, London, on 14 March 1759 and married Ann Mason at St Mary's, Marylebone, on 11 April 1789. He became an officer in the 1st Life Guards - Captain 1787, Major 1795, Lieutenant-Colonel 1800 - and disappeared from the Army Lists 1810-12.

TALBOT - e 1788. Possibly George Talbot who played for White Conduit, Moulsey Hurst, MCC, etc, 1785-89. This could have been George (1761-1850) who succeeded his brother as 3rd Baronet 1812.

PETER TAYLOR - first recorded in club minutes when proposing Sir Richard Worsley on 3 August 1773. Also in 1773 he was present at the two-day Andover Races with his son, Robert Paris Taylor, and several fellow members of the Hambledon Club when 'on each day Mr Taylor gave a turtle'. Born at Wells, Somerset, on 11 November 1714, the younger son of Robert Taylor, a grocer, and orphaned at 13, he married Jane Holt in 1740 and by 1755 worked as a silversmith in London. There he struck up an acquaintance with the corrupt politician Henry Fox, later Lord Holland, Paymaster-General from 1757 to 1765, and his accomplice, the army agent and contractor, John Calcraft, which led to his appointment as Deputy-Paymaster in Germany during the Seven Years War (1757-63). Following his associates' example, he embezzled enormous sums from the public funds and after five years on the Continent, during which time £150,000 a month was said to have passed through his hands, he returned with a huge fortune (one estimate £400,000) with which he bought the estate of Burcott near Wells in 1764 and soon afterwards Purbrook Park north of Portsmouth where he spent nearly £100,000 building a large 'universally admired' mansion at the foot of Portsdown. A Hampshire JP by 1770, he represented Wells in Parliament 1765-66 and Portsmouth 1774-77, dying at Wells on 3 November 1777. There is an inscription to Peter and his wife Jane (d 1770) in the parish church near Purbrook. One of the executors of his will (proved PCC) was Charles Wolfran Cornwall (1735-89), Speaker of the House of Commons 1780-89, a former pupil of Reynell Cotton's at Hyde Abbey School and a steward of its inaugural Old Boys' reunion dinner in 1774. In 1781 Purbrook Park with its 'large, elegant, new built, capital Mansion House' was advertised for sale (*Hampshire Chronicle* 13 August) and the following year Taylor's estate was called upon for a settlement of a shortage of funds for which he stood surety while Deputy-Paymaster. His son (1741?-92), formerly Sheriff of Somerset 1765-66 and MP for Berwick-on-

Tweed 1768-74, was ruined and spent his last ten years as a debtor in Fleet Prison.

ROBERT THISTLETHWAYTE— e 1779, president 1780 and 1785. Born on 24 May 1755, son of Robert of Norman Court, Hampshire, he succeeded his father in 1767 and his uncle of Southwick Park in 1771 before going up to Queen's, Oxford, in 1772. In 1778 he married Selina, daughter and co-heir of Sir Thomas Frederick Bart, when they were painted by Gainsborough in what appear to have been two marriage portraits. The *Hampshire Chronicle* on 18 June 1781 announced: 'Mr Thistlethwayte intending to give a ball on the last day of the Winchester Races, will think himself honoured by the company of the Ladies and Gentlemen of the County'. He sat as MP for Hampshire 1780-90 and died on 22 October 1802.

PETER THRESHER - e 1780, by 1785 styled Captain Thresher, r 1791 as Captain Thresher. There were three generations of Peter Threshers at Fareham. One who married Jane Rolfe there in 1728 was far too old to have become a captain between 1780 and 1785. To a lesser degree the same applies to his son, baptised Fareham 14 April (and 5 May) 1729 and died 4 May 1794 aged 65 (MI). The third Peter, nephew of the last and son of William Thresher (1736-85), was baptised Peter Joseph at Fareham on 26 April 1761. During the 1780s he appears in army lists as a half-pay lieutenant of the 77th Foot, but could have gained a higher rank in the Militia. On 1 May 1792 he married Ann Percy at Catherington and died on 19 November 1800 aged 39 leaving four children: Henry, Thomas, Charlotte and Mary Ann. It will be remembered that a Henry Thresher married Tom Sueter's daughter, Sally, and that it was in his house at Emsworth that the cricketer died in 1827.

TOOKER - e 1773. Perhaps James, Lord of the Manor of Daubney two miles east of Hambledon.

ROBERT TURNER - mentioned in club minutes 1773, steward 1777. During the summer of 1779 he attended club meetings regularly, also the dinner at the *George* on 21 September. He died on 24 March 1780. Turner lived at the Hermitage in Hambledon, a mile from Broadhalfpenny Down, which was advertised for sale four months later in the *Hampshire Chronicle* of 17 July:

To be LETT, the unexpired Lease of that well known and commodious house, called the HERMITAGE, late in the occupation of GEORGE (sic) TURNER Esq; deceased, situated in the parish of Hambledon, near Broad-Halfpenny, of which there are ELEVEN years to come, at a very moderate rent, consisting of a drawing-room, dining parlour, study, and store-room on the ground-floor: five bed-chambers on the first floor, and good garrets, cellars, coach-house, stabling for six horses, dairy, wash house, brewhouse, &c. with an exceeding large garden planted with the choicest fruit-trees in full bearing, and other trees and flowering shrubs and about twenty acres of arable and pasture land contiguous to the house; in a fine sporting country, where several packs of hounds are kept, and a most agreeable neighbourhood, within one mile of Hambledon (a good market town), 62 miles of London, 14 of Portsmouth, 14 of Winchester, and 8 of Petersfield. The situtation is not only pleasant and desirable but the premises have been completely fitted up, and considerable additions made to them by the late possessor.

The whole may be viewed by applying to the gardener on the spot, and further particulars known on application to Mr William Augustus Bettesworth, attorney at law on Portsmouth Common.

The 'several packs' mentioned here must have included the one belonging to Thomas Land. His house was actually more like two than one mile from the village centre. One of his servants was noted in the parish registers under 13 September 1779 - the burial of Charles Brown 'son of the cook at Turners'. His will of 3 March 1780 was proved in the PCC the following 20 April. It divided his estate between his sister, Elizabeth Turner, and three nieces, Margaret, Jane and Elizabeth Turner, daughters of his late brother John, with a further note that 'as a mark of my opinion of my niece Robina Hough daughter of the said John and of my niece Margaret, the daughter of my brother Thomas I bequeath to each of them the sum of five guineas'. His executors were John Spooner of Mottisfont,

Richard Oswald of Ayr, Scotland; Robert Udney of Hook in Titchfield and George Rose of the Tax Office, Old Palace Yard, London. Robina was the widow of Captain Samuel Hough (see page 164).

TYRWHITT - e 1775, r 1777.

BENNETT WALLOP - e 1772. Born 29 January 1745, son of Viscount Lymington, he was possibly 'Young Wallop' seen by John Baker at a Hambledon match at Guildford in 1772. Died 12 February 1815.

WARREN - e 1773.

JOHN WHALLEY - e 1779, president 1783. Born 22 June 1743 and baptised at St Giles', Oxford, son of Robert of Blackburn and Oxford by Grace née Gardiner. He entered Oriel, Oxford, in 1760 (BA 1764) and assumed the name Gardiner after Whalley on 11 November 1779 when he succeeded a maternal relative as owner of Roche Court, Fareham. In 1787 he took the name of Smythe between his other surnames after succeeding to a Smythe relative's estate at Cuddesdon, Oxon. He was elected MP for Westbury 1780-84, appointed Sheriff of Hampshire for 1785-86, created a baronet 1783 and died on 18 November 1797.

THOMAS WILLIAM WHALLEY - e 1788, steward 1792. Younger brother of John (see above), baptised at St Giles', Oxford, on 30 September 1754; 'gone' entered against his name in the 1795 subscription list.

WILLIAM WHITE - e 1783, r 1785.

GEORGE FINCH, Earl of WINCHILSEA - e 1786, president 1787 and 1789. Born at St James's, Westminster, 4 November 1752, died South Street, London, 2 August 1826. No Hampshire associations, but for a useful account, including his cricketing income and expenditure in 1789-99, see Snow 1976-77.

EDWARD WOOLLS - e 1785, r 1789. According to Ashley-Cooper he resided at Farringdon and died in 1824.

JOHN AUBREY WOOLLS - e 1785. Baptised at Fareham on 26 May 1752, son of Thomas Appleford, fifty years the vicar, he went to Pembroke, Oxford, in 1770 (BA 1774) and served as vicar of Fareham from 1790 until his death on 29 March 1811.

Sir RICHARD WORSLEY Bart - e 1773. Born 17 March 1751, educated at Winchester and Corpus Christi, Oxford; MP for Newport, Isle of Wight, 1774-84, Newtown, Isle of Wight, 1790-93 and 1796-1801; Controller of the King's Household 1779, PC 1780; sometime Governor of the Isle of Wight. His *The History of the Isle of Wight* was published in 1781. In 1782 he brought an action against George Bissett, an officer in the Hampshire Militia, claiming £20,000 for criminal conversation with his wife, but received only one shilling damages. Soon afterwards, around 1784, he settled in Rome, travelled to the Middle East and for a while served as British Resident in Venice. He returned with a large collection of antiquities which he exhibited at his country seat, Appuldurcomb, on the Isle of Wight where he died on 8 August 1805 (see *DNB*).

WRIGHT - e 1774. Of Barton Stacey.

YALDEN – e 1778.

POSTSCRIPT

Though ignored by most historians until recently, considerable documentation exists for Hambledon cricket during the fifty years following the demise of the old club in 1796. Details of matches against East Meon & Meonstoke in 1800, Emsworth in 1802, Winchester in 1807, Portsea in 1814 and 1815, Havant in 1815 and Portsmouth & Portsea in 1818 are given by Buckley (1937 pp. 37-106). Several entries relating to Hambledon cricket between 1818 and 1824 appear in the published diary of the Revd E.Y. White. (*Sports Quarterly Magazine* No. 16 1980) And, more importantly, Hampshire County Record Office at Winchester owns the original Hambledon C.C. records covering the years 1808 to 1826. There was also a record book for a slightly earlier period in the possession (in 1879) of Colonel Butler (1798-1885) of Bury Lodge, a Hambledon cricketer of the mid-19th century. But its present whereabouts (if still extant) are unknown. All we have is the extract from the minutes for 1804 which was reproduced in *Sports Quarterly Magazine* (no. 12, p. 2) in 1979:

> Aug 15., 1804. Moved by General Clavering, seconded by Mr. Poulter, That, in conformity with the practice of the old club, it is desirable the club should nominate players for any match to be played distinct from the Gentlemen of the club, the following men be considered as the Players for the club in any such match, in addition to those already in the habit of playing on the Down - J. Bennet, Bennet, Freemantle, Poynter, Button, Pink, Windebank, White, J. Small, Barnett, Morant, Hammond, Lear, Holland.

Twelve of the fourteen were among those advertised by the *Hampshire Chronicle* of 10 September for a match on Windmill Down on the 20th 'made by Thomas Bonham, Esq. and Charles Clavering, Esq. for 50 guineas each side', the wickets to be pitched at 9 o'clock and begin play at 10 precisely'. Others listed were Knight, Boys, Clay and Littlefield, with three unnamed gentlemen making up the eleven on each side. It was also noted that 'on the following day the anniversary of the Hambledon Club will be held at John Stewart's, the *New Inn*. - Dinner on Table at six o'clock'. Bonham was a subscriber to the old club as far back as 1778, ten years before Poulter joined in 1788. On the playing side Freemantle and Small were also survivors from the 1780s. They and several others - the two Bennetts (presumably the noted John and James), Pointer, Windebank, Button and Holland - represented Hampshire and in some cases England during the 1800s. Charles and Brigadier-General Clavering were sons of Lieutenant-General Clavering (d 1777), the former Commander-in-Chief of Bengal who fought a bloodless duel with Hambledon member Richard Barwell.

According to a letter written by Thomas Smith of Droxford in 1857, quoted in *Scores and Biographies* (vol. I, pp. 114-5), the playing strength also included 'Brown, the fastest bowler then known, Beagley, Carter, Bowyer, Garrat, &c., some of whom were paid 10s. per day by the Club as bowlers'. Apparently this refers to a slightly later period, around 1810-20. From the same letter we learn that members continued to gather at 'the old club-house' on Windmill Down, built by Tom Sueter back in 1783, in a room where they held club dinners beneath an ancient bat hung as some kind of trophy above the table. This relic of former days survived until the year 1819 'when a member of the club, after dinner by way of frolick, took it down and insisted on having one hit with it, and before it could be prevented he rashly proceeded to do so; the consequence was it fell all to pieces, being quite rotten and worm eaten, causing great dismay and annoyance to all'. In 1814 the club paid 2s for mending its thatched roof and six years later had some of its woodwork repaired. Even so, Smith tells us that it had fallen into decay by about 1825 when 'many members left the neighbourhood' and the club was no longer well supported.

Both the club (or at any rate a newly-formed club) and the ground survived for several more years. *Bell's Life* for 16 July 1826 reported that the previous monday ten of Hambledon lost by four wickets to the same number of Cold Harbour Lane, Emsworth. Hambledon played Midhurst on Windmill Down in 1829 - the scores of both games, home and away, can by found in *Scores and Biographies* (vol. II, pp. 78-9, 83) - and brief details of several more Hambledon Club matches on the old Windmill Down ground down to 1836 are provided by Squires' *Pre-Victorian Sussex Cricket*. This may have been the club, still flourishing in 1844, whose matches against the South Hampshire Club are given by Haygarth (Vol. III, pp. 231, 249). That season its notices in *Bell's Life* refer to 'the Hambledon ground' being 'in the village of Hambledon' - which, if taken literally, means another must have replaced Windmill Down, which is situated on a hill well outside the actual village. However a continuity with 1804 on the catering front is indicated by a report for 1844 that when Hambledon entertained South Hampshire 'the dinner provided by Mr J.G. Heath, of the *New Inn*, gave general satisfaction'.

In conclusion it may be worth noting some of the players who turned out for Hambledon or the Hambledon clubs between 1800 and 1850. During the first two decades we find the names H., J. and W. Boyce, C. and T. Clay, Frankham, Friend, P. and W. Garrett, Hale, Hamilton, Hatch, B. and W. Hedger, Huested, Humphrey, Knight, J. Jarman, H. Littlefield, F. and H. Stewart, Smith esq and Warren. In 1829 the team comprised Pay, Hammond, J. Bulbeck esq, Foster esq, Boyce, Friend, Etherington, Gale, Bligh, Downman, Garrett - plus in the return Purnell, Richards, Luiville, Boniface, Clark. And playing in the match Married *v* Single of the Hambledon Club in 1844 we have (for the single) H. Gilder, Gamon, Littlefield, J. Bulbeck, E. Hale jun, Morgan esq, G. Higgins, J. Foster esq, H. Kennett jun, Allans, W.H. Moody esq; (for the married) Colonel Butler, H. Barkworth, Hall, H. Kennett, S. Moody, Greentree, T. Smith, H. Munns, Lunn, Perkin, J. Kennett (*Bell's Life* 21 July 1844).

(This postscript was written before the publication of the books by David Underdown and Neil Jenkinson)

NOTES

1. For example by the prize-ring historian J. Ford (1972), C. Brookes of Leicester University (1978), the social historian D. Birley (1979, 1993, 1999), Oxford's T. McLean (1987), M. Marqusee (1994) and the Hambledon specialist A. Mote (1997).

2. The *criquet* chimera was exposed and fully explained by L. Hector: 'The Ghost of Cricket Walks the Archives', *Journal of the Society of Archivists*, 4.7 (1973) pp. 579-80. Nevertheless both Birley (1979) and Marqusee continued to maintain that the first certain record of cricket was the French *criquet* in 1478. In fact Marqusee's version of cricket's early history – the one approved by British academe - is based entirely on this and that other notorious canard, the 1668 cricket field at Clerkenwell when the local rate book, which supposedly rated the landlord of *The Ram Inn* for this cricket field, was badly misread.

3. D. Malcolm: 'Cricket Spectator Disorder', *The Sports Historian*, 19.1 (1999), pp. 16-37.

4. The Centre's thesis follows the opinions put forward in *Sports Spectators* (1986) - 5 citations in the endnotes - by A. Guttmann of Amherst College, USA, a prolific but not wholly reliable writer on sports history. Within British academic circles Guttmann is viewed as a leading authority on cricket, especially the work of John Nyren - notwithstanding that he consistently refers to cricket players as 'cricketeers' and that his source for Nyren is not a copy of the 'Young Cricketer's Tutor' itself but references which appear in a certain Hans Indorf's *Fair Play und der "Englieshe Sportgeist"* published in Hamburg in 1938 (Guttmann p. 200, note 133).

5. Among many other things, the Centre claims that unlike the 18th century there are no records of crowd disorder between 1802 and 1866. Incidents which it chooses to ignore include (to take just one six-year period) the Hinckley players assaulted by a mob armed with stakes and stones at Nuneaton 1827;the coach of a visiting club stoned at Southborough 1831; Leamington New Club attacked by a crowd of about 400 at Coventry 1833; and a riot involving both players and spectators when Reigate played on Richmond Green in 1833.

6. *Kentish Gazette* 23.11.1782, 14.8.1773; K.J. Cole: *Two Hundred Years of Dorking Cricket* (1969) p. 10; J.Goulstone, 'Fresh Light on Kentish Cricket'; *The Cricket Quarterly* 6.4 (1968) p. 193.

7. According to the Centre for Research's own list of references no original texts or archival material - not even the essential Haygarth, Waghorn and Buckley - were consulted by its experts during the

course of its research into 18th century cricket. In fact only three pre-War publications are listed - Pycroft's *The Cricket Field*, under the date 1851, Mitford's *Our Village*, which the Centre insists was written in 1879 (pp. 17, 34, 35), and Nyren's *locus classicus*, which the Centre throughout calls *The Young Cricketeer's* (or *Cricketeers'*) *Tutor*!

8. Proof that the game had spread sixty miles west of Hambledon by the 1730s is provided by an advertisement for Ridgway Races near Dorchester in the *Sherborne Mercury* for 9.5.1738:

    Friday, Twelve Dorchester Men challenge 12 Men from any other Place to play at Cricket for 12 Pair of Gloves, Value One Shilling a pair: Every Man to pay 6d at Entrance, and begin at One o'Clock in the Afternoon.

    The Entrance-Money to be paid to John Cox at Ridgway.

9. 'The Goodwood Score Sheet', *Sports Quarterly Magazine* 5 (1978) pp. 8-10; and note 23.

10. Richard, son of Richard and Silvester Kates (sic), baptised at Naunton, Glos, 30.7.1731; as Richard, son of Richard Keats, 'pleb', of Harford Bridge, Glos, entered Magdalen Hall, Oxford, 30.5.1749 aged 17 (BA 1753, MA 1756). By his wife Elizabeth, Richard had eight children baptised at Chalton: Richard Goodwin 1757, William Bouchier 1758, William 1759, Elizabeth 1762, Mary 1764, John 1772, Ann 1770, Silvester 1774.

11. By his will, witnessed by John Lancaster, Elizabeth Colwell and William Newell, Thomas Land sen left £40 apiece to his grandchildren Francis Foster and Betty, wife of George Gay; 5s apiece to his daughter, Betty Foster, and his sister Martha's daughter (maiden name Binna Dennes); £1 apiece to his nephew George Dennes' four children; residue to his son Thomas, sole executor, who had to provide for the education of George, Francis and John, sons of his grandson, George Foster. The next meeting of the manorial court for Hambledon noted 'the death of Thomas Land, a customary tenant of this manor who died since the last court and his son Thomas Land (is) the next heir'. His nephew was presumably the George Dennis who witnessed a marriage at Hambledon in 1762.

12. Knight (1997) p. 20.

13. Elizabeth Tulip (born Hambledon 1749) had an illegitimate child by Thomas, son of Thomas Pratt, husbandman of Hambledon, who had to pay for its upkeep from 1775 until ceasing to be a charge on the parish. A year after her inheritance she became the wife of the Richard Mathews who witnessed Land's codicil. Both appear in the marriage register as paupers (she signing x), though according to a 1793 directory Richard was a farmer.

14. There was at least one other George Foster in mid-18th century

Hambledon - who had a son George baptised 1758, married Frances Coleman 1765 (both signing x), and as menial servant to Thomas Land was appointed gamekeeper in 1769.

15. Waghorn 1899 p. 63, Haygarth Vol. I xix, *London Evening Post* 6 October 1767.

16. Rait Kerr; Bowen; Birley 1979, 1993, 1999.

17. He was followed by Carew 1723, Ann 1726, Henrietta Maria 1728, John Daniel 1730, Francis 1731. The third of the four brothers became a schoolmaster at Newbury and minor poet.

18. Ashley-Cooper p. 147.

19. Charles Richards, born c1754, son of Charles sen of Bradninch, Devon, entered Oxford 1772 (BA 1781, MA 1783) and was father of James Cotton (c1792-1814) and Charles junior (c1783-1835); vicar South Stoneham; rector and patron of Chale and master of Hyde Abbey School. Charles senior and junior were two of the executors of leading club member John Richards senior.

20. Buckley 1935 p. 212.

21. Later instances include: 'Mr Charles Holloway of Winchester, with Mr Mitchell of Easton as a look-out mate' (*Salisbury Journal* 5.6.1820); '11 from Nursling and Millbrook, with one given mate' (*Bell's Life* 12.9.1824); 'he got 75 runs at his first innings, and went in, the last mate, for seven runs' (*ibid* 22.4.1827); 'Evans, Thumwood, and another mate of the Old Andover Club' (*ibid* 11.7.1830); 'G. Jolliffe, the celebrated player of Candover, given as a mate' (*ibid* 5.9.1830); 'ten of Overton, with a given mate' (*ibid* 4.7.1838); 'Alton parish were to have "Beagley", and "Tollfree" as given mates' (*ibid* 12.8.1838); at Southampton 'the superior bowling of the given mates' (*ibid* 25.7.1841). The word also appears in the writings of Mary Mitford (born Alresford 1787): 'Joel Brent ... ran out his mate, Samuel Long' (*Lady's Magazine* 1823), etc.

22. Sarah, daughter of Rev William Stevens, vicar of Hambledon, was buried 12.12.1783. Their children were William Stevens, born 6.10.1771; Sarah baptised 24.12.1772, John baptised 23.2.1774. The last was perhaps John who married Frances Padwick at East Meon 1793 and whose widow (?), Frances Bayton, was married at Hambledon 1805. William Stevens, matriculated from St Edmund Hall, Oxford, 1794, conducted marriages at Hambledon 1795-96 (while curate?) became rector of Ford, Sussex 1807-48, and vicar of Madehurst (adjoining Slindon) 1815-48, and died 'at his residence in the Hornet, Chichester', 17.1.1848.

23. T.J. McCann: 'Edward Aburrow, Cricketer and Smuggler: another link between Slindon and Hambledon', *Journal of the Cricket Society* 10.2 (1981) pp. 17-19.

24. Regarding Frances Nyren, John's granddaughter, Mary Nyren of Folkestone, told E.V. Lucas that 'when she was an old lady, still living in Hambledon, she dressed in a soft black silk dress, with a large Leghorn hat tied on with a black lace scarf, and held a gold-headed cane when out walking. She went out only to church and on errands of mercy ... Mrs Nyren, when a widow, found a happy home in her son John Nyren's house till her death at over ninety years of age'. But assuming she was about the same age as her husband, this means her death occurred sometime during the 1820s or 1830s, which contradicts a memorandum book kept by Richard's grandson, Henry Nyren, according to which she died in 1808.

25. Samuel Maunder (1785-1849), the publisher and lexicographer, was co-proprietor of the *Literary Gazette* along with William Pinnock (1782-1843), the latter a native of and sometime schoolmaster at Alton, ten miles north of Pertersfield. The 2nd edition of *Death's Doings* (1st Edition 1826), 'consisting of numerous original compositions in verse and prose, the friendly contribution of various writers; principally intended as illustrations of thirty copper-plates designed and etched by R. Dagley' was published in 1827. Maunder's *The Game of Life* occupies pp. 69-72 and an essay by 'Barnard Batwell', accompanyimng an etching, 'Death and the Cricketer' in which a skeletal bowler is about to bowl underarm with a bearded, scythe-bearing Father Time keeping wicket, pp. 73-84. John Small's memior, signed 'S.M.', is inserted in the form of a continuous footnote to *Verses in Praise of Cricket* by The Revd M. (sic) Cotton between pp. 72 and 73 and is unpaginated. It forms the basis of an account of Small by 'A Hampshire Bowler', dated Winchester May 19, published in *The Annals of Sporting* in 1827, pp. 323-26, and reappears in *Pierce Egan's Book of Sports and Mirror of Life* (1832) pp. 338-39.

26. Mote, p. 42, has a picture of the "original lodge" (a stand for spectators) on Broadhalfpenny "built each spring by T. Sueter." Several versions of this picture were shown at the Swaffham Museum at an exhibition there in 1997 where it was attributed to Swaffham in 1797 (v England): it is shown in Yaxley's *History of Norfolk Cricket* (Nostalgia Publications 1997, p. 6). In the picture the bowler and the striker appear to be based on Shepheard's well known drawings of David Harris and Tom Walker c. 1790. Neither player appeared at Broadhalfpenny and in any event Sueter's building was on Windmill Down.

27. William Tyner, born Croydon April 1763, educated Tonbridge School and St John's, Cambridge (BA 1785, MA 1806), ordained 1786, curate Little Berkhamstead, Herts, 1786; married at St Mary, Portsea, 1792 Nancy Maria Howell (children baptised Portsmouth 1793-95, Hambledon 1796, Chalton 1798-99), married 1811 Sarah Colston of Croydon; vicar of Compton with Upmarden, Sussex, 1806-54; died Lee Park, Blackheath, Kent 26.9.1854.

28. Within a few weeks of Paine's reported appearance at Hambledon H.M. Government sent Henry Swinburne to France on an unsuccessful mission to negotiate the release of prisoners. Swinburne dined with the diarist John Baker at a cricket match at Henfield in 1772 (see also note 33).

29. J.S.Penny: *Cricketing References in Norwich Newspapers 1701 to 1800* (1979) pp. 5 and 10; *St James's Chronicle* 15.9.1764: 'Yesterday afternoon, at the great Cricket Match behind Montague House, a well-dressed man had his pocket picked, and while the offender was conveying (sic) to the Horse Pond, the Accuser was deemed by some of the Mob as the guilty person, and underwent a more severe ducking than the real criminal'. According to J. Carter, 'Cricket Matches 1731-1773' , *The Cricket Quarterly* 2.3 (1964) pp. 161-171, no matches were recorded in London or Middlesex in 1764, though in every subsequent season. The annual hurling contest, Munster *v* Leinster, held in the Artillery Ground since at least the 1740s was banned from the ground in 1764 and switched to the fields behind Montague House (roughly the site now occupied by London University). Whether cricket was similarly proscribed is not known.

30. A 'dulce lenimen' was also provided for the steward in 1787. There is no such word in the *OED* but it must derive from *dulce*, 'sweet', and *leniment*, 'something which appeases or assuages', therefore denote some kind of convenience. It may be noted that on 22.5.1787 the club 'ordered that a convenient box for the inclosure of a convenient utensil be provided'.

31. Hambledon scored 176 & 123, the twenty-two 138 & 142. The return, 'the great cricket match between the Hambledon 11 and 22 from the neighbourhood of Liphook', on Cold Ash Hill near Bramshott, finished on Saturday 2 August: Hambledon 157 & 101, Liphook etc 61 & 122 (*Hampshire Chronicle* 11.8.1777).

32. When Hampshire played at Lord's the spectators were liable to include ladies of a quite different class. Thus a number of 'trulls' were reported among the crowd at the six a-side match, Hampshire *v* England, on 21-23 August 1788 (see Buckley 1935, p. 223).

33. Mrs Swinburne met her husband, whom she married at Aix-la-Chapelle in 1767, while 'a young lady with a good fortune, who was being educated at a convent by Ursuline nuns'. In Vienna 1780-81 she received the order of La Croix Étoilée from Maria Theresa while Emperor Joseph stood godfather to her son Joseph; in France 1786-88 Marie Antoinette enrolled her eldest son as one of her pages (see Henry Swinburne in *DNB*).

34. Compare the exchange between Lord Tankerville and Sir Horace Mann in J. Duncombe's *Surry Triumphant* (1773): 'Hedge now thy bets, said Tankerville … To the Earl the Knight replied, Thy counsel

I do scord; I with no Surrey man will hedge That ever yet was born ....'

35. Compare P. Norman: 'Great matches in those days (c1830) were often said to be for £1000 or a thousand guineas a side, and bills to that effect used to be placarded about, although no money changed hands' *(Scores and Annals of the West Kent Cricket Club* 1897 p. 34); 'Viator' (F.Gale?): in the 1830s 'the hundred guineas a side was a myth, and only represented a private guarantee given by wealthy patrons of the game against loss in case of bad weather' *(Kentish Gazette* 10.8.1880).

36. N. Pickard: 'In Search of a Cricketing Ancestor', *The Journal of The Cricket Society* 7.1. (1974) pp. 17-19; J. Pennington: 'Noah Mann of Northchapel (1756-1789): a local hero', *West Sussex History* 66 (2000) pp. 3-6.

37. The IGI has a Thomas Walker baptised at Thursley 26.11.1765.

38. Although said to have died aged 76 (in 1835) the IGI records a John son of William Wells baptised at Farnham 29 July 1768. If this was the cricketer it would mean he began to take part in the great matches when aged almost 19 rather than 28 as currently believed.

39. He is recorded in the 'List of the Cricket Club' which forms part of a large printed sheet in the Finch MSS, Leicester County Record Office, bearing the date 1784. However from internal evidence it is clear that the list cannot date from before 1786. For example one member is named as 'Lord Dare'. There was no such title: the entry can only be a misprint for 'Lord Dacre'. In 1784 this would have meant Thomas Barrett-Lennard (1717-86) who 'was a martyr to rheumatic gout, being entirely crippled by it for many years before his death'. Therefore the member must have been his nephew, Trevor Charles Roper (1745-94), who succeeded to the title on 6.1.1786 (see G.E.C.: *The Complete Peerage* IV, 1906, p. 16).

40. His only son, Ulick John (born Belmont, Hants, 1802), the next Earl of Clanricarde and sometime Under Secretary of State for Foreign Affairs, Ambassador to Russia and Postmaster-General, ran a gambling syndicate designed to separate wealthy young men from their fortunes. One early victim, the cricketer Vinny Cotton, lost a reputed £13,000 at two sessions of cards. Their racket came to public notice when John Auldjo went to court after being swindled by the Clanricarde set whom he met during a match at Lord's in 1826 (see *Sports Quarterly Magazine* No. 6, 1978, pp. 14-17).

SELECT BIBLIOGRAPHY

ALTHAM, H.S. *A History of Cricket*, George Allen & Unwin, London, 1926.

ARNOLD, Ralph. *A Yeoman of Kent: An Account of Richard Hayes 1725-1790, and the village of Cobham*. Constable, London, 1949.

ASHLEY-COOPER, F.S., *The Hambledon Cricket Chronicle 1772-1796*, Herbert Jenkins, London, 1924.

BOWEN, R., 'John Baker's Diary', *The Cricket Quarterly* 3.4 pp. 235-45., The Author, Eastbourne, 1965.

BUCKLEY, G.B., *Fresh Light on 18th Century Cricket*, Cotterell & Co., Birmingham, 1935.

—— *Fresh Light on Pre-Victorian Cricket*, Cotterell & Co., Birmingham, 1937.

—— 'The Hambledon Club', *The Cricket Quarterly* 7.4 pp. 164-69., Roland Bowen, Eastbourne, 1969-70

BIRLEY, Derek. *A Social History of English Cricket*. Aurum, London, 1999.

COBBETT, W. *Rural Rides*, Everyman's Library, Dent, London, 1912.

[COKAYNE] G.E.C. *The Complete Peerage of England, Ireland, Great Britain and the United Kingdom extant, extinct or dormant*. The St. Catherine Press, London, 1959.

DAGLEY, R. *Death's Doings*, J. Andrews, London, 2nd Edition 1827.

GOLDSMITH, J., *Hambledon*, Phillimore, Chichester, 1994.

GOULSTONE, J. and ARROWSMITH, R.L., 'The Hambledon Membership Roll', *Sports Quarterly Magazine* 4 (1977) pp. 15-18.

HAMPDEN J. (ed) *An Eighteenth Century Journal: Being a record of the years 1774-1776*. Macmillan, London. 1940.

HARRIS Lord and ASHLEY-COOPER, F.S. *The History of Kent County Cricket*. Eyre & Spottiswoode, London, 1907.

—— *Kent Cricket Matches 1719–1880*, Gibbs & Sons, Canterbury, 1929

HAYGARTH, A. (compiler), *Frederick Lillywhite's Cricket Scores and Biographies*, Longman and Co., London, Vols I-II, 1862; Vol. III, 1863.

KNIGHT, R.D., *Hambledon's Cricket Glory*, The Author, Weymouth, 1975-date.

LUCAS, E.V., *The Hambledon Men*, Henry Frowde, London,1907.

MOTE, Ashley, *The Glory Days of Cricket*. Robson, London, 1997.

——, *John Nyren's The Cricketers of my Time: The original version*. Robson, London, 1998.

NYREN, J., *The Young Cricketer's Tutor*, Effingham Wilson, London, 1833.

PAGE, W., DOUBLEDAY, H.A. (eds) *Victorian History of the County of Hampshire and the Isle of Wight*, Constable. 1900-14.

PAGE, W., SALZMAN, L.F. (eds) *Victorian History of the County of Sussex*, Janes Street, Constable, OUP. 1905-7, 1935-53, 1987.

PENNY, J.S., *Cricket References in Norwich Newspapers 1701–1800*, The Author, Norwich 1979.

PYCROFT, J., *The Cricket Field*, Longman, Brown, Green and Longmans, London, 1851.

RAIT KERR, R.S., *The Laws of Cricket*, Longmans, Green and Co., London, 1950.

SNOW, E.E., 'Extracts, Relating to Cricket, From the private Accounts of the 9th Earl of Winchilsea 1788-99', *Journal of the Cricket Society* Vol. 8.1 pp. 26-31, Vol. 8.2 pp. 35-36. The Society, London, 1976 & 1977.

SPENCER, A. (ed). *Memoirs of William Hickey*, Hurst and Blackett, London, 1913-1925.

SQUIRE, H.P. and A.P. *Pre-Victorian Sussex Cricket*. The Authors, Henfield, 1951.

UNDERDOWN, David, *Start of Play*. Allen Lane, London, 2000.

WAGHORN, H.T., *Cricket Scores, Notes, &c. From 1730-1773*, William Blackwood and Sons, London, 1899.

—— *The Dawn of Cricket*, The Marylebone Cricket Club, London, 1906.

WILMOT, Eardley, *Reminiscences of the late Thomas Ashetton Smith Esq.*, Routledge, Warne & Routledge, London, 1862.

INDEX

210

Clark, Francis, 7
Clarke, Hambledon member, 154.
  See also Jervoise, T.C.
Clavering, General Charles, 197-8.
Clay, Charles, 91, 197.
Clouts, cricket-ball maker, 31.
Cobbett, William, 59.
Coles, Charles, Hambledon member, 154.
Coles, Henry, Brewer, 29, 38, 59, 60, 94, 102.
  death, 61.
  family tree, 60.
Colwell, Elizabeth, bequest, 6.
Compton, Sussex, 95.
Conway, Capt. Hugh Seymour, Hambledon
  member, 154-5.
Cooley, Revd William, Hambledon member,
  155.
Cosham, 67.
Cotman, xiii, 59.
Cotton, Revd Reynell, Baptised at Rudgwick,
  17.
  Copyhold house in Hambledon, 18.
  Sale of, 18-19.
  Cricket Song, 17-25, 41, 70-1.
    basis of other songs, 20.
    earlier version not extant, 20.
    100 copies in 1781, 20.
  Died, 18.
  Educated Winchester College, 17.
  Hambledon member, 4, 14, 155.
  Hyde Abbey School, 17.
  Married at St.Martin-in-the-Fields, 17.
  Oxford, Corpus Christi, 17.
  School in Winchester, 15.
    Reunion, 17-18.
Court, 102.
Court Lodge, 10.
Coxheath, 1.
  Cricket Society, 91-2.
Crondall, 133.
Crookham, 130.
Crosoer, 80.
Croydon, 9.
Cricket's alleged beginings, criquet, xi.
Criquet, xi.
Cuddy, see Curry.
Curry, also known as Cuddy, 1, 22.
  real name Edward Aburrow, 23.
  See also Aburrow, Edward.
Cussans, John, Hambledon member, 14, 155.

Dampier, Revd John, Hambledon member, 156.
Darnley, Lord, Hambledon member, 91, 111,
  112, 120, 156.
Dartford, 2, 3, 50, 113.
  Brim/Brent, 2, 37.
  Club, 1.

Daulering/Durling, 2.
Davis, 121.
De Burgh, Henry, Hambledon member, 158.
  see also Dunkellin, Lord.
De Burgh, John Thomas, Hambledon member,
  14, 156.
Dehany, George, Hambledon member, 156-7.
Dehany, Philip, 14, 89, 92, 94, 112.
  Hambledon member, 157-8.
Denmead, Manor of, 53.
Denmead Molyns, 5.
Dog, lost, 1, 50, 100-1.
Dorset, Duke of, 21, 24, 34, 42, 47, 52, 72, 74,
  75, 76-7, 78, 80, 92, 98-9, 101, 104-5,
  110, 111, 112, 113, 114, 118, 119.
  Nancy Parsons, Mistress of, 105.
  wielding bat, xii, 97.
  See also Sackville.
Droxford, 198.
Drummond, Revd Henry Roger, Hambledon
  member, 158.
Duke of Dorset, see Dorset and Sackville.
Dulce Lenimen, 91, 102.
Dunkellin, Lord, Hambledon member, 15, 89,
  158.
Dyson, Jeremiah, Hambledon member, 158.

Eartham, 36.
East Meon, 66, 94.
  and Meonstoke, 66, 197.
Easton, 144.
Edmeads, 24.
Edmonds, John, 3.
Edwards, John, Hambledon member, 158-9.
Egham, 71.
Elvetham, 130.
Emsworth, 54, 197.
England, 1, 20, 24, 27, 31, 37, 38, 42, 49, 51, 52,
  55, 63, 70, 71, 72, 73, 74, 75, 76-7, 78,
  80, 81, 89, 92, 93, 98-9, 100, 103, 104,
  108, 110, 111, 112, 113, 118, 120, 123,
  125, 126, 129, 134, 135, 136, 137, 140-1,
  144, 145, 198.
  five of, 32.
Esdaile, Edmund, historian, 36.
Essex, 123.
  Cricket Club, 91.
Eton College Magazine, The Microcosm, 84.
Everitt, Capt. Charles Holmes, Hambledon
  member, 159.
Everitt, Capt. Thomas Cooper, Hambledon
  member, 159.
Ewshot, 131.

Falmouth, 104.
Fareham, 5, 21, 34, 67.
Farnham, 24, 124, 131, 133, 134, 135, 139,
  140, 142, 143.

218

HAMBLEDON CRICKET GROUNDS

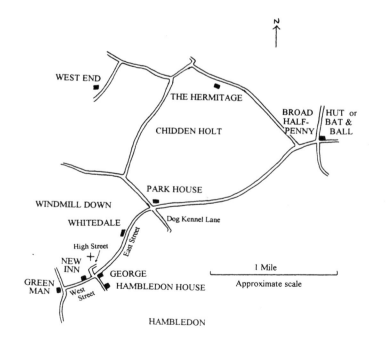

HAMBLEDON